Philip Phillips, Alexander Clark

Song Pilgrimage Around and Throughout the World

Embracing a life of song experiences, impressions, anecdotes, incidents, persons, manners, customs, sketches, and illustrations throughout twenty different countries

Philip Phillips, Alexander Clark

Song Pilgrimage Around and Throughout the World
Embracing a life of song experiences, impressions, anecdotes, incidents, persons, manners, customs, sketches, and illustrations throughout twenty different countries

ISBN/EAN: 9783337213251

Printed in Europe, USA, Canada, Australia, Japan

Cover: Foto ©Thomas Meinert / pixelio.de

More available books at **www.hansebooks.com**

Yours in Faith & Song
Philip Phillips.

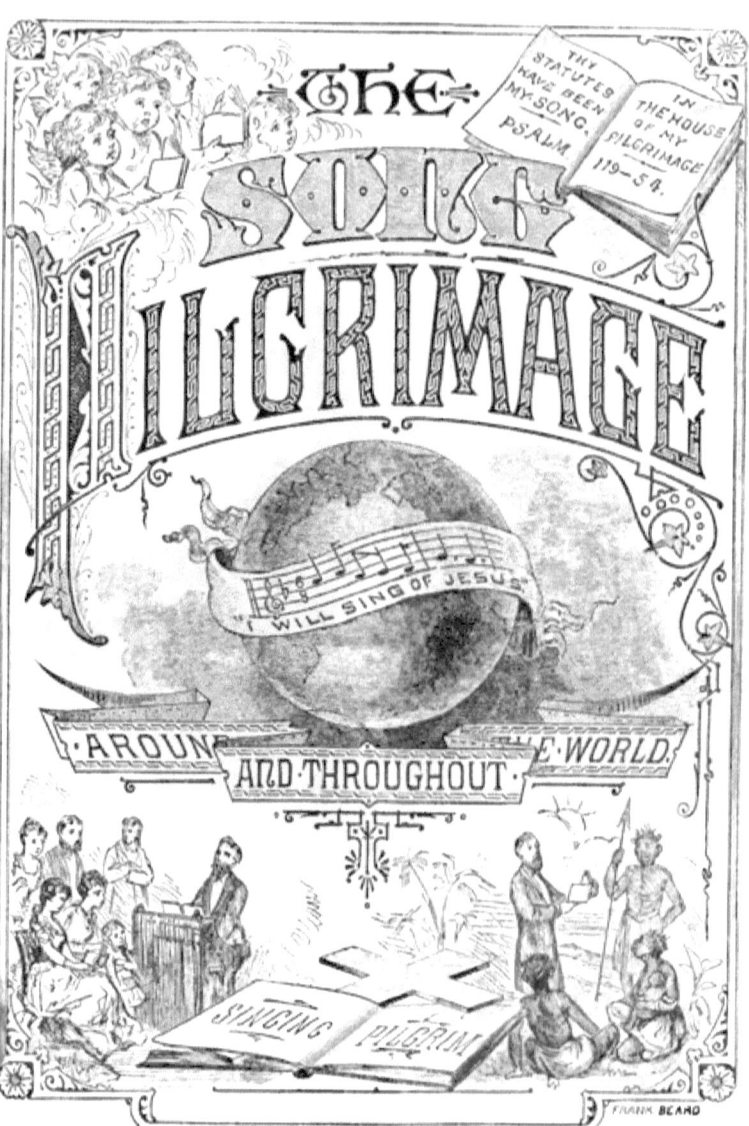

SONG PILGRIMAGE

AROUND AND THROUGHOUT THE WORLD,

EMBRACING A

Life of Song Experiences, Impressions, Anecdotes, Incidents, Persons, Manners, Customs, Sketches, and Illustrations Throughout Twenty Different Countries.

By PHILIP PHILLIPS.

INTRODUCTION BY

Rev. J. H. VINCENT, D.D.,

WITH A BIOGRAPHY BY THE LATE Rev. ALEXANDER CLARK, D.D.

CHICAGO:
FAIRBANKS, PALMER & CO.

NEW YORK, E. B. TREAT.   CINCINNATI, WALDEN & STOWE.
SAN FRANCISCO, J. P. HILL.   FOND DU LAC, WIS., G. L. BENJAMIN.

1880.

DEDICATION.

TO MY WIFE,

Olive M. Phillips,

WHOSE CONSISTENT LIFE, TIMELY COUNSELS, UNSELFISH SPIRIT, UNWAVERING DEVOTION, AND AFFECTIONATE COMPANIONSHIP HAVE EVER MADE MY LIFE AS A SUMMER MORNING AT HOME.

TO MY ELDEST SON, JAMES,

WHOSE BOYISH CURIOSITY, FILIAL LOVE, AMBITION, AND READY SERVICES IN THE LONG JOURNEY CONDUCED TO ITS COURAGE BY THE WAY; AND

TO MY YOUNGEST SON, PHILIP,

NAMESAKE AND PET OF THE PARTY, WHOSE CHILD-LIKE WAYS, WHOSE SONGS AND CRIES WERE ALIKE MUSIC TO US ALL, WHO SO OFTEN PUZZLED US IN THE BREAKING DAWN, BY ASKING "PAPA, MAMMA, WHERE ARE WE NOW?" WHOSE PRATTLE AND PLAY GAVE US THE REAL HOME FEELING ABROAD.

PREFACE.

The Author, in the following pages has attempted a narrative of his somewhat eventful life. From childhood providence seems to have appointed him to the service of song. His earliest recollections are precious memories of praise to the dear Redeemer, sung by a beloved mother; and hymns of gladness, as when the Christian dispensation was announced by the angels of heaven to the shepherds on the Judean hills, have echoed through his soul from the morning of his life until his maturer years, making the gospel itself a never ceasing song of delight.

Music is as essential as theology in the Christian system. It is an inherent element of the redemptive economy. It was a prominent part of the Hebrew ritual, in the Mosaic dispensation, as the Psalms of David grandly witness. The Lord was magnified in the temple service by the sound of psaltery harp and organ, as well as by the still richer tribute of that most wonderful of all instruments, the human voice. God has always been well pleased when His children recognized Him, and honored His name by psalms and hymns and spiritual songs, and by the sound of the trumpet, timbrel, stringed instruments and organs. He invites His creatures, animate and inanimate, to give praise, to sing, to rejoice, and to come into the harmony of divine worship. Mountains, hills and trees; sun moon and stars;

young men, maidens, old men and children; angels and archangels, "everything that hath breath," all are invited to join the concert of universal adoration.

Music is the heavenly occupation and the earthly joy. It is a cardinal doctrine among the doctrines of revealed religion, as well as a science; it is dominant among the distinctive principles of the "faith once delivered to the saints." It is the golden link between the natural and the spiritual kingdoms.

While others may write books of theology, philosophy, polity, and pious experience, all admirable in their way; and while there may be no end to the making of many books touching the history, purposes and prospects of the Christian church, it became the writer's choice to prepare a volume relating to the central and the sweetest of all themes of earth or heaven—the song-service of the Lord's redeemed.

The circumstances which prompted the author to consecrate himself to this special department of religious duty, are incidentally related in the pages which follow. The impressions of the spirit indicating what line of thought and life to pursue; how to use the passing hours in the promotion of God's glory by the potent agencies of music; how to magnify the office and power of sacred song in the sanctuary and in the home; how to utilize the voices of the masses, the occurrences of the times, the opportunities of every day and every soul; how to bring all silent and inharmonious conditions into responsive, accordant and universal thanksgiving to God; these have been some of the hopes entertained by the writer, as possible to witness in realization among the glorious achievements of the latter day. The author does not lay claim to any great or speical gift as a writer, singer or evangelist. He simply gives expression to the inmost meaning of his soul when he sings; and now, as he writes, it is only that some words, possibly, on the printed page, may serve as helps to inquirers at the cross, for whatever of incident, expression or doctrine is related here is but the sincere language of a soul in accord with the gospel of the Son of God, and uttered in expectation of blessing others as he who writes has himself been blessed, a thousand times and a thousand fold, in confessing hearty allegiance to Jesus Christ, the Lord of all.

CONTENTS.

DEDICATION	3
PREFACE	5
ILLUSTRATIONS	8
GENERAL CONTENTS	9
INTRODUCTION (By J. H. Vincent, D.D.)	15
THE PHILLIPS FAMILY	19

BIOGRAPHY.—(By the late Alexander Clark, D.D.) Birthplace—First Public Singing — His First Song— Wandering Pilgrim—First School Teacher—His Mother—Memorial Incident, His Mother's Death and Funeral—Philip and his Brother Joshua leave Home—Mabel Forbush—The Grant Indenture—His Work the Year Round—Aunt Sallie Smith—First Singing School—His Conversion—A Narrow Escape—Ambition for Musical Training—His First Teaching—A Band of Indians—His First Horse—A Most Gracious Revival—Goes to Ohio—Marries Miss Olive M. Clark—Burning of His Store in Cincinnati—Goes to New York—First Trip to England—First Service of Praise and Bible Reading—First State S. S. Convention in California and Oregon...... 25

CHAPTER I.—SINGING IN NEW YORK AND SUBURBS—Singing in the Great Academy of Music—Singing in the Slums of New York— New York Suburbs — City of Brooklyn — Greenwood Cemetery—Staten Island—Long Island—Northern Suburbs. 69

CHAPTER II.—SINGING IN THE SOUTHERN STATES—Philadelphia—Baltimore—Delaware—Washington, D.C.—Alexandria—Fredericksburg—Richmond—Petersburg — Raleigh—Norfolk—Goldsboro—Wilmington — Columbia— Charleston—Augusta—Athens—Savannah — Atlanta—Opelika—Selma—Florida—Jacksonville—Tallahassee— Montgomery—Mobile—Macon—Meridian—Jackson—Vicksburg—New Orleans — Galveston— Houston—Austin—Brenham—Waco— Dennison— Sherman—Dallas—Shreveport—Jefferson—Little Rock—Memphis — Brownsville—Nashville—Chattanooga—Knoxville—Greenville—Old Kentucky—Lexington—Frankfort—Louisville—Covington 79

CHAPTER III.—SINGING IN THE CENTRAL STATES—Cincinnati—Marion—Western New York—Pennsylvania—Oil City—Harrisburg—Lancaster—Pittsburg—Williamsport, Etc., Etc...... 122

CHAPTER IV.—SINGING IN NEW ENGLAND.—Maine, the Pine Tree State—New Hampshire, the Granite State—Vermont, the Green Mountain State—Connecticut, the Nutmeg State—Rhode Island, the Little Sister... 130

CHAPTER V.—SERVICES IN THE BRITISH AMERICAN PROVINCES. The Province of Quebec and Ontario—The Pilgrims' Mission—Montreal—Quebec—Hamilton—Ottawa—Toronto—Petrolia. 139

CHAPTER VI.—SINGING IN THE WEST.—Michigan—Detroit—Jackson—Adrian—Grand Rapids—Saginaw City—The Lumber and Mining Districts—State of Wisconsin—State of Minnesota—St. Paul—Minneapolis, Etc.—Indiana, the Hoosier State—State of Illinois—Chicago—State of Iowa—Great State of Missouri—State of Kansas—State of Nebraska............................ 146

CHAPTER VII.—COLORADO AND THE PACIFIC COAST.—Territory of Utah—Singing to the Mormons—California, the Golden State—Sacramento—Oakland—San Francisco—In the Gold Fields—State of Oregon—Portland—Salem........................ 157

CHAPTER VIII.—THE START FOR AUSTRALIA.—Westward to the Golden Gate—Embarked for a Foreign Shore—Flying Fish—Passenger, etc.. 161

CHAPTER IX.—THE HAWAIIAN OR SANDWICH ISLANDS—Honolulu—American Missionaries—The Natives—The Products and the King—House of Parliament—Unbounded Hospitality.. 167

CHAPTER X.—OFF FOR NEW ZEALAND.—New Passengers—Man Jumps Overboard—"Crossing the Line"—180th Meridian—The Southern Cross—Australia as Seen Through Our Eyes—The The Colony of Victoria—The City of Melbourne—A few Solid Facts... 173

CHAPTER XI.—SINGING IN AUSTRALIA.—The Mayor's Welcome—My First Night of Song in the Metropolis—Melbourne Press—First Song Sermon in Melbourne—The Trip to Ballarat—Visit to Creswick... 181

CHAPTER XII.—SINGING IN AUSTRALIA CONTINUED.—Religious Liberty in the Colonies—The Wesleyan Conference and its Management—Gospel Chariot—In the Suburbs of Melbourne—Visit to Geelong—The Great Australian Evangelist—Castlemaine, the Old Gold Fields—An Authorship Dinner—Nature and Self in Duet—Sandhurst and its Gold Rocks—A Father in the Role of Domestic Economist—The River Murray—Australian Amazon 191

CHAPTER XIII.—SINGING IN AUSTRALIA CONCLUDED—A very Bird-Like Home—Song Sermon to the Children of Melbourne—Across the River Murray—The Ovens District—The Australian Eldorado—Tea Meeting at Kilmore—From the Country to the City—Another Visit to the Interior—Free Thought Newspaper—My Services in the Smaller Towns—An Earnest Christian in Harness 202

CHAPTER XIV.—DEPARTURE FOR THE WESTERN DISTRICTS.—Warnambool—A Surprise Dinner—Chasing Kangaroos—My Song Campaign—New South Wales—Some Facts Concerning the Colony—Jokes and Jealousy—The City of Sydney—Celebrating our National Birthday............................... 212

CHAPTER XV.—THE COAL FIELDS OF AUSTRALIA.—The Granary of the Colony—Back to Sydney and its Suburbs—Over the Hills—A Missionary Family—Orangeries and Vineyards—The Author of Boomerang—Farewell Service in N. S. Wales—Illuminated Address.. 219

CHAPTER XVI.—AN EXCURSION DOWN BOTANY BAY.—Departure for South Australia—The City of Adelaide—A Pleasant Ride—A Stage Journey Inland—A National Whistle from a Magpie—Final to the Interior—Farewell Address to Mr. Phillips... 227

CHAPTER XVII.—TASMANIA, OR VAN DIEMAN'S LAND—A Few Facts Concerning the Colony—The City of Launceston—A Christian Philanthropist—Stage Journey to Hobart Town—The Tasmania Capital—Delightful Natural Scenery—Our Last Day at Melbourne—Farewell Address......................... 237

CHAPTER XVIII.—OFF FOR THE INDIAN OCEAN—Storm at Sea—King George's Sound—The Colony of West Australia—The Genuine Aboriginal and his Boomerang—Laughable Opinions—Crossing the Equator................................... 249

CHAPTER XIX.—THE ISLAND OF CEYLON—The Missionary's Life Insurance Policy—Song Service in Ceylon—The Heathen City of the Gods—Our Visit to Columbo—Men Wearing Combs.. O'er Hills with Verdure Clad—The Peredenia Gardens—The Coffee Estate of Rosenath—Service in a "Rest House"—The Grand Old Ship Mirzapore............................ 255

CHAPTER XX.—TO AND AT CALCUTTA—The Hoogly or Ganges—Calcutta, the City of Palaces—Our First Days in Hindostan—The Great Banyan Tree—Revival Services—Industrious Scenes and Localities—Description of the Idols—The Burning Ghats—None to Believe Him but Jesus—Arrival of the Prince of Wales 269

CHAPTER XXI.—NORTH INDIA, INCLUDING BENARES, LUCKNOW, AGRA, CAWNPORE, ETC.—Song Service at Noon—The Fakirs—The City of Allahabad—Riding on an Elephant—The Trip to Agra—Taj Mahal—The City of Delhi—Lucknow, the Capital of Oude—The Grave of Havelock—North India Conference at Cawnpore—Sunday Morning Conference Love Feast—Pagan and Christian Gatherings.................................. 285

CHAPTER XXII.—BOMBAY AND VICINITY—The Worshipers of the Sun—Missionary House at Byculla—Fragmentary Facts.. 305

CHAPTER XXIII.—MADRAS AND LEAVING BOMBAY—Services at Madras—Secunderabad—Bengalore, Etc.—Back to Bombay—Farewell Service in Bombay................................ 312

CHAPTER XXIV.—EN ROUTE TO PALESTINE—Suez Canal—Joppa and the Holy Land—Onward to Jerusalem—Services in Jerusalem—Our trip to the Jordan and Dead Sea—Departure from Jerusalem 316

CHAPTER XXV.—EGYPT AND CROSSING THE MEDITERRANEAN SEA—Sights in and about Cairo—A day at the Pyramids—Back to Alexandria—Cleopatra's Needle 329

CHAPTER XXVI.—ITALY AND AUSTRIA—At Sea Again—Island of Sicily—Mt. Etna—Messina—The Queen City of the Sea—Pompeii and Naples—Mt. Vesuvius—Rome, the Eternal City—Florence, the City of Art—The City of Turin—Vienna, the Capital of Austria—The City of Milan—Quaint Old City of Prague 334

CHAPTER XXVII.—GERMANY AND HOLLAND—Leipsic, the Publishing City—City of Berlin—Beautiful City of Hamburg—City of Bremen—City of Amsterdam—The Hague or Capital—City of Rotterdam... 346

CHAPTER XXVIII.—OVER THE SEA. SECOND VISIT TO ENGLAND—An English Welcome................................. 352

CHAPTER XXIX.—SINGING IN ENGLAND—Torquay—Plymouth—Exeter—Bath—Yeovil—Swansea—Merthyr Tydvil—Worcester—Kidderminster—Chester—Manchester—Still I am Singing—Huddersfield—Ireland................................ 361

CHAPTER XXX.—SINGING IN SCOTLAND—Aberdeen—The Interdicted Organ—Cauper Angus—Johnny Groat's Land—Edinburgh—Perth—Inverness—Dundee—Wick—Dumfries—New Castle-on-Tyne—Scarborough and Hull—Lincoln—Sheffield—Nottingham—Banbury—Bedford—Cambridge...................... 375

CHAPTER XXXI.—THE ENGLISH SUNDAY-SCHOOL UNION—Second Farewell Meeting to Mr. Phillips........................... 386

CHAPTER XXXII.—BRIEF ACCOUNT OF THE THIRD ENGLISH TOUR—Third English Welcome—Colchester—Louth—Boston—Newark—Peterboro—Derby—Dewsbury—Leeds—Manchester—Chesterfield—Stockport—Mexboro—Southport—Belfast—Nervey—Lisburn—Londondery—Carrickfergus—St. Helen's—Burton—Walsall—Birmingham—Worcester—Hereford—Swansea—Pembroke Docks—Gloucester, Etc., Etc.—Song Service in London—Conference Hall—City Temple—Mr. Phillips' Third Farewell to England—Arrival at Chautauqua.................... 396

CLASSIFIED INDEX OF PERSONAL MENTION................. 461

INTRODUCTION.

But few words are necessary in introducing this volume to the "wide, wide world" of general readers, and especially to that large part of it made up of persons who have listened to the songs of the singer himself—Mr. Philip Phillips—a world-wide traveler, who has compassed the globe, reaching, perhaps, a larger number of hearers than any other religious singer of our day.

There is a realm of classic music in which success has been sought and achieved by gifted and ambitious singers. They have subjected their vocal powers to the severest training, under the great masters of voice culture on two continents. They have been able to perform vocal feats rivaling in boldness and wonder the achievements of the athlete. They have studied for immediate effect. They have sought human applause, and have won it. The triumphs of a single concert have compensated them for years of patient toil and frequent failure. Amidst the ringing plaudits of enthusiastic auditors, they find reward for persistency, fatigue, expense and patient waiting.

Art in its highest forms is to be glorified. Art may indeed be of man, but man is of God; and true art is but the evolution, through human purpose, energy and skill, of the divine conception and ideal. It is legitimate and praiseworthy to seek the highest attainments in whatever line of life one has a peculiar aptitude, and to which he is by natural endowment called; for thus man may glorify his creator.

Men sometimes achieve success in specialties of thought and labor without protracted preparatory training. Native taste and tact sometimes produce the most delicate and powerful effects of high art. This is true in oratory as in music. John Summerfield, without the training of the schools, held the multitudes who thronged to hear him, spell-bound by his matchless eloquence. An Everett might well have coveted the magnetic power and peculiar grace of that young Methodist orator.

Bailey says, in "Festus," that "love is the art of hearts, and the heart of arts." The burning eloquence of Summerfield, while resulting from natural power, was also dependent largely upon the intensity of the divine love which dwelt within him.

Many of the early preachers of Methodism in England and in the far West and South of our own country, derived their success from this two-fold endowment—inborn tact and divine impulse. Some of the finest oratory ever heard on this continent has been of this natural sort—developed entirely outside of the schools.

In music we discover the same law. Culture exalts mediocrity. An ordinary voice well trained gives pleasure by its clearness, accuracy, and the perfect control in which it is held. Where genius enjoys culture, the largest results are secured; and where genius and a certain divine inspiration are combined—the inspiration of tender, genuine love—we find, even where culture may be lacking, the success already mentioned.

The modern religious awakenings on both sides of the Atlantic, as well as the enthusiasm enkindled during our civil war, now happily lying in quite a remote past, were largely attributable to the power of song—the song of the individual singer, or of great choruses, or the thunder of song from the enraptured multitudes. Mr. Moody owes a large part of his success to Mr. Sankey. It is doubtful whether he could ever, by any powers which he possesses, have achieved a tithe of his success but for the musical inspirations excited by his compeer, and the immense choirs which he had the wise policy to organize. Among the human instrumentalities which God has so abundantly blessed in this great revival movement, the principal one is the in-artistic, uncultivated, fervent singing of Sankey and his associates. In the honors to be awarded in the future by a grateful republic, the writers and singers of our most popular war songs will receive a share of the glory now bestowed so lavishly—and none too lavishly—upon the war president and his successful generals. The old "Glory, glory, hallelujah!" "Your mission," "Tramp, tramp, tramp," and others of our patriotic songs stirred the hearts of the people to their very depths and rallied the masses of the people around the banner of the nation.

In this department of naturally endowed and inspired singing we must place the subject of the present volume. In the war time and its revival services, at Sunday-school conventions and elsewhere, he has been a great blessing to the church and the nation. Untrained in the schools, as indifferent to the laws of high art in vocal performance as was John Summerfield to the mere theory of elocution, MR. PHILLIPS has perhaps done more than any man of his time for the promotion of congregational singing in the churches —the kindling of fervor in public conventions. He has been criticised by foe and friend, but he has gone steadily forward singing his simple melodies, publishing books, crossing continents and oceans, and inciting many a heart to renewed consecration and holy service.

No one claims perfection for MR. PHILLIPS; but from a personal knowledge of him for nearly twenty years, from intimate association with him in Sunday-school and church work, from long weeks of travel in his company on both sides of the continent, I am glad to be able to pay this willing tribute to his genuineness as a man, his earnestness, fidelity and conscientiousness as a Christian, his simplicity and effectiveness as a singer for the cause of humanity and Christ.   J. H. VINCENT.

PLAINFIELD, N. J., April 10, 1880.

PHILIP PHILLIP'S BIRTH-PLACE.

THE PHILLIPS FAMILY.

MR. SAWYER PHILLIPS, the father of our subject, was born at Ashfield, Massachusetts, May 16, 1791. He was a man of vigorous physical constitution, indomitable energy, and sincere practical piety. He emigrated to Chautauqua County, New York, in the year 1816, in company with his father, Philip Phillips, and consequently was one of the first settlers of the county. Western New York was, at that time, accounted one of the frontiers of civilization. Two years later he married Miss Jane Parker, a woman of superior personal qualities, with whom he spent many happy years. He became the father of fifteen children, eight of whom are living at the time of this writing. In the then new country of that far west, farming and the cooper business were most lucrative. Both vocations were understood by Mr. Phillips; by out-door and in-door industry he was ready to serve the best interests of his cherished household; and, therefore, by following one or both of these honorable occupations he managed to make a comfortable living for his numerous family. He died at Cassadaga, New York, June 4, 1871, the bride of his youth having preceded him to the better land by twenty-seven years. *Of these fifteen children, brothers and sisters of Philip, the Song Evangelist, we may venture a few words in passing, for the purpose of making the reader feel at home in the family.*

ALONZO PHILLIPS, the first born, died when a lad of five years old. He was a gentle, affectionate child, and his death was a heavy blow to his fond parents.

THOMAS D. PHILLIPS was born in 1822, married twice, has three children, practiced dentistry for many years, and has always resided at Cassadaga. The dignified appearance and pleasing address of this senior brother combine to make him the one whom the family delight to honor.

WILLISTON PHILLIPS was born in 1824; he also was twice married and has four children. He is a busy citizen and manufacturer, conducting a well-established country merchandizing in connection with a village hotel at Cassadaga. There the whole generation of Phillips are wont to gather in occasional family reunions, for it is a home of cheerfulness and plenty, abounding in everything substantial, and where the atmosphere has never been tainted by the fumes of strong drink.

ROSINA PHILLIPS was born in 1825. She was a most interesting and promising child, but was "early crowned," being called home in 1836.

ALONZO PHILLIPS was born in 1826, became a physician, and married in 1850—has three children. After practicing medicine for a number of years in the State of New York, he retired from the profession, and removed to Fredonia, where he how resides. He has decided literary tastes, has read extensively, is a student and lover of nature, and has sympathies as generous as his culture.

WILLIAM W. PHILLIPS was born in 1828, married in 1850; has four children; is a farmer and cooper, a man of generous impulses, and a rich fund of genuine humor, always ready to turn a joke in his own favor, but never to wound the most sensitive nature. He resides, at present, in Cassadaga.

CHARLES PHILLIPS was born in 1830 and married in 1858. He was for many years a teacher and merchant; and, for some time past has held the office of Justice of the Peace at Cassadaga. He enjoys the confidence of all who know him. He honors the Savior by a consistent life. His counsels are esteemed by the living, and his prayers and presence are a comfort to the dying.

SAWYER PHILLIPS was born in 1831 and died in 1854. This young man had a cheerful, sunny spirit, and for his genial manners and obliging disposition, was beloved by a large circle of acquaintances.

JOSHUA PHILLIPS was born in 1833 and died in 1850. He was a great sufferer during the last years of his short life; but all his pain was endured with patience and Christian resignation.

PHILIP PHILLIPS was born in 1834, married in 1860; has two children; is an author and singer. For six years after his marriage he resided in Ohio, then removed to the city of New York, which is now his home.

ROSINA PHILLIPS was born in 1836; married in 1862 to Milton E. Beebe. She has one child and resides in Buffalo, N.Y. Her husband is an architect, and president of the City Council. She is the only living sister, and is a sweet-spirited Christian. She cheerfully devoted herself to the care of her father to the closing moments of his life, thereby not only proving her own filial affection, but winning to herself the peculiar love which the entire family have ever bestowed upon her.

BENJ C. PHILLIPS was born in 1838 and died in 1840.

ALPHONSO R. PHILLIPS was born in 1839 and died in 1841.

G. HARRY PHILLIPS was born in 1841, married in 1865, and has five children. He is diligent in business, fervent in spirit, serving the Lord," and has an open hand toward every known duty and worthy object of need. He resides in Springfield, Ohio.

Z. BARNEY PHILLIPS was born in 1843, married in 1866, and died in 1879. He has four children. He served three years in the Federal army during the civil war; traveled considerably with his brother Philip in his musical tours, and was thus brought into closest sympathy with him in this lifework. He was the youngest of the family. Nature endowed him with superior taste and tact, with rare talent for making and keeping friends, and his Christian integrity sustained him in secular affairs. The home paper (*Springfield Republican*) thus speaks of him:

"The deceased was long known in Springfield as a successful business man, of generous impulses, honor, and the strictest integrity, always carrying his Christian principles into his secular affairs.

"He was an active member of the High Street M. E. Church, and was for years a very successful superintendent of the Sabbath-school with that organization. He was everybody's friend—always courteous, pleasant and helpful, and was therefore, very popular personally, and universally beloved.

"He was very patient throughout his long illness, and died at last very peacefully, trusting in his Savior. His last letter was written to his brother Philip, wherein he stated, 'My faith is sure and steadfast, anchored in Christ. No storm can shake me or cause it to drag.'"

The surviving members of the Phillips family are all healthy, industrious, and well received in the communities where they dwell. A common trait of character among them is good humor. From their parents they received a practical and vigilant instruction; but there was no rigid domestic exaction, no severe discipline, such only as military or police regulations warrant toward inevitable law-breakers. There was a sunny freedom every day in the Phillips home.

Some new joy dawned out of every new morning the whole year round. Love was the ruling impulse. The children were early made to feel their individual responsibilities, and to understand their relative duties toward each other and toward their parents. There was the utmost confidence reposed by father and mother in their offspring; and this loving trust challenged the best behavior, secured a uniform obedience, and kindled an ever-brightening affection. And through all the home administration there shone a constant cheerfulness. It was a household where song and joy prevailed. And hence the intensity of life which beams in every Phillips face. It is the gospel-loving kindness; and its sure sign is a smile, even in the test of a great sorrow, or in the depth of a sore bereavement. It feels most keenly every grief; it is sensitive to every untoward influence and circumstance; it can weep freely; but it surmounts trouble, and gets forward with agile step and with thanksgiving.

BIOGRAPHY.

BY REV. ALEXANDER CLARK, D.D.

IN Chautauqua County, New York, in a plain farm house, at the foot of a wooded hill, Philip Phillips began his song—in a minor key. For he was a minor of minors himself. The time was August 13, 1834. This first song was perhaps, nothing new or strange in the Phillips household for this noisy youngster was the seventh in the squalling scale. The six other children as they came in their regular order of about one year and a half apart, no doubt had introduced themselves by the same key. Philip's lungs, however, tradition informs us, proved to be as elastic in this first exercise as those of his stoutest baby predecessor; and why not? He was the prophet of his own career.

When about five years of age he used to be frequently called upon to sing by the neighbors who dropped in to visit the parents. Before complying with such requests, he would always settle himself in the family cradle, and then rock himself vigorously all the time he sang. This rocking accompaniment seemed to be necessary to his success, as well as to his own enjoyment of the exercise.

FIRST PUBLIC SINGING.

When he was yet a very small boy, Philip made his first public appearance in sacred song. It came about in this way: His father had taken him to the village church, one day, when it so happened that some difficulty arose about the singing. The minister, the Rev. Mr. Peckham, gave out the familiar hymn,

"When I can read my title clear,"

And the choir attempted to sing it to a tune somewhat new. All were not artists, of course, in that country choir, and, after some scrambling around among tones and half-tones, they made an utter failure on the first verse. Now, the minister had chanced to hear Philip sing this same attempted tune at home; and, either for a just rebuke to the singers for their lack of preparation, or as an easy and novel way of getting all parties through the emergency, he came down to the pew and asked the little fellow if he would not sing the hymn. Philip accordingly stood up and sang it all through *alone*. The effect can be more easily imagined than described.

Even in these tender years the boy had a mind well stored with religious songs, taught him by his father around the family hearth; and they, no doubt, have been very powerful agents in moulding his life, and in giving it the special bias for sacred song, which has so greatly blessed the world. Many of the old-time hymns are as fresh in the mind of Mr. Phillips to-day as when learned, years ago, beside his father's knee. Among his other favorites was an old hymn now rarely seen in our collections, which seems to have made a deep impression upon the young singer's mind. On account of the peculiar suggestiveness of the words, when taken in connection with his pilgrim life, we reproduce the quaint stanzas as a rest in the narrative at this point.

"WANDERING PILGRIM."

Come all ye wandering pilgrims dear,
  That's bound for Canaan's land,
Take courage and fight valiantly,
  Stand fast with sword in hand.
Your Captain's gone before you,
  Your Father's only Son,
Then pilgrims, dear, don't let us fear
  But boldly travel on.

We've a dark, howling wilderness,
  To Canaan's peaceful shore.
The lands are drought, and pits and snares,
  And chilling winds do roar.
But Jesus, He'll go with us,
  And guide us on our way,
If enemies examine us,
  He'll teach us what to say.

Good morning, brother traveler
  Pray tell me what's your name,
And where is it you're going to,
  Also, from whence you came.
My name it is Bold Pilgrim,
  To Canaan I am bound,
I'm from the howling wilderness,
  To the enchanting ground.

Pray, what is that upon your head
  That shines so clear and bright?
Likewise the covering of your breast,
  So dazzling to my sight?
What kind of shoes are those you wear,
  On which you boldly stand?
And what's that shining instrument
  You wave in your right hand?

'Tis glorious hope, upon my head,
  And on my breast, my shield,
With this bright sword I mean to fight
  Until I win the field.
My feet are shod with gospel peace,
  On which I boldly stand,
And fight I will until I die,
  I'll win fair Canaan's land.

You'd better stay with me, pilgrim,
  And give your journey o'er,
Your Captain, He is out of sight
  His face you'll see no more.
My name it is Apolyon,
  This land belongs to me,
And for your arms, and pilgrim dress,
  I'll give it all to thee.

Mistaken fiend, the pilgrim said,
  Your offer I disdain,
A glittering crown of glory I
  Shall shortly there obtain.
If I but hold out faithfully
  To my dear Lord's command,
I'll jointly there, be with an heir,
  Of Canaan's promised land.

It has been said, and often quoted, "let me make the ballads of a country, and I care not who make the laws." Music takes a firmer hold upon the public heart than almost anything else; and the quality of a nation's popular songs will greatly determine its moral and political force among its neighbors. No wonder Philip Phillips became a traveler. His earliest songs speak of pilgrimage and journeying; and as he learned to sing he was unconsciously but inevitably led into a love of travel. Living in the country, Philip, as a matter of course, attended the country district school, and for many summers his voice was the leading one in the school songs, as he was wont to sit among the smaller children on the low front seats.

FIRST SCHOOL TEACHER.

This first school teacher—Miss Romina Jennings,—after thirty years, thus writes to him: "Are you the little Phillips boy who used to sing so loud and sweet the song, 'Try, Try Again?'" She had heard of the Singing Pilgrim and the great success of his "Evenings of Song," and wondered if it could really be her former pupil who had made such a worthy fame in the world. That God had made him instrumental of so much good in the use of his early gift, must indeed, have been a source of much gratification to the faithful teacher. Mr. Phillips says, in speaking of her letter: "There it is again! Although you *do* forget the singer, you can not forget the song." This has been the philosophy of Mr. Phillips' entire musical pilgrimage. We felt that he had been ordained to his new ministration of the gospel, in the natural gift of his voice, and that though the people all around the world might forget his name and face, yet the gospel news would remain with them, and bear fruit in God's good time. And is it not a mark of true advancement, in the people of this age, that they have learned to avail themselves of the avenues of man's great and universal passions, in order to carry divine truth into the soul? Only when the fruit of every faculty, and the outcome of every taste shall be something to add to the best thought of God in the world, will He be fully glorified by men. But let us return to Philip. Our thoughts have been on pilgrimage. His mind received its first impressions of duty and of God from

HIS MOTHER.

What can equal the consecrated influence of woman in the most holy of all sanctuaries, the home!

Save to us the motherhood of the race, and you have saved the race. When every mother in the land shall feel her children to be the gift of God, and shall instruct them by word and example, in the Christian life, then truly will the kingdom of God be near at hand: for He cannot break His promise to those who dedicate themselves and their children to Him in faith.

Though greatly burdened by domestic cares, often crying cares, indeed, as there was almost always a babe in the family—Philip's mother was in the habit of taking each one of the children to her room, separately, and there asking God's blessing upon its precious life. She did this even when they were yet very young, but the holy influence of those sacred moments alone with mother and God, has extended over the whole lives of some of that home-circle of brothers and sisters. Though Philip was only nine years of age when that devoted mother was called to heaven, her prayers and teachings are fresh in his mind to this day.

MEMORIAL INCIDENT.

One little incident is remembered well by him, which shows what tact she possessed in seizing upon small opportunities for impressing religious truth. It was hay-making time. The little fellow was out in the lot where one of his brothers was mowing, and coming too near the scythe in his pranks, had cut his foot pretty badly. In great terror at the sight of blood, which began to flow profusely, he ran limping and screaming to the house. It was not that he was in so much pain that he manifested such alarm, but that he believed he would die from the wound. He always supposed blood to be a *sure* forerunner of death, and he did not wish to die. On reaching the house and explaining the accident, he found the ever-sympathetic mother ready to soothe and help, as no one else could do. While dressing the wound, he tremblingly put to her the all-absorbing question: "Mother, how soon will I die?" No doubt she was surprised at the strange question, not being able to read what had been passing in the boy's mind since seeing that blood, but with a quick sense of the favorable moment for doing her child good, rather than of merely comforting him, she answered: "Oh, Phillie, I don't know. Don't you think we had better pray?" Thus she taught him that "God is a refuge and strength, a very present help in trouble." How indelibly this little interview was engraved upon the young mind! It has recurred to him over and over again, when in the midst of danger; and the gentle words of his mother: "Don't you think we had better pray?" have followed him everywhere, and fallen like a benediction into his soul in many a trying time. He remembers, of the occurrence, only this mere fragment of the conversation. He does not recollect whether his foot hurt him much or not; but this counsel on the matter of prayer will go with him to the end of his life. Mothers often excuse themselves from a careful religious teaching of their children upon the plea of their numerous domestic duties, and think they have fully canceled their obligations to God if they send the little ones, once a week, to the Sunday-school. It is a vain hope. A child dressed up in all its Sunday finery is not in the receptive condition in which the mother might find it a dozen times through the course of the week. Little Philip Phillips had a very different feeling in his heart, there in that farm-house kitchen, having his cut foot doctored, and believing that he would die, than any Sunday-school teacher could have aroused in him when everything seemed going right. The morning and the evening prayer, the Christian talks with the children, day by day, as they were tempted to do wrong, and all the numberless loop-holes by which the mother is enabled to look into the soul of her child, give her peculiar advantages for doing them good in spiritual things. She is pre-eminently the true religious teacher of youth. Nature has constituted her such. The Sunday-school teacher can supplement the work of the mother, but should not be expected to atone for its loss. And as for the "cumbering cares" of mothers with large families, the case of Mrs. Phillips shows plainly that if there be the spirit, the opportunities will soon be discerned; yes, and they can be improved without loss of time, in the busiest days. A child does not need to be continually lectured or prayed with; but let it know that there is the deepest sincerity on the part of the parents, and a very few words will suffice to impress it. All mothers can find an occasional corner of time to be thus employed if they desire the privilege of such service.

HIS MOTHER'S DEATH.

As before mentioned, Philip was only about nine years old when his mother died. This was certainly the saddest bereavement that could have befallen him. It was even worse for the five children who were younger than he, and who so much more needed his mother's care. The last babe was just a year old the month that the mother was called upon to resign it to other arms, leave it to theirs and the Heavenly Father's care. Ah, who can picture the desolation of that family when the heart-broken father sat in sorrow beside his motherless babes, in the darkened home?

What an outlook for him, when nearly all were too small to be trusted to themselves, and all boys but one. He felt that indeed his hour of trial had come, and that all that could be done was to

> "Bow the knee and kiss the rod,
> And perfect grow through grief."

HIS MOTHER'S FUNERAL

Mrs. Phillips was well known through all the country around; and being held in high esteem, her loss was felt in the entire neighborhood. Many of nearer acquaintance felt it to be a personal bereavement. Consequently, when the hour for the funeral arrived, vehicles and mounted riders came from all directions to attend the sad service. Every public road, and every by-road furnished carriages or wagons to the long procession, which moved slowly and mournfully from the family residence to the village church, three miles distant, over the hills. In this sad company were an unusually large number of women, who thus testified to their departed sister's worth. Reaching the church, this mile-procession found the space already crowded by the people of the village who came to mingle their tears with those of the stricken friends and family from the country. It was a memorable funeral.

The sermon, preached by the Rev. Remington, was based upon Psalms xlvi. 10, "Be still, and know that I am God." The providence seemed so unusually dark, considering the helplessness of the family, that there was a special fitness in these words, as calculated to remind men, that when God works, human opinions should be deferred until such time as He should make His wisdom understood. It gave a rest to the spiritual feet, where everything else seemed to be slipping away. The hymns sung upon the occasion were these:

> "Sister, thou wast mild and lovely,
> Gentle as the summer breeze."

> "Thou art gone to the grave,
> But we will not deplore thee."

> "Why do we mourn departing friends,
> Or shake at death's alarm?"

Philip felt that, in the music, his dumb sorrow found voice. Those old-fashioned hymns have ever since occupied a sacred place in his memory.

At this funeral were representatives of three generations of the Phillips family, the grandfather of eighty years, the husband of the deceased, and his eleven motherless children. Philip has since attended the weird orgies of many a foreign burial, but none ever impressed him so deeply with the solemnity of death as this leaving of his mother among the dead.

PHILIP AND JOSHUA LEAVE HOME.

After the funeral plans were discussed among the relatives, who decided that Philip and his older brother Joshua should go and live with their uncle, Clark Parker, twelve miles away. They left the old home with all its hallowed associations of Mother, and a thousand dear domestic joys, feeling for the first time in their lives, probably, the indescribable loneliness of orphanage. Though going among kind relatives, they could not forget the sudden calamity which had sent them there and the new made mound in the village burial ground. Poor little Philip took the change so much to heart that, after a short time he was compelled to return home. In speaking of this sad time afterward, he said that it often appeared to him that he should die of sheer homesickness. Ah, brother Philip, other souls than thine have felt this bitterness! Others, too, have experienced, some time or another in life, this first heart heaviness that even tears will not relieve. This is the utter desolateness which now we know by its proper name—home-sickness. It is the process of inoculation which makes us only liable to a mild form of the disease ever after. No doubt Philip Phillips endured more positive agony, twelve miles from home, in that experience, than he has at any time since with continents and oceans between him and his loved ones. And it is well that the heart can outlive its childhood's sorrows.

MISS MABEL FORBUSH.

An old family friend who had been with Mrs. Phillips some time previous to, and through her illness, consented to remain awhile and help keep the house in order. She seemed a special providence to the children, with her careful forethought and tender sympathy. The world is more deeply indebted, perhaps, than it is willing to acknowledge, to the class of women which Miss Forbush represents. Having renounced, for themselves, the closer relationships of love and home, they give their lives to the general good of the communities where they dwell, filling up gaps made in other homes, and by their heartsome presence and unselfish ministrations, banishing many a cloud of grief from stricken souls. Is it not, indeed, upon such patient, chastened faces all over the land, that the Master's smile floods down to-day, as He marks the agony that is crushed out of sight for others' sake? Truly, such women are ministering angels, and "great is their reward in heaven."

After his father married the second time, the new mother came into the home with her four children, making an already large family still larger by the accession. Each one of the children was brought in upon the memorable occasion, and introduced separately to their new relative. When it came Philip's turn, his strange emotions proved too much for him. Upon coming into the presence of his stepmother he burst into a passion of tears. He had never felt before how absolutely his own mother was lost to them. After a time he felt inclined to go and live with a neighbor, Joel Fisher, do chores and go to school. His father consented reluctantly to the arrangement, and accompanied his boy upon his new venture. Although he had another attack of home-sickness, it did not approach, in magnitude, the first one, and he soon became accustomed to the change. He remained here for more than a year, attending to farm matters in the summer, and going to the country school in winter. Then occurred the death of Mr. Fisher, when Philip again went back to his father's house, where he remained a year or so, with something of the old home feeling restoerd.

About this time a neighbor, Benjamin W. Grant, proposed that Philip should come and board with him, help about the farm and the dairy, and attend school. To this plan he readily consented, as he could thereby go to the same school, where his brothers went, and therefore would not be virtually separated from them. Giving good satisfaction, his employer desired him to remain after the school had closed, and, persuading him by better inducements, he again assented to the proposition. Mr. Grant promised that if Philip would remain with him until he was of age, assisting in the work as required, that he should be "set off" with one hundred dollars and two suits of clothes. This seemed a very fair offer, and after consulting his father, the arrangement was closed, and an indenture drawn up and carried out in full. But Philip's father could not sign it after all, yet Philip, at the time supposed he had done so. As a specimen of the transactions of other days, and as suggestive to boys of the present, who, favored and protected at home, sometimes complain of parental restraints, this indenture is herewith submitted.

THIS INDENTURE WITNESSETH:—That Philip Phillips, of the town of Stockton, in the county of Chautauqua, and State of New York, now aged fourteen years, by and with the consent of Sawyer Phillips, his father, endorsed hereupon, hath voluntarily and of his own free will and accord put and bound himself apprentice or servant to Benjamin W. Grant, of the town, county and state aforesaid, to learn the art of farming and also that of manufacturing cheese, and as an apprentice to serve from this date for and during and until the full end and term of six years and three months next ensuing, or until the said Philip Phillips shall have attained the age of twenty-one years, which will be on the thirteenth day of August in the year fifty-five, during all which time the said Philip shall serve the said Grant faithfully, honestly, and industriously; his secrets keep; all commands everywhere readily obey; at all times protect and preserve the goods and property of his said master and not allow or suffer any to be injured or wasted. He shall not buy or sell or traffic with his own goods or with the goods of others, nor be absent from his master's service without leave, but in all things behave himself as a faithful servant ought to do during the said term, and the said Grant shall clothe and provide for the said Philip in sickness and in health, and supply him with suitable food and clothing; and shall use and employ the utmost of his endeavors to teach or cause him to be taught or instructed in the art of farming and dairying, and also cause the said Philip within such term to be instructed in the general branches of education taught in the common school by providing him with such books as shall be necessary for the same. And also by sending him to school three months in each year during the said term, and at the end of the said term give the said Philip a new Bible. And also the said Grant agrees to give to the said Philip when he shall arrive at the age of twenty-one years two suits of clothes; one to be of a common quality, and one to be a handsome suit; also the said Grant further agrees that if the said Philip should enjoy his health during said term as well as the average of persons at that age he will at the end of said term pay to the said Philip the sum of one hundred dollars.

And for the true performance of all and singular the covenants and agreements aforesaid, the said parties bind themselves each unto the other, firmly by these presents.

In witness whereof the parties aforesaid have hereunto set their hands and seals, the —— day of May, in the year of our Lord one thousand eight hundred and forty-nine.

Signed, sealed, and delivered } BENJAMIN W. GRANT. [L.S.]
in presence of } PHILIP PHILLIPS. [L.S.]

Dated the 15th day of May, 1849.

Philip greatly respected this family, and with it found a most comfortable home. Mrs. Grant and her daughter Myra, now Mrs. Webb Warren, were both exceedingly kind to him; Mr. Grant was strict, dignified, systematic, but always self-possessed and considerate. Here the boy had all the healthful employment of a dairy farm for several years,—milking, plowing, chopping wood, making maple sugar, and such odd chores as are common in quiet country life. This helped materially to give him the healthy constitution which is to-day, apparently, as vigorous as in his boyhood. If young persons, these days, could mix such energizing occupation with their college and high school courses, we should soon have a race of intellectual giants where now we see but weaklings. The mind is directly dependent upon the body for its supplies of power; and a good digestion does much more toward making a lad in school a great man by-and-by than a dozen professors. A certain modern writer puts it in this emphatic way: "The first requisite to success in life, is to be a good animal;" and tersely adds, "A weak mind in a herculean frame is better than a giant mind in a crazy constitution." Young men who covet great learning would do well to bear these thoughts in mind. Let them adopt the surest method of reaching their desired end, viz: by attaining to as perfect physical health as is possible, upon which to feed the mind.

Mr. Grant was considered one of the most successful dairy farmers in Chautauqua county, and while with him our young singer mastered the art—that of butter and cheese making, he used to go after the sixty or eighty cows (all of which he knew by name) and bring them from the pasture for milking. He usually milked ten, night and morning, and almost invariably sang as he milked. The cows actually seemed to expect the singing, and would grow restive if they did not hear it, so greatly had the pleasant habit influenced the dumb creatures. His milk-yard songs came to be remarked by the neighboring farmers who passed that way; and when rallied upon the point, the lad would modestly reply: "The cows kick and hook if I do not sing— and sometimes they hook and kick all the same if I do."

HIS WORK THE YEAR ROUND.

Young Phillips' regular work for the year was divided about as follows: from March to the end of April, sugar-making—Philip collecting the sap from seven hundred and ninety trees, with a two horse sled. From the end of April to July, plowing, sowing, hoeing, and making fence. From July to October gathering the hay and harvesting. October and November were usually more or less occupied by felling trees, chopping wood, making rails, and preparing for winter. From November to March was the only time for attending school. Such was our young singer's yearly work while on the farm. A distant relative of his mother, familiarly known to them as

AUNT SALLIE SMITH,

was a near neighbor to Mr. Grant. She used often to call Philip in and have him sing for her, and then, during the interview, she would talk with him about his mother. Her sympathetic nature was drawn out toward the boy, and she did much, during that formative period of his life to cheer him on his way. It was his delight, after a day of depression, to step over to "Aunt Sallie's," and spend an hour or two in talking things over, and in getting back that home feeling which kinship alone inspires. She was one of the greatest blessings of his boyhood. Her piety and kindness kept his heart from growing close, and his judgment hard, in that important era of his life. A peril touches every child somewhere, and at this peculiar crisis when verging upon the years of manhood or womanhood, the necessity for a judicious and confidential friend is indeed imperative.

"Aunt Sallie" lived to a good old age. She has since joined Philip's sainted mother in heaven; but the memory of her Christian counsel will abide in the Singing Pilgrim's soul forever.

FIRST SINGING SCHOOL.

In the fall of 1850 Mr. Samuel Howard organized a singing class in the neighborhood. Mr. Grant gave Philip an opportunity to attend; so after his day's work, he would walk two miles twice a week to learn the rudiments of music. Mr. Howard had a good voice, and understood what he was teaching. The "Dulcimer," by I. B. Woodbury, was the first book used, and after that the "Shawm," by W. B. Bradbury, was introduced. Our young singer became greatly interested in his studies, and would occasionally interrupt the singing of the class to ask for a fuller explanation, so determined was he to become an adept in the science he so greatly loved. In a short time he had become so proficient in reading music, that he was invited to become a member of the church choir, which was one of the best in that country. Thus, at the age of sixteen, he had gained one of his early ambitions.

HIS CONVERSION.

In the winter of 1851, a protracted meeting was held in the Baptist Church at Delanti, New York, under the pastoral charge of Rev. B. C. Willoughby. Philip Phillips was first attracted to the meeting by the singing, as well as by the usual love of novelty and excitement, common among young men of quiet country places. His interest deepened, however, as the days passed on, and he became thoughtful and anxious about his soul. He began to feel the need of a personal Savior. At last he opened his heart to Henry, Mr. Grant's eldest son, who, it seems, had also been under conviction. The two boys agreed to go forward among the seekers at the next meeting, each one promising to go if the other would do the same. These partnerships of inquiry do not always magnify individuality of character; but it is because self must be minified, humiliated and forgotten before the matchless love of Christ Jesus who is all and in all. The joint approach of two or more confiding friends, toward the foot of the cross, is always beautiful; for so the loving disciples grouped about Calvary and the garden in the days of our Lord's passion and victory.

Well! the set time came. The next evening found our two interested young friends in an audience of mixed motives and varied emotions, but resolute to do their duty at the cost of whatever criticism. Philip, however, was seized with strange misgivings. He thought he was resolute; but in the moment when most he needed that grace, his courage forsook him. He felt that he could not face that great congregation. The minister announced and the people sang the following well known hymn:

> "I'm a pilgrim, and I'm a stranger,
> I can tarry, I can tarry but a night.
> Do not detain me, for I am going
> To where the fountains are ever flowing;
> I'm a pilgrim, and I'm a stranger,
> I can tarry, I can tarry but a night.
>
> "There the glory is ever shining ;
> Oh, my longing heart, my longing heart is there,
> Here in this country so dark and dreary,
> I long have wandered forlorn and weary,
> I'm a pilgrim and I'm a stranger,
> I can tarry, I can tarry but a night.
>
> "There's the city to which I journey ;
> My Redeemer, my Redeemer is its light,
> There is no sorrow, nor any sighing,
> Nor any tears there, nor any dying;
> I'm a pilgrim, and I'm a stranger,
> I can tarry, I can tarry but a night."

All through the singing of this hymn Philip was filled with chaotic emotions. At its close the minister said, with great solemnity, "I feel that some persons here to-night are grieving the spirit. Let us repeat the last verse." The trembling boy, touched by this remark, received it as addressed to him alone. With crimson face and beating heart, he pressed to his place among the bowing penitents. It was a hard struggle with his pride, but he gained the victory.

Philip walked home alone that night. It was December. The ground was covered with snow; but above him the moon and stars were shining. He walked along meditatively through the snow. He felt that he had done his duty. In his heart he was waiting for the Lord. And who ever sought the Lord earnestly and failed to receive a gracious response?

Was that a word dropped from the clear skies above him? He could not tell; but it fell right into his expectant soul: "Go in peace; thy sins are forgiven thee." He felt uplifted to the very throne. The new song which was put upon his lips then filled his raptured heart with gladness; and it is the song which he has been singing ever since, with sweeter and deeper gratitude with every added year of blessing.

The meetings continued; and many of young Philip's friends and neighbors were made sharers in the spiritual joy which he had experienced. At the following covenant-meeting, Philip with others, made a public confession of faith, was baptized in the creek near by, and united with the Baptist church. His parents were members of this church, and here he had always attended service. That was a winter never to be forgotten.

A NARROW ESCAPE.

Early the next summer Philip had a narrow escape from drowning. A large company of young people assembled at Cassadaga for a picnic on the lake near by. There is an island across the lake, and on it was a grove, where the pleasure-seekers meant to hold their festivities that day. Some of them were to go over in skiffs and flat-bottomed boats, while the others would drive or walk over by way of the bridge. With all the usual merriment of such occasions the party met at the shore of the lake. A small skiff, containing six persons, started out first in the mimic fleet; and this was followed soon after by a flat-boat, in which were fourteen ladies and seven gentlemen. The number was greater than should have been admitted into the boat; but there was a reluctance to leaving any behind; therefore the fatal risk was taken. The weight of the passengers brought the top of the boat almost to the water's edge. But the surface of the lake was smooth as glass, not a ripple responsive to the almost imperceptible breath of the air. All went well until they had reached the middle of the lake, when, by some mishap or mismanagement, the smaller boat capsized. This accident created consternation in the larger boat, which was so heavily loaded and so ill adjusted for confused movements on board. By a sudden movement of the passengers, the boat dipped water, lurched to one side and sank to the bottom, leaving its frightened occupants all struggling in the water. The boatman and six ladies were drowned. Many of the gentlemen, being good swimmers, succeeded in dragging several of the ladies to the shore, and thus saved them from drowning; but all could not possibly be rescued. The disaster was indeed a fearful one. Philip was so exhausted by swimming the long distance to the shore, that he sank down even when near enough to land to have walked out in safety, and would certainly have been drowned had not his brother Charles come to his assistance. He was taken immediately to his brother Williston's house, in Cassadaga, where lay upon the parlor floor the dead bodies of three of his companions.

Night fell, and with it the dark curtain of a thunderstorm. Pealing thunder echoed around the horizon of the fatal lake, or moaned dismally over the watery graves of the dead. In the lightning's glare, which, at fitful intervals, lit up the lake and shore, could be seen the forms of eager searchers, dragging the treacherous waters for the missing bodies. It was a strange, weird scene of horror, a night of gloom, the shadows of which have never been fully lifted away. The funeral was solemn and impressive. Eight coffins side by side! The pale sleepers were representatives of the youth and beauty of the place. Their launch into eternity was a sudden surprise, a startling prov-

silence, and the neighborhood was appalled. Seven of the young people who met this untimely death belonged in and about Delanti, where their bodies now rest in the slumber of one common grave, in the village church-yard. The lesson of this direful calamity, whatever may have been the momentary pang, has lingered in gracious influences in many hearts, to this day.

AMBITION FOR MUSICAL TRAINING.

As the months came and went, Philip's desire to advance in music increased. He urged Mr. Grant to get him a violin. He, however, gave him no encouragement that he would do so; and hence the boy was left with his longing unsatisfied. About this time a Mr. Adams Davis began a singing school in the village. Philip became a member of his class, and made rapid progress. The teacher was agent for George A. Prince's melodeons, and sold a number of these instruments to the parents of his pupils. One day when Philip went home from school, he found Mr. Davis at the house, and a new melodeon standing in the room. He was surprised, indeed, to see that when the agent was ready to leave, he made no motion to take the instrument along with him. "Is he going to leave his melodeon?" whispered Philip, aside, to Mrs. Grant. The kind motherly eyes could no longer conceal the secret. She looked into his eager face, and anticipated his joy, while she said, "Well, Philip, what's the use of having money if you cannot use it? we have bought this melodeon for you, but you must not neglect your work or studies on account of it." The lad's gratitude can scarcely be imagined. His heart was filled to overflowing. (Not having any particular information on the subject, the reader may conclude from the typical "boy" that he celebrated the event by dancing all over the kitchen floor, cracking his heels together, or by turning any number of matchless hand-springs, and possibly one or two successful summersaults in honor of the occasion.) At any rate we know from his own lips since, that he was actually so happy that he could not sleep. Such an over-joy as this was to Philip does not often come to any human life.

And we may rest assured that his work did not linger on his hands, after this, but was dispatched in incredibly short time, that he might rush to his practice. Every moment was occupied, and very soon he was able to accompany his voice with the instrument in several tunes. He was patient and persevering. Little by little he overcame the intricacies of flats and sharps, white and black, and began to discover possible depths of sweetness and harmony beneath the arbitrary conditions of the key-board. For the scale is an alphabet, the spelling, the reading, and the rhetoric of music are possible only to him who masters the letters. This Philip did. He began at the beginning. He touched the radical resources of the science at the right place and time, and was consequently an inventor of accordant combinations, as well as a performer of written harmonies. After four months diligent practice, our young enthusiast, like most sanguine musicians in their teens, felt himself prepared to play in the church. It was indeed a great moment for him, when, with the eyes of all the people upon him, he started out with the choir on a hymn, a greater moment, when he found himself fumbling wildly over the key-board in his efforts to "catch up." *He had gone back to correct a mistake*, and the choir had gone on complacently without him! He soon learned that playing for himself at home, and playing for a choir at church, were two very different things.

About this time a Mrs. Paulding came into the town to give lessons on the piano and melodeon. Philip was too poor to pay ten dollars a term, much as he needed and desired the instruction. His brother, Williston, however, came to his aid and told him, one day, while at Cassadaga, that he would advance him ten dollars, and let the debt stand until he could conveniently cancel it. Accordingly the arrangements were made, and Philip began his first lessons in figured bass. His faithful attention to the study soon made him a fair country player.

The organization of Good Templars first began to arrest attention at this time, and Philip became popular as a singer of temperance songs. His fine voice helped much to call out the people who knew his gift. When thus drawn together, new lodges were formed, or the old ones strengthened by new members. In this way he spent several months, going from place to place, and singing his temperance songs. His talent increased under the stimulus of these exercises, and the desire to devote himself exclusively to music grew stronger every day. Mr. Grant must have marked his uneasiness under the routine of farm work; for he soon proposed that Philip should sing and teach, as his fancy directed, and with the proceeds, pay a man to take his place on the farm. This suited him exactly; and so, the supply being obtained, our hero-student went at his music heart and soul.

HIS FIRST TEACHING.

At the age of nineteen, he began his first singing school at Allegheny, New York. Through the influence of his brother, who was the leading physician of the place, and the Rev. E. F. Crane, he succeeded in organizing a large class. This he taught with great satisfaction for several terms. He sold Prince's melodeons, also, and received a per centage on all his sales. He closed his singing school with a public concert, which elicited high encomiums from the entire community, and which, no doubt, had no inconsiderable influence on the work of his after-life.

A BAND OF INDIANS.

Just after his school had closed, a band of twelve Indians

itinerated through the place. They were under the conduct of a minister by the name of Raymond, and were engaged in giving concerts in various towns, for the benefit of an Indian school near Towanda, New York. Philip trained them in singing, and, being pleased with his methods and manners, they and their agent desired him to accompany them to New York City, offering him one hundred dollars a month. The opportunity, promising not only a handsome remuneration, but also a sight of the great metropolis, seemed too good a one to be lost, and after consulting with his brother, Alonzo, it was decided that he should go with them for a short time at least, and in the meantime he would write the particulars of the arrangement to his father, and ask his advice about retaining the position. When information on the wisdom of this proceeding was received from home, it was to strongly urge him to abandon so novel a scheme, and return. His father feared the associations which might be brought to bear upon his boy, therefore after spending a few days with them he returned, and resumed his teaching, continuing this business in connection with that of introducing musical instruments into the homes of the people, until he became of age. He now thinks that his father did a very wise thing in dissuading him from the tutorship of the roving Indian band; for with his youthful ardor and inexperience, there is no telling into what temptations he might have fallen.

When Philip came to settle with Mr. Grant, he found that the interest on the sum paid for the melodeon left him in his guardian's debt twenty-five dollars. He gave his note for this amount and paid it when it became due; so his capital at the age of twenty-one was—his music. However, having had such success in his early attempts in the prosecution of his art, he was enabled to go on with courage and vigor in the way he had planned for the future. Soon after attaining his majority, a gentleman highly respected, and of influence in the neighborhood, proposed to enter into the music business with Philip. The bargain having been made, a substantial and somewhat ornamental wagon was fitted out, and a fine span of horses obtained, prospective of the musical tours throughout the adjacent country. The intention was to sing, to sell instruments, and, perhaps, to arrange for singing classes. But as the preparation went forward it was plainly seen that Philip had made an unfortunate choice of a partner. It seemed impossible for him to rid his mind of the idea of speculation. He bought fruit, produce, etc., etc., which he thought they could dispose of to a profit through the country. Of course, this was out of the line of the original business contemplated by the co-partnership. Philip was greatly annoyed by the evident mistake he had made. He could not think patiently of degrading his music by peddling it out along with other wares of speculation; hence, after a free discussion of the subject, the partnership was mutually dissolved. There was no personal alienation, however; it was a matter of business which righted itself by each man diverging, naturally, toward his legitimate calling. The result of the settlement was a maturing of better plans by which Philip should go alone.

His ideas were not extravagant. One small buggy with an arrangement for carrying a melodeon behind the seat was deemed sufficient for the purpose. The next thing was to purchase a horse. One of the neighbors, a deacon, had an animal to sell. Now Philip had always a great reverence for deacons in general, considering them a degree above ordinary church members in example, and in authority, and in piety. At least such was the conception of the young musician. When, therefore, this deacon, the venerated leader in spiritual affairs, enlarged upon the fine qualities of his horse, and assured Philip that his was exactly the animal he needed, the meek listener believed all he heard, and readily bought the horse for one hundred and twenty-five dollars. He was delighted with his purchase. As soon as the technicalities of the transaction were ended, Philip went to the deacon's pasture for his horse, caught him easily, and mounted and rode him into the village without bridle or bit.

It having from time immemorial been the custom among the rural population to include in every sale of a horse a halter also, and none having been furnished in this instance, Philip asked the deacon about it. "Oh," said the deacon, "This horse is so gentle that he needs no halter," and therefore, on the plea of the animal's amiability, he refused to supply it. A hitching strap was necessary, however and obtaining one, Philip put it upon his horse. It was then that the extraordinary qualities of the animal began to be apparent; for no sooner had the strap been placed upon his head, and hitched than he began to plunge, and pull backward with all his might. Indeed so violent were his exercises in this line, that Philip feared he would pull his head off; so his new owner cut the strap, letting the beast fall heavily backward. While he was righting himself, however, and developing more and more of those "excellent qualities" which the deacon had attributed to him, an alien thought crept into Philip's mind: *What if he had been cheated in his bargain?*

His first thought was to go to the deacon, which he immediately did. He felt that something needed explanation. He was disheartened, and slightly provoked. He was in a mood to be advised and comforted. It was a serious business with him, for it involved other questions, and very much depended on the truthfulness of the deacon's word. Philip found the deacon who greeted him with that placid, pious smile which is peculiar, if not to the just man, at least to just such men, and the professionality which assumes the place of conscience.

The discomfited Philip explained the case to him, told of the remarkable actions of the horse which he had bought as free from blemish, and inquired what it meant. The deacon heard his story with unmoved countenance, and then laughed softly as he remarked, " I told you the horse did not need a halter, he always stands without." This was the sum total of his consolation from the deacon. Some one then told Philip to get a strong rope, and tie it around the horse's neck. He did so; but no sooner did the wary animal find that he was hitched than he began to pull as frantically as before. His owner stood mute with amazement, discouraged, and with a lurking suspicion of the integrity of horses and deacons generally, for that wandering thought again came into his mind: *Had he been cheated ?* If so, what next ?

Presently another proposition was made to him. A Mr. Fisher suggested that he take his horse down to the lake and hitch him to a boat-post there; when if he pulled contrariwise, he would go back into the water, and an immersion might prove more efficacious in the case of the horse than it seemed to have done in the case of the deacon. For it was a question whether this trick of the horse or that trick of the deacon should be the more difficult to correct. Advice was what Philip wanted just now, his own resources being exhausted; so down he went with his horse to the lake. But there was no singing! The place for the experiment was selected, the boat-post found, and preparations made for the proposed feat of educating a horse into proper behavior by an application of cold water. Philip led the horse to the spot, and amid a breathless hush in which nothing could be heard save the lapping of the listless waves upon the shore, essayed to put the rope over the horse's neck, with much trepidation. This was accomplished with a degree of success which surprised even himself. He then proceeded to tie the fractious quadruped to the post. An experienced equestrian might have understood the animal's action under such circumstances; but Philip did not. Whether there was something in the lake scenery which had soothed his nerves, or the soft eddying of the waters that calmed his stubborn spirit, no one could discern; but here, when the horse was ardently expected by owner and spectators to indulge in his habit of stretching halters to their utmost tension, he stood as gracefully and as quiet as a lamb, looking benignantly around as docile as the deacon had predicted. That he was hitched was a fact too insignificant for his lofty consideration just now. He proved again that he was a horse of extraordinary qualities, a tangible illustration of the deacon's veracity. But this new gift for standing, so recently developed, only brought back that ugly thought, stranger than ever, to Philip's mind, that the deacon had *forgotten* to tell him of the animal's gift for pulling at both ends. The case was discouraging enough, and Philip felt that, "being his own man," did not, for him, mean making fine bargains; so forgetting his grand, preconceived notions about " manhood," he went again to his brother, Williston, and asked him what he should do. This brother had helped Philip before, and his resources did not fail him here. He took the remarkable animal which the deacon had sold to Philip, and traded him away. Then another animal was purchased which did not pull at the head; and the young singer finally got started on his musical expedition.

In passing through the country he would stop at the most prepossessing houses, take out his melodeon and music, and sing his songs to the honest farm people. In this practical way he advertised the music which he had for sale, the melodeons, and himself inevitably. In the villages he did the same, and with very creditable success. This gave him opportunities for finding out the most enterprising towns in which to come again and establish winter classes. Thus he spent several summers, teaching in the winter time, and giving what leisure he could control to private study. At the end of this time he entered into co-partnership with Mr. D. J. Cook, and they together opened a large room in Fredonia, N. Y., for the sale of pianos, melodeons, music, etc. Here they worked with great energy, according to well devised plans, and with profit in every way to themselves and others. They received their supply of goods from Messrs. Sage & Sons, of Buffalo, until that firm became involved in business complications, and could no longer furnish them with instruments. This threw Philip once more upon his own resources, and he resumed his singing and teaching services.

A most gracious revival, in connection with Rev. A. Wheelock, D. D., began in the Baptist church of which he was a member. As he had charge of the music, he gave up his entire time, for several months, to real revival work. It was here that he first began singing his sacred solos, in public religious gatherings, which have since become the life and power of his religious meetings. After the minister had ended his discourse, Philip, imbued with the spirit of the subject, would deliver the same message in song. Many a conscience which could not be aroused by the sound reasoning or the fervent appeals of the sermon, was suddenly stirred under one of these sweet songs which followed. The solo was sung just before the invitation to penitents was given; and it, no doubt, had much to do with the increasing numbers that pressed forward from evening to evening, for prayers. After the meetings, Philip would frequently invite unconverted young men to his room, and there pray with them and urge them to become Christians. Several souls are ready to witness the beginning of their religious experience from those little personal interviews in Philip's room. It was a most effectual awakening, and many were brought into the church. In this distinctive feature of evangelical service, Philip Phillips evidently is the pioneer. When these meetings had closed he began holding musical conventions throughout western New York and Pennsylvania. Sometimes these conventions continued three days, sometimes a week, and occasionally two weeks. While teaching the science and practice of music, Mr. Phillips was never forgetful of the deeper significance of this accomplishment, and the gospel was always honored by a share of the time. He had considerable success in selling instruments during these conventions, educating the tastes of the young people, and worthily appealing, by the merits of the subject, to the pecuniary possibilities of parents. For music is an enlightener of homes, a protector of society, and a promoter of civilization, and all who labor to magnify its influence are public benefactors. Philip followed this sphere of duty for several years, conscientiously, diligently, and with ever-increasing fame as a singer, until his name was known in adjacent states, and even in distant towns and cities. One day a Mr. E. B. Olmstead, from Marion, Ohio, came to hear Mr. Phillips sing. He was so greatly pleased that he invited the singer to come to Ohio, promising to give his personal influence, which was not insignificant, to the stranger and to his new ideas of music in worship. Mr. Olmstead was himself the superintendent of the public schools of Marion; and Philip having had an order for a church melodeon from the same place, decided that he would visit Ohio, with a view of remaining a few months if circumstances should warrant.

GOES TO OHIO.

Accordingly he went, and his first introduction to the people of the Buckeye State was an evening of song at the Baptist church in Marion. At the close of the meeting a large class was organized, which Philip taught every week for two consecutive terms. He also gave lessons in instrumental music, and sold melodeons, thus filling in the whole time with zealous industry. He almost always closed his class labors by a public concert. At Marion he met with a Mr. Davis who had a rich and resonant bass voice, who afterwards accompanied our friend and sung with him in many places, the two singers everywhere producing a profound impression. At no point hitherto in his career, had Mr. Phillips met with such signal success as during his two month's stay at Marion. After returning to western New York, and making another singing tour through many small towns, he made a second visit to Marion. Here he brought out the "Cantata of Esther,' and gave it several times with eminent satisfaction to the public. It was during this second visit that Philip began to permit a touch of romance in his music. He suddenly discovered that he had a very interesting pupil in one of his classes in instrumental music, a Miss Clark, whose father had recently purchased one of his melodeons. Indeed, there is some reason to believe that this young lady was the fair attraction which lured our hero so soon from New York to the west; at any rate, the interest increased, and has ripened into a mutual intimacy which has been sweeter every hour since that auspicious moment when it began.

From Marion, Philip went to Bellefontaine, Ohio, where he sang and taught for six months; from Bellefontaine he went to Sydney, in the same region of the state, and remained, occupied by his chosen profession for four months; from Sydney to Muncie, Indiana, for six months; from Muncie to Chillicothe, Ohio, for one term; and from this ancient town, the oldest in the state, back to Marion.

On the 27th of September, 1860, Mr. Phillips (and we drop his boy-name from this point, as we have been tempted to do for several pages past), led to the altar the "interesting pupil" before mentioned, Miss Ollie M. Clark, the last unmarried daughter of Harvey Clark, Esq. Mr. Clark had for many years been a successful farmer and drover. He and his estimable wife were sincere Christians, and the parents of ten children of the highest respectability. The daughters were all liberally educated at Delaware, Ohio, and other places, and were subsequently married to men of position and honor in the community. The best fortune that parents can possibly confer upon sons or daughters, is an education. Nor can too much care be taken in the selection of the institutions where character is moulded for life and for eternity. After his marriage Mr. Phillips bought for himself a little house for one thousand dollars, at Marion, Ohio, in which he resided for two years. As there was no regular Baptist church in Marion, he felt it his duty to join the Methodist church, of which his wife and friends were active members. Accordingly, at morning "love-feast," in the year 1860, he handed his letter to the pastor, Rev. Isaac Newton, and has ever since been an active member of that organization. About this time he brought out his first book, "Early Blossoms." His opportunities for selling this book were not large, yet twenty thousand copies were sold. He also opened a music store, and sold sewing machines in connection with his musical merchandise. He engaged to teach a few select music classes also, at Delaware, Bellefontaine, and other adjacent places. About this time he happened to make the acquaintance of Wm Sumner, of Cincinnati, of the firm of Messrs. Sumner & Co., and was induced to go and occupy a part of their large and elegant store in Pike's Opera House on Fourth street. After talking over the matter with his wife and friends it was decided that Sumner & Co. should furnish the capital, while Mr. Phillips managed the business, sharing profits and losses according to a stipulated basis. Accordingly, he made temporary disposal of his little Marion home, and went to Cincinnati, which move proved a stepping-stone to future success and usefulness. Wm. Sumner and John R. Wright were among the most prosperous men of the west, possessing large capital and wielding a wide influence in business circles. Here Mr. Phillips was the chief agent in working up an extensive trade in large portions of three States.

But while pushing his business his voice was allowed but little rest. He was invited to sing in the city or vicinity almost every night. This he did gratuitously. He sang, also, in the Sabbath-schools, in soldiers' hospitals, and in connection with the United States Christian Commission.

After a year or two of busy life in the " Queen City," Mr. Phillips brought out his second book, " Musical Leaves," which commanded an immense sale. It was circulated largely in the army, as well as in the Sunday-schools— among the strong, stalwart men of battle, as well as among the multitudes of innocent little ones at home. The music of these bright pages seemed to meet responses everywhere. There were words and chords for all human conditions. The " Musical Leaves" were leaves of healing and blessedness. They dropped in among homes, and camps, and schools, and churches like breaths of inspiration. The sweet and charming melodies thus broadcast over the land were indeed a gracious influence in those days of war and alienation and bitterness ; its circulation was upwards of 700,000 copies.

Next appeared the " Singing Pilgrim," a most unique and methodical complication of sacred songs. In this work, the author brought out the very original idea of using pictorial illustrations in connection with the words and music of the hymn. The story of John Bunyan's " Pilgrim" suggested topics of thought, and afforded an impressive blending of Bible teaching and religious poetry in the beautiful allegorical account of the Christian life. The book was enthusiastically received by the public, and had an extremely large sale in all parts of the country. The calls upon Mr. Phillips for " Services of Song" came from all directions. He became widely known by the publication of his " Singing Pilgrim."

This explained, no doubt, the increased number of invitations received by him to sing in various places. He responded to as many calls as his attention to business would allow. About this time came the closing scenes of the war. Mr. Phillips was invited to be present at the final anniversary of the "United States Christian Commission," held in the hall of Representatives, Washington City. In the course of the evening he sang the song entitled "Your Mission," which was most flatteringly received by the brilliant assembly. The lamented *President Lincoln* was present, as well as many high state officials; and all seemed borne along by the exquisite sentiment and heart-felt rendering of the words. So much was President Lincoln impressed by the song, that he handed the following request to the chairman of the meeting, the Hon. W. H. Seward: Near the close let us have "Your Mission" repeated by Mr. Phillips. Don't say I called for it. A. Lincoln. As many of our readers may have forgotten it, we will reproduce the song, just here, for their benefit. The charm of the composition consists in its pure Gospel Spirit. The teaching of Christ is touchingly embodied in the verses; and the music is admirably adapted to express the inmost meaning of the truth conveyed. It is simple, but immortal:

YOUR MISSION.

(*As sung by Mr. Phillips at the request of President Lincoln.*)

Words by MRS. E. H. GATES. S. M. GRANNIS.

1. If you can not on the ocean
   Sail among the swiftest fleet,
   Rocking on the highest billows,
   Laughing at the storms you meet;
   You can stand among the sailors,
   Anchor'd yet within the bay;
   You can lend a hand to help them
   As they launch their boats away.

2. If you are too weak to journey
   Up the mountain, steep and high,
   You can stand within the valley,
   While the multitudes go by;

    You can chant in happy measure,
      As they slowly pass along,
    Though they may forget the singer,
      They will not forget the song.

3 If you have not gold and silver
    Ever ready to command;
  If you can not t'wards the needy
    Reach an ever open hand;
  You can visit the afflicted,
    O'er the erring you can weep,
  You can be a true disciple,
    Sitting at the Savior's feet.

4 If you can not in the conflict
    Prove yourself a soldier true,
  If, where fire and smoke are thickest,
    There's no work for you to do;
  When the battle field is silent,
    You can go with careful tread,
  You can bear away the wounded,
    You can cover up the dead.

5 If you can not in the harvest
    Garner up the richest sheaves,
  Many a grain both ripe and golden
    Will the careless reapers leave;
  Go and glean among the briars,
    Growing rank against the wall,
  For it may be that their shadow
    Hides the heaviest wheat of all.

6 Do not, then, stand idly waiting
    For some greater work to do;
  Fortune is a lazy goddess,
    She will never come to you.
  Go and toil in any vineyard,
    Do not fear to do or dare;
  If you want a field of labor,
    You can find it anywhere.

Those were wonderful days—the April of 1865. Never, perhaps, in the history of any nation, since the world began, were so many thrilling events crowded into the calendar of a single month. Joy and grief, exultation and lamentation, bells of rejoicing and wails of sorrow, alternated in bewildering echoes through the land. Shortly after the occasion above described, President Lincoln was assassinated. He was suddenly taken from us—he who had so heroically accomplished his own mission in the face of such utter discouragement; and recalling his unusual interest in this song, the mourning public called upon Mr. Phillips to go in all directions and sing before them the song that their lost leader had loved so well. So numerous were these requests that he was obliged to decline many of them. State Sunday-school conventions were, after this, held in many of the States, and at almost every one the author of " The Singing Pilgrim" was solicited to afford a service of song; and, as he used his own book in these exercises, the newspapers seized upon the coincidence of his musical tours and this appellation, and unanimously gave him the name, "Singing Pilgrim," which, however distasteful to himself, will follow him through life. Indeed, this was enterely contrary to Mr. Phillips' desire. It seemed to place him in an ungracious light of an advertised piety, an attitude which all his tastes and feelings most emphatically denied.

BURNING OF HIS STORE IN CINCINNATI.

In the year 1865 his music store took fire and was destroyed. This was a most calamitous circumstance, as it left our friend entirely without capital. The very night his property was swept away by fire, he was singing, in Leavenworth, Kansas, for his opening song:

>"Can there overtake me
> Any dark disaster,
> While I sing for Jesus,
> My blessed, blessed Master?"

He believed that had he been content to follow the path which God had so signally opened to him, and let secular business alone, the sentiment of the song would have proved true. But there was his mistake. He had a call, surely, to preach the gospel in song; and God pursued him with anxieties and losses until he was willing to follow the divine purpose, rather than his own. It is the old story of man's blindness, and the Father's infinite love in the sorest extremes—the affliction of the child for its own good. Trials and losses are thus, in His hand, made the instruments of joy to the afflicted one. But how difficult it is to see this at the time of tribulation! The soul does not comprehend that it is being called away from a gross, self-chosen employment, to one glorious and elevated above the highest conception. The nets and the fishing should be forsaken, now, as at the beginning of gospel ministry, *straightway*, when the Savior calls to higher work. What are earthly emoluments, compared with the " twelve thrones," the " hundred fold," and the " everlasting life!"

Just here we may anticipate somewhat, and borrow an incident or two from Mr. Phillips' experience further on, in witness of the better than material rewards for dutiful service. It seems that, while in England, Mr. Phillips had occasion to visit Bristol to hold a service of song in Colston Hall. The journey had been a long one, and as the hall was very large, and nearly 3,000 tickets had been sold, Mr. Phillips felt somewhat discouraged at the difficult task that awaited him. Notwithstanding his duties, however, he felt that he must visit the world-renowned Orphan Asylum. He did so, and after a few moments' converse with Mr. Muller, was shown over the building. Entering one of the schoolrooms the children sang to him, " Courage, brother, do not stumble; Trust in God and do the right." The surprise of being cheered by one of his own songs had the best effect, and courage revived. After singing a song to the children he left the building, but, before doing so, was met at the door by a number of little ones, who each presented him with an article of needle-work of their own making. The Bristol Orphanage, which is a marvelous institution, providing food, clothing, and education for 2,000 orphans, was founded on and is supported by simple faith, no man having ever been asked to contribute to its sustenance, and perhaps it is but natural that those who visit it should have their courage strengthened and their faith revived. In providing for his enormous family, Mr. Muller has always relied with a quiet faith upon the promises of the Heavenly Father, " in all things, in prayer and supplication, making his requests known unto God."

But there is small occasion for any explanation of this wonderful institution here, for it is world-renowned. It stands in evidence of the sure rewards that follow a life of trust. After Mr. Phillips had completed his tour through Ireland and Great Britain, and was on the eve of sailing for home, a pleasant farewell surprise was tendered him by the Sunday-school Union at the Jubilee building. The occasion was one of rare delight. During the evening the following resolution, beautifully illuminated and framed, was presented to him:

Resolved, That the most cordial thanks of this Committee be presented to Mr. Philip Phillips, of New York, for his indefatigable labors in conducting 100 Services of Song, on behalf of the Continental Mission Fund, whereby the sum of £889 was realized on account of this important object. In closing this engagement, the Committee desire to offer to Mr. Phillips a slight expression of their appreciation of his valuable services; and, with this resolution, beg his acceptance of a Drawing-Room Time Piece, with the assurance of their best wishes, that his valuable life may be long spent in singing for Jesus, and that he may be instrumental in doing a great work for the Savior.—WILLIAM GROSER, AUGUSTUS BENHAM, FOUNTAIN JOHN HARTLEY, JOHN EDWARD TRESSIDER, ALFRED SHRIMPTON, MATTHEW W. RICHARDS.

The testimonial, which was entirely unexpected, was briefly acknowledged by Mr. Phillips, who started the next morning for the United States.

But to resume our biographical outline. After Mr. Phillips' great misfortune at Cincinnati, the fiery trial of his business purposes, he rented a store in New York, and began again his sale of instruments and music; but as he followed his old practice of singing for churches, Sunday-schools and benevolent organizations of all kinds, he was obliged to leave most of his business in the hands of clerks and agents.

This again proved disastrous. He had to become responsible, personally, for large expenditures which the profits of the trade as reported to him, did not cover. A shrinkage was apparent; and, before long, the secret was explained. A more suspicious man would have been saved many of his trials; but Mr. Phillips was singularly generous in his judgments of men. He took for granted that every man was a gentleman, until he showed himself a knave. He met a loss of $5,800 by one man alone. This startled him into a more careful examination of his affairs, which ended in the decision to look up a responsible partner, who could have personal interest in the business with himself. Accordingly an arrangement was made with Mr. William Edsall, of New York. They rented a fine store on Union Square, for five years, and designed continuing the sale of instruments, and at the same time publishing Mr. Phillips' books from year to year. In this way he hoped to find more leisure for musical composition, and for holding his song services, into which his heart entered so fully. But the new plan did not prove satisfactory. Mr. Edsall was a man of ability and uprightness; but the music trade was not familiar to him. Being unacquainted with the technical ins and outs of it, the sales of the goods fell off deplorably.

After two years trial they found that it still required Mr. Phillips' copyrights and singing to pay the expenses of the concern. The proceeds of these resources, were, in fact, the main part of his income, and seemed to belong more personally to Mr. Phillips. Of course such a drag and drain was not policy; and after due deliberation, they mutually agreed in the best of spirit to dissolve the partnership; Mr. Phillips was to assume all the liabilities, pay the store rent, and allow Mr. Edsall a generous sum for his time spent in the business. Very seldom does the settling up of a firm's affairs answer to the high expectations indulged by the proprietors in the beginning. So it was in this case. Mr. Phillips had to become responsible for the balance of the lease, $5,000 per annum, and pay the losses of bad debts beside, all out of his own income. This, with the increasing hard times, would have left him worse than bankrupt had it not been for his voice. His nature generated hope to such an extent that he always caught a glimpse of the "silver lining" while singing his way out, even in the darkest and most threatening clouds of misfortune.

GOES TO ENGLAND FOR THE FIRST TIME.

In the year 1868, he first visited Europe. His main object in making the trip was to obtain rest and see the country; but he soon found that his fame had preceded him. After a tour of sight seeing on the continent, he came back to London, where he was invited to give some of his song services, vague ideas of which had floated over the Atlantic to the English people. With his accustomed readiness, he complied.

His first appearance was before the Sunday-school Union Committee, in the Jubilee Hall; subsequently he sang at the great Temperance Fete, in the Crystal Palace, to forty-two thousand people; at Mr. Spurgeon's Metropolitan Tabernacle, and also among the outcasts in Effingham Theatre, White Chapel. The net proceeds of his evening at Spurgeon's Tabernacle were given to the orphanage of the church.

From London he went northward, visiting the leading cities and towns of the United Kingdom, delivering in all, at this first stay in the country, sixty-seven services of song.

It was during this musical campaign that he was waited upon to compile a book of sacred songs, for publication by the British Sunday-school Union. This he did before leaving London. The book was entitled, "The American Sacred Songster." It has had a sale in England of over one million and one hundred thousand copies. His services of song, all over the kingdom, became very popular.

This was the first introduction of the sacred solo into religious meetings, as defined worship; and the delightful innovation spread like glad tidings of great joy all over the country. So much were our English neighbors pleased, that four years later, Mr. Phillips was invited to again visit England, and conduct one hundred services in aid of the Continental Sunday-school Union Fund, for establishing Sunday-schools on the continent of Europe. The people of Great Britain are wide awake on the missionary question, and, glad to forward so grand a cause, our Singing Pilgrim again left his native land, in 1872, and applied himself to his loved work abroad. He gave the stipulated one hundred services in consecutive order, without a single failure or delay, and left in the hands of the treasurer of the Society, almost one thousand pounds sterling, ($5,000) to be donated to the designated object.

After fulfilling his regular engagements, he was induced to give fifty more evenings before leaving England. This was now the second time that the English public had an opportunity of testing the power of simple gospel singing, and so forcible was the impression, that Mr. Phillips carried away with him over four hundred applications for song services to which he was not able to respond.

Subsequently came the marvelous work of Messrs. Moody and Sankey, emphasizing the teaching and approving the method of the Pilgrim who had preceded them, and whose story of the cross was one with their own. While in London he had a very urgent call to return to America, and give his song services in the Presbyterian Tabernacle, San Francisco, California. He was offered $4,800 a year, the largest salary, probably, ever offered a singer in regular church service. But he felt that he could not confine himself for all the Sundays of the year. He therefore arranged with the church in San Francisco for twenty Sundays, at the same rate, instead of the calendar fifty-two; and on his return from England went forthwith to California, and settled at the Golden Gate from April to September. During the evenings of the week, he gave his services of song up and down the Pacific coast, always returning at the end of the week for his engagement at the Tabernacle. It was at this time that he first combined Bible readings with his musical deliveries. These have since become very attractive and popular.

FIRST SERVICE OF PRAISE AND BIBLE READINGS.

Here, also, his first Song Sermon was published, and it was given in this Tabernacle in 1873. This was the second time that Mr. Phillips had visited the Pacific coast. A year or so previously, in company with J. H. Vincent, D.D., the Sunday-school apostle, and Dwight L. Moody, the famous evangelist, he had spent several weeks in Sunday-school and revival work in these same sunset regions. It was about this time that Mr. Moody decided to devote himself exclusively to preaching. This decision may perhaps have grown out of his marked success while laboring in San Jose, San Francisco, Salt Lake City, Denver and other western towns. At the meetings which he held in these places, Mr. Phillips conducted the singing, and would often sing his solos in connection with Mr. Moody's earnest appeals. This union of song and speech so eminently blest of God in this tour, was doubtless the precedent which was followed by the gospel partnership of Moody and Sankey, the influence of whose dual evangelism the world has acknowledged as divine. In all this wonderful achievement Mr. Philip Phillips will stand recorded on history's page as a pioneer and leader, giving tone to the new movement and uniformly aiding every consecrated worker in this great white harvest field of souls. Dr. Vincent and Mr. Phillips then went to Oregon, where they conducted the first Sunday-school Convention ever held in that state. These meetings in California and Oregon were pronounced, by those who attended them, as exceeding in power and interest anything ever known hitherto in the west, especially the one at San Jose. So great was the religious awakening, that Messrs. Moody and Phillips remained some days after the close of the

FIRST STATE S. S. CONVENTION IN CALIFORNIA
And continued the meeting with special reference to its revival features. Many souls were converted, and many more aroused to active religious work. After Mr. Phillips' engagement in San Francisco had been filled, he returned to New York, holding his "evenings of song" in various places through the east, and thence on to the British provinces of Canada.

There had been some correspondence previous to this time between Mr. Phillips and an Australian committee on the subject of his coming to that country. It was renewed and as a result our pilgrim brother promised one hundred nights of song in that far away sea land, Australia. This engagement was made good in 1875, with forty-one extra nights following. While in Australia, he made still another promise, to return to England for one hundred nights, under the auspices of the Sunday-school Union. Of course this opened his way around the world, as the London religious newspapers made announcement of this third engagement for England, and these periodicals circulated freely through India, Ceylon and the East, as well as over the European continent.

Missionaries in foreign fields were pleased to avail themselves of this opportunity of securing his services for gospel singing, while he was *en route* to London.

These engagements between Australia and London,

were given gratuitously, in almost every instance, and were enriched by special evangelistic work on the part of the happy traveler. He was a pilgrim indeed, whether he would or not. What hope and courage he brought to the disheartened and home-sick toiler for Christ in those desolate heathen lands! What a privilege to see his sunny face, to grasp his brotherly hand, and to hear such sweet messages of comfort in their own native tongue as those simple gospel hymns brought to them. They came, indeed, as an evangel of hope, to those faithful servants of the Master. In this way he spent nearly one year between Australia and London, singing to the people of every church and class. Reaching England at last, he began his musical entertainments early in August, 1876.

Here he gave one hundred consecutive "evenings of song," (excepting Saturdays and Sundays, although he frequently sang on these days also,) without a single break in his programme, from sickness or other causes. When this series was completed he remained to sing another hundred nights for local Christian objects. As upon the two former occasions, he left England with many necessarily unanswered applications to sing in various parts of the kingdom. The details of Mr. Phillips' travels will be given more at length in the department of this work, "Singing Around the World." Suffice it to say that he has never given a single service where admission has been charged, but that he has divided the proceeds with different Christian objects. This always left some financial benefit to the immediate cause for which he sang. And just here, it is but simple justice to say of Mr. Phillips, that certain volunteer censurers be answered who have ungenerously spoken of him as "singing for Jesus at one hundred dollars per night." The criticism is unjust. The very wording of the sentence is malicious, irreverent and coarse, and no fair-minded Christian should be guilty of such speech.

Mr. Phillips has, during his life-time, sung forty-three nights at one hundred dollars a night; and the parties who engaged him for those forty-three services, at one hundred dollars a night, received a net profit of over $4,500; while he has sung over three thousand nights when he shared equally with the object for which the service was given, taking risks on himself. At least one-fourth of these nights have not paid more than his necessary expenses; but, at the same time, the societies have always made a profit. No lecture committee has ever gone down into its pockets to pay him for his work. He pays his own expenses and leaves a profit besides; and this being his exclusive work, absorbing all his time and taxing his strength, unsalaried, even as an ordinary Methodist preacher, who is sure of support; he is doing much less for himself than many prominent pastors of the day who lecture at from fifty to three hundred dollars per night, and yet receive large or sufficient salaries beside. This supplementary service is repeatedly undertaken by ministers, and very little mention is made of it in the way of unfavorable criticism. The public is not informed as to just what private channels these immense lecture fees are turned into; nor does it care particularly, or busy itself to inquire. The work of Mr. Phillips surely deserves equally patient consideration. He feels that his duty lies in this direction, and that he can no more avoid it and have peace within than a minister can flee from his call to preach the gospel. Neither can he follow out the providential promptings to bear the message of salvation to widely separated people, but by making the work self-sustaining, as we have tried to show.

Of course, much of the work must be gratuitous, or nearly so; and these few one-hundred dollar engagements would scarcely make up the deficiency. "The laborer is worthy of his hire," and it would be a very sentimental religion which could deny its advocates a fair chance with their own honestly-earned money. Because Mr. Phillips prefers independent management of his own affairs—because he does not go before the public as a beggar, indeed, shall it be said that, therefore, he is not "singing for Jesus?"

The wonderful interest displayed in his meetings, the revivals of religion which have grown out of them, and the many letters received from persons who have been deeply impressed by his songs, all would combine to deny the truth of the statement, if such statement could be even unwittingly made.

This much we think due to our friend, in explanation of his course.

CHAPTER I.

SINGING IN NEW YORK AND SUBURBS.

IN reviewing the many interesting points of my musical tour around the world, I have thought to recount some of the incidents which may be entertaining to the public; and in doing so, I shall begin with my own country, America, where the journey began.

My sacred solos were first given before audiences in the United States, where God's blessing so richly attended them, that I was encouraged to carry this gospel in song, on to a wider circuit. Friends at home will bear with me, in a brief recital of the pilgrimages made in our own states, by me, in this work; for they will not forget that interested persons in Great Britain, Australia, India, and, indeed, in all the various countries visited by me, are anxious to learn something of my own country, America, and the spirit in which I was received there. My notes, accordingly, shall be so arranged, that readers may easily refer to those most interesting to them, relating to my labors in their own, or in foreign countries. In the year 1866, I began my pilgrimages of song in earnest, although I had for a long time been accustomed to singing around the country in Sabbath-school conventions, revival meetings and musical institutes.

I now decided to devote my whole time and best energies to this work of evangelization by sacred songs, to which I felt divinely called. No other employment seemed proper for me; in no other one was I so happy or successful. So, following the Master's leading, I devoted myself to the writing and singing of simple gospel music, and His blessing was ever upon me. From the first I determined not to cater to the popular taste by indulging in anything light or frivolous in my singing. I made no pretensions toward the classical in song, as I deemed that plain sweet melodies reached the popular heart sooner, because they were of Nature and not of Art.

I felt a binding duty upon me to preach the gospel in this way, and in following up this duty, three objects were kept in view by me, which I will here mention in the order of their importance:

First:— To cheer and uplift Christians by the sweet Bible promises;

Second:— To lure the erring or indifferent to Christ by the charm of lofty sentiment and pleasing melody; and

Third:— To provide an honest living for myself and family, in such a way as to be able to aid many Christian enterprises, without being a burden to any organization for my expenses.

The year 1866 was a very eventful one to me. It was during that year that I left Cincinnati,—after having my business burned out,—and went to reside in New York city. Eighteen sixty-six, was, our readers will remember, the centennial of American Methodism, and I was called from one end of the country to the other to sing at anniversaries. The requests were so numerous I could accept only those from the largest cities. Ah! that was a glad year for us all, and the followers of good John Wesley fell to singing all over the land. The principles of an experimental religion, planted in a new soil, and watered by faith and prayer, had yielded an abundant, a wonderful harvest, and Methodists must needs rejoice; so we all sang and praised our God.

It was during this year, also that I set our denominational Hymn Book to music, as a thank-offering. The exclusive singing of church choirs always gave me a great deal of pain. I felt that God's way was to have the *whole congregation* sing, and worship him, rather than to give this part of public worship out to a few paid singers. It seemed a terrible desecration of God's gifts, and I did all I could to influence the people to a more Scriptural style of singing, as I went from church to church at their call.

"Let the *people* praise Thee, oh, God, let all the people praise Thee," sang the sweet singer of Israel. By and by, some of the churches adopted congregational singing, then others, until now choirs in our largest Methodist churches are the exception, rather than the rule. In some cases the choirs are still kept up, but only for the purpose of *leading* the congregation in singing. Oh, how the soul surges with emotion at the sound of a vast assembly joining with one accord in

"All hail the power of Jesus' name."

It makes one feel something of the exultation of the redeemed in heaven, as they rejoice in great companies around the throne! What if there *are* old women's voices, high and cracked, in that chorus; boys' voices shrill and discordant; the harmony of the whole is perfect, and each soul has its chance to praise the Lord in the assembly of His saints! Truly this must be a better way than for a few to monopolize the whole service of song.

SINGING IN THE ACADEMY OF MUSIC. NEW YORK.

Among my other invitations was one to sing at the anniversary of the Christian Commission in New York city. This I accepted; but never shall I forget my trepidation in going before that brilliant audience at the great Academy of Music, with my simple gospel songs; for hours before the time I was filled with nervous fear, and could only flee to God for support in my weakness. This was *His* work, not *mine*, and He gave me the needed courage, and then favor with the people. The *elite* of the metropolis were present—an audience of over 3,000 persons. I came before them with trembling, but soon the responses from the audience reassured me, and I felt that I was safe. The sentiments uttered in song were finding answers in many other hearts, and the applause was frequent and hearty. All through the evening's exercises I was constrained to thank God in my heart for this happy ending of the duty which I so greatly dreaded. Even the New York press ventured next day to speak in approving terms of this " new departure" in sacred song. In referring to my evening at the Academy of Music the New York *Tribune* remarked: " Since the days of the Wesleys, there has probably been no man who has been so popular a leader and singer of sacred song as Mr. Phillips." But grateful as I was to the *Tribune* for its generous comments, I made no pretentions to leadership of any kind. I only wished the people to adopt God's method in their church singing; and if I could spread His truth, in some degree, by my own voice, this would be honor enough for me. I was entertained on this occasion by a most excellent Christian gentleman, Mr. Bishop, a man of great wealth and deep piety. Being a plain man myself, and unused to the luxury of such surroundings, I should have felt embarrassed and awkward, but for the simple-hearted hospitality of my host. We are apt to think of the poor as having the monopoly of this virtue, but Christ's religion makes such sweet charities abound in all stations. The rich man who has bowed at the feet of his Savior, feels the yearnings of brotherhood for all who have named the blessed Name in love. He is one with them in heart and in sympathy. The Master had been entertained as an honored guest in this elegant home, and made all hearts tender ere the coming of my pilgrim feet to their door. Since this, my first singing in the metropolis, I have given upwards of seventy evenings of song in the same city, besides conducting the music in one hundred and forty religious meetings. These efforts were received with favor, and I believe attended with blessing, also. The most satisfactory work, to my own soul, which I have ever done, was

SINGING IN THE SLUMS OF NEW YORK.

In connection with Rev. William Booles' and Jerry McCauly's mission Water Street is well known as one of the vilest quarters in New York. Here a plain mission room stood amid the filth and crime, while a small band of noble souls were laboring to save the falling through its services. One Sunday evening the little mission hall was crowded with the Magdalenes, and other of the most vicious characters of the fourth ward. I was to sing for that strange audience:

About time for the exercises to open, the famous Kit Burns headed a band of about thirty "roughs," and, marching up the aisle, took a position immediately in front of me.

I feared we should have trouble with him before the evening was over, but, trusting in God, began the services as usual. For a time, all went well. Kit and his companions listened with marked attention through several songs. Then some one called out from the door: "Kit, you are wanted." Rising at once in his seat, Kit sent back his ready answer; "Tell 'em to go——" and I went on singing of Jesus and his love. Again the rough shouted from the door: "Kit, you're wanted outside." This time our hero stood up once more and in his hoarse voice called back "Tell 'em this is the first Jesus meetin' I ever attended, and I shall stay till its out." This seemed to settle the matter, and we had no more trouble from outside. During the evening I gave a short exhortation, pleading with the unconverted to come to Christ, and begin a better life. So close was the crowd as they sat around me, that I could hear some of the women say, "We will do better! Yes we will!" No doubt they were sincere in those promises, but only God and the poor chained soul can fully understand the galling bondage of habit. Many a woman there could weep with remorseful emotion over the tender allusions to to "little baby fingers," and all the motherhood in her be aroused to pledge itself for her own darlings; yet, when tomorrow came, the bad associations drew so powerfully, that the old neglect and sin went on. While I sang "scatter seeds of kindness," it all seemed quite possible, but the tomorrow's test too often found them unequal to it. Sin had left its mark of irresolution upon them. Only by sovereign grace, alone, can such poor weakened souls be held to a better purpose and life.

A few days after this, one of the women who attended the meeting on this Sunday evening, was found drunk on the street. The Matron of the Mission, seeing her condition, managed to get her into the mission room, that she might be saved from the idle gaze of the crowd until she came to herself. For some time she lay in a drunken stupor on the floor, and then the influence of her dram began to pass off. Raising herself on her elbow, she looked around, and, thinking she was in the " Tombs " or " lockup," thus began to soliloquize: " Now I'll have to stay here thirty days"—that being the penalty for drunkenness on the street—" my business will all go to sticks! I know the policeman, d—n him! When I get out I'll show him;" but just here looking about more closely, she perceived her mistake, and muttered, "I *aint* in the Tombs, after all. Where am I?" Then after a moment: " Oh, I'm in tnat place where they scatter seeds of kindness." She remembered the song of the Sunday night previous. The Matron, overhearing her words, came to her and said, "Yes, I found you on the sidewalk, drunk, and I knew the policeman would soon get you into the Tombs, so I brought you in here to rest. Now, won't you come with me, and have a good wash, and cup of tea?" "Oh, I am too dirty," was her reply, as she surveyed her bedraggled clothing and soiled hands. "No, come; it will do you good," still argued her new friend, and by her winning kindness the poor woman was persuaded to go in, wash herself up, and have a cup of the good matron's tea. While the abashed woman sat there, a few earnest Christians dropped in, and a short prayer meeting ensued, in which she was hopefully converted to God. She held fast her profession of faith, and, after three months, died in the triumphs of the gospel. During her last days, she thanked God that she had ever heard the songs at the Water Street Mission.

MISSION HALL.

So impressed was I that much good could be done by singing the gospel to the outcasts of this great city, that I then resolved, God helping me, that I would sometime be instrumental in building a Mission Hall in New York, for this purpose. I thank my Father above that in His providence I have been enabled to commence the undertaking, although it may take years to complete it. In anticipation of the end, however, I find much joy and inspiration. I shall continue singing, praying, and trusting for the success of my plan. Through my own labors, and some unsolicited donations, I have already fifteen hundred dollars secured for the enterprise, and am quite hopeful of obtaining the remainder. Gradually this new order of simple gospel singing became so well received that I was called upon to sing my solos at the anniversaries of missionary societies, Sunday-school institutes, and at the close of sermons, in the most popular churches of New York, Boston, Philadelphia, Chicago, Cincinnati, St. Louis, Baltimore, Washington City, San Francisco—in fact, my invitations came from all parts of the United States, both city and country. The style of singing was then new, and we suspect had a touch of novelty about it. But God made it instrumental of good, not only through my humble efforts, but those of many others, who have since adopted this method of preaching the Word; and I praise God for it. The sacred solo has become one of the most effective agents employed in evangelistic work.

NEW YORK SUBURBS.

It was usually supposed that any entertainment given in the suburbs of New York would prove unsuccessful, but I found it otherwise. My evenings of sacred song were given in many of the halls and churches outside of the city proper, and always to audiences sufficient to leave a fair profit with the societies employing me. Our readers abroad may be interested to learn something of the magnitude of the suburbs of this our great metropolitan city, New York. Prominent among the settlements which have sprung up around the central point of commerce and trade, is

THE CITY OF BROOKLYN,

With its forest of churches, and its great suspension bridge connecting it with New York. Brooklyn has a population of over half a million souls. There is constant communication kept up with the mother-city, by means of the various bridges, ferries, and tunnels of East River, which separates the two busy marts. The city of New York for many years discouraged the building of wharves, piers, docks, or warehouses on the Brooklyn side, being anxious to concentrate its own commerce on its own shores. But this has not stopped the spirit of the daring enterprise. Since 1844 there has been $125,000,000, in private capital, expended on docks and warehouses along the Brooklyn shores. These furnish a dockage of twenty-five miles. An immense commerce is carried on here. Over 5,000 men are engaged in the one business of warehousing. In the houses of the Atlantic Dock Company, it is estimated that grain and other commodities are stored to the amount of $261,000,000 worth annually. Brooklyn, a suburban town of New York, as we often speak of it, is not only the "city of churches," but also the greatest grain market in the world. The value of the boats engaged in the grain carrying trade alone is over $18,000,000. But we cannot stop further to give statistics, but jot down these for our friends abroad. From this whirring, busy city, let us pass into the sacred shades of

GREENWOOD CEMETERY.

Which every tourist tries to visit in going to New York. It is probably the most beautiful resting place of the dead in the world. It comprises 400 acres of ground, and vast sums of money have been expended, both by the city and private individuals in decorating this place of sad memories. Then there is PROSPECT PARK, whose quiet, cool retreats, furnish a rare solace to the tired brains, who toil so many hours of the day amid the whirlpools of trade.

STATEN ISLAND

Is also a beautiful place of homes; has a population of 40,000, is thirteen miles wide and twenty long, reposing quietly on the bosoms of the harbor of New York Bay. This island-city is almost a realized "El Dorado" in the summer season, with its lovely drives, groves, magnificent residences, and the fragrant fruits and flowers that greet the eye on all sides; yet the numerous great flat-boats plying about the shores in all directions, and at all hours, give it an air of business, as well as of romance. The island is well provided with churches of every denomination, in many of which I have given my services. The people here are, as a rule, more conservative than in New York—not so changeable or extravagant in their notions.

LONG ISLAND,

At whose extreme south-western end we find the city of Brooklyn, has special interest from the many watering places along its shores. It comprises a territory of one hundred and eighteen by twenty miles, and has a population of over half a million. The people are rather of the staid, Knickerbocker style, generally rich, and having a fancy for attending to their own affairs, rather than those of their neighbors. Many of our literary characters have country seats on this island. William Cullen Bryant, our lamented poet and journalist, here chose out the beautiful retreat of "Roslyn," where he passed his last quiet years. Here, also, the "Prince of Merchants," A. T. Stewart, purchased a whole township and laid it out for a garden city. His houses are rented to moderate livers, who cultivate the rich land surrounding their dwellings. The soil in the center of the island is rather barren and sandy, but toward the east and west ends it is very fertile. Here we find minds who make choice of the best literature and the most cultured social pleasures. An audience honors the one who comes before it here, less by its noisy demonstration than by its deep attention and quiet appreciation.

NORTHERN SUBURBS.

Leaving New York and passing northward, I sang in the historic towns of Irving, Sing Sing, Tarrytown, Nyack, and others, situated on the beautiful Hudson River. This river has been very appropriately styled the "Rhine of America." We are prone sometimes, when sailing along its placid waters, past the lovely villas, sloping lawns, parks, woodland, hill and vale, to imagine that its attractions *exceed* those of all other rivers of the earth.

CHAPTER II.

SINGING IN THE SOUTHERN STATES.

AFTER singing in various parts of my own city, New York, and its suburbs, I bent my course southward, making my first stop at the capital of New Jersey, Trenton. New Jersey is one of our smaller states, having an area of some 7,500 square miles. Historians do not agree as to what people first made settlements here. It is certain that there were colonizations made by the Fins, Swedes, and English, so that having such a mixed ancestry, it is not strange that we find the people of this state distinguished by some striking characteristics.

That quaint essence, "a Jersey man," has an almost world-wide reputation for oddity. New Jersey was much forward of the times in 1776, when her state constitution provided for universal suffrage among her voters—white, colored, male and female sharing equal rights at the polls. This, however, was modified in 1807.

My first appointment in the state, was to sing before about four hundred Methodist ministers at a reunion conference then sitting in Trenton; and right here I will insert an article written by Rev. E. H. Stokes, D.D., in regard to this meeting, and which appeared in one of the local papers.

"The New Jersey conference of the Methodist Episcopal Church for the year 1865, was held in Green Street Church, Trenton, N.J. Nine years before, by the action of the General Conference, the Newark Conference had been created, and all ministers north of the Raritan Bay and River fell into that body at the conference of 1857. We had therefore been separated for a period of eight years. A reunion had been arranged, and was looked forward to with much interest by both bodies.

At the proper time, a delegation went to the depot to receive their brethren of the Newark conference, whose session was held at that year in Rahway. They formed a line and marched down State Street, entering the church two abreast, headed by Bishop Janes, their president, while the members of the New Jersey conference, under the direction of Bishop Ames, arose to receive them, and as they passed up the aisles to their seats, sang in tender tones:

"And are we yet alive
And see each other's face?"

The song rolled on, and the interest was intensified as these war-scarred veterans of the Cross looked each other in the face, after a separation of so many years; and they continued to sing:

"What troubles have we seen,
What conflicts have we past,
Fightings without, and fears within,
Since we assembled last."

Bishop Ames gave the address of welcome, which was nobly responded to by Bishop Janes. Then followed remarks by those on both sides of the line, full of personal reminiscences, which absorbed the mind and thrilled the heart. The tide of emotion ran strong and high. Then Bishop Ames, whose eye is always keen to perceive the exact manner and moment when everything can be turned to the best account, said: "I have now a rich treat in store for you all." Then turning, bowed to a rather small, slender, dark-haired and dark-eyed young stranger, who instantly arose, and stepping upon the platform, sat down in front of a small cottage organ. "I have the pleasure," said

Bishop Ames, "of introducing to you Philip Phillips, of Cincinnati."

The name was new to most, and besides the bishops, perhaps none of that vast congregation had ever seen his face. During the introduction he sat like a timid child, while not less than two thousand eyes were intently fixed upon him, and expectation was so high that it seemed as if an angel could hardly meet it. Silence followed; then the feet of the stranger touched the pedals of the instrument, while his fingers swept over the keys, and a melody was born, so soft, and sweet, and tender, that every heart was moved, and words as smooth as drops of molten silver fell upon the ear:

> "If you cannot on the ocean
>   Sail among the swiftest fleet,
> Rocking on the highest billow,
>   Laughing at the storms you meet,
> You can stand among the sailors,
>   Anchored yet within the bay,
> You can lend a hand to help them,
>   As they launch their boats away."

When the first verse was ended, there was a long breath drawn, as if the heart during its singing, pressed with an over-measure of sympathy, had forgotten its functions, and the sigh now bursting gave it temporary relief. The singer proceeded with his song, while the listeners, oblivious to everything around, drank in the strains as the traveler in the sun-scorched desert drinks of the cooling streams.

By referring to the date at the beginning of this article, it will be seen that the time was just before the close of the late Rebellion. When the fifth verse was reached—

> "If you cannot in the conflict
>   Prove yourself a soldier true,
> If where fire and smoke are thickest,
>   There's no work for you to do;
> When the battle-field is silent,
>   You can go with careful tread,
> You can bear away the wounded,
>   You can cover up the dead"—

By this time every eye was a fountain of tears, and every bosom heaved with irrepressible emotion, strong men, including the Governor of New Jersey and other state officials, wept like children, and old and young were alike borne on the resistless tide of song.

Amid the stifled, yet only partly suppressed sobs of the multitude, the singer by a nice art arose a little in the last verse from the depths of sympathy to which he had carried them, and with a slight touch of the exultant in his tones, struck the last verse:

> "Do not, then, stand idly waiting
>   For some greater work to do;
> Fortune is a lazy goddess,
>   She will never come to you;
> Go and toil in any vineyard,
>   Do not fear to do or dare,
> If you want a field of labor,
>   *You may find it anywhere!*"

With the repetition of the last line so skillfully managed, and so nicely adjusted to the condition of his audience, every face bathed in tears, and every heart wrought to the highest degree of enthusiasm, felt ready for any service or any sacrifice; but as the last two lines were dying away on the singer's lips—

> "If you want a field of labor,
>   You may find it anywhere."

Bishop Ames, less emotional, perhaps, than many, or having a thought of the practical that he knew must soon come upon that noble band of ministers, said, with solemn emphasis, yet with a slight twinkle of good nature in his eye, "I hope the brethren will remember that when they get their appointments." It was like a thunder-clap to bring us back from the delicious dream into which we had fallen, and were made to realize that we were still upon the earth and among the real.

The whole scene was one of unparalleled interest, and as fresh in memory as of yesterday. In passing out of the church at the close of service, a minister said to one of his brethren, 'What did you think of that singing?' 'Think of it?' said the brother addressed, 'I cried so I had no time to think.'"

From that day the name of Philip Phillips has been with us a synonym for all that is pure and beautiful in the realm of song.

Since then three persons have written me, saying they dated their conversion at that conference and the spiritual influence of those hymns. I can but humbly praise God that I have been thus honored as His instrument in promoting Christ's cause. Since that time I have always been welcomed by good audiences, and sympathetic hearts, in the various churches of Trenton. Passing on to

PHILADELPHIA.

In the state of Pennsylvania, I filled an engagement at the American Academy of Music. Many of the friends abroad, will remember Philadelphia as the city in which our great Centennial Exposition took place during the year 1876. It comprises a population of about eight hundred thousand, largely of Quaker extraction—staid, quiet, God-fearing, and law-abiding people. The Quaker city is distinguished for the regularity and width of its streets, its extreme cleanliness, and the wealth, and refinement of its citizens. It has a proud history, having been the birth-place of American Independence.

My audience at this time was four thousand people. I was introduced by that noble Christian gentleman, George H. Stuart. While presenting me, he remarked: "Although my friends say I have no taste in music, yet I have eyes that could weep with President Lincoln, when Mr. Phillips sang his touching songs in Washington." I then sang the song by which our lamented President had been so much impressed and was encored again and again. Although Quakers are somewhat averse to singing, I find them quite interested in this simple gospel style; for, since that time, I have sung many times in the different churches of the city, and never to small audiences. It was here that I first met that good man, R. Pearsall Smith, who has since scattered his notes on the "Rest of Faith" over our own land, Great Britain, and even up into the palace of the German king. It was after one of the "services of song," which I held at Ebenezer church, that this noble man called me aside, and gave me some words of strong encouragement. His remarks have been a great blessing to me ever since. Shortly after this, Mr. Smith wrote me a very urgent request to visit his father's house, and there sing some of my songs. He said, "My father is a good man, but although all his children are Christians, he has never made a profession. Now, Bro. Phillips, I have faith to believe that if you will go there, and sing some of your hymns, he will give his heart to Christ." Such was the entreaty; so I fixed upon a date, and went. Most of the family were present, and nearly all in the sombre garb of Quakers. Pearsall Smith had taken the forethought to invite that saintly man, Alfred Cookman, to be present, but he and I were the only ones there, outside the family. Upon our arrival, we found the aged sire sitting in his beautiful parlors.

For sometime I felt considerably at a loss to know how to introduce my singing to Quakers, who do not favor music or form. Finally I said, "I see you have a little organ here." "Oh, yes," was the reply; "and," added Pearsall Smith, "please sing us one of your hymns." Accordingly I sang. The old man, with white locks, listened attentively, and after I had finished one piece, said to me: "Will you please sing that over again?" So I sang the hymn, "What hast Thou done for me?" again, just to please his fancy.

Every person in the room seemed to be engaged in silent prayer, as I could see by glancing around while singing.

The moment, I felt, was fraught with tremendous issues to the human soul within that bending frame. The spirit of God came upon me, and I sang to my own tune, the following verse of the hymn:

> "I spent long years for thee,
>   In weariness and woe,
> That one eternity
>   Of joy thou mightest know!
> I spent long years for thee, for thee,
> Hast thou spent *one* for Me?"

The father of seventy years was weeping as I closed. "Let us pray," said Alfred Cookman. They all knelt, and he *did* pray—yes wrestled—with God for the old man's salvation, and that prayer was heard above! Then and there the old man had born within him a hope of eternal life. He gave himself up to Christ who had given his life for him, as the hymn said, and we all rejoiced together. Speaking aside to R. Pearsall Smith, in the course of the evening, I said: "How strange this is!" "Why so?" he returned. "I expected it, just as I wrote you, for I felt that God would honor the means." This was one of the happiest evenings of my life, for it was one of song and salvation.

DELAWARE

Was the next region I visited. This is a thrifty little state lying southeast of Pennsylvania, and washed all along its eastern shore by the beautiful Delaware Bay. The whole state comprises only an area of about 2,100 square miles, and most of the soil is sandy. However, the Delaware farmers have studied the science of soils, and know just what crops will flourish best there; consequently, many of our choicest fruits and vegetables come from this section. Delaware peaches are considered especially fine. The people, also, do an extensive business in the oyster-beds, which are found all along the coast.

Dover is the capital of Delaware, and Wilmington its chief city. Here I held a service of song in a hall. I did not feel very well, but went through the programme as best I could, and the audience endured like good soldiers! Cheers for Wilmington!

After resting several days I felt more in the mood for singing, and so continued my pilgrimage. I found that my art, though essentially spiritual and intellectual, was much dependent upon the physical nature, as this would constantly react upon the higher one. I therefore sang with most satisfaction when in good health. Upon leaving Wilmington I held services in all the larger cities and towns of the state, everywhere finding the people hospitable and appreciative. Singing on in my course I soon found myself at

BALTIMORE,

The "Monumental City," and largest city of Maryland. This state lies directly west of Delaware, and is pierced by the Chesapeake Bay. The area is about 9,300 square miles. The western part of the state is hilly, or mountainous, but as it slopes eastward it becomes level.

The Bay forms a most excellent avenue of commerce, and furnishes the state with other important resources. Baltimore is famed as a beautiful city, all over the world, It contains a population of about 300,000 souls. My first appearance here was at the anniversary of the Missionary Society of the M. E. Church. This style of music was altogether new to Baltimoreans, and they seemed quite entranced with it. Some in the audience even fell to shouting over it. There is no city in our country more Methodistic than Baltimore, nor scarcely another equal to it in its hospitality to strangers. I went from church to church, here, and sang to gathered crowds, and over seven thousand children collected, to listen to my songs, at Market Hall. I stood on a stand and sang until I was tired and hoarse. Afterwards I was requested to give a service in one of the Baptist churches. I readily complied, as I worked with all denominations alike.

The programme of the evening was just about half finished, when the good Rev. Griffith Owen, (now deceased) came to me and asked if I would allow an interruption for a few moments. Of course, I willingly consented, and seated myself to rest awhile. There was a slight rustle in the congregation, and in a moment a couple stood before the altar to be married. Why they had chosen this time for the beautiful ceremony, I do not know; but it seemed most appropriate to celebrate so glad a sacrament, in the midst of joy and song. At the close of the ceremony, I sang a nuptial hymn, and they went on their way rejoicing. It formed a very pleasant little episode in our meeting, as one may imagine.

From here I was invited to give about twenty-five services of song through the state, under the auspices of the State Sunday-school Association. These were given in connection with Rev. Mr. Owen, its State Secretary. We visited Fredrickstown, Cumberland, Hagerstown, and all the principal points in the state, and left a fair surplus in the hands of the State Sunday-school Treasurer.

WASHINGTON, D.C.

This is our Capital City—the center of our government. It contains a population of about 150,000, and is much admired for its elegant buildings, tasteful decorations, and wide, clean streets. My first singing here was in the Hall of Representatives, in presence of the national dignitaries, Mr. Lincoln and most of his cabinet. My songs were very kindly received.

The simplicity of the melodies, combined with their lofty

sentiments, touched those great minds, wearied with the tangled affairs of state, and for a time seemed to bring comfort and rest. Mr. Lincoln seemed particularly pleased with "Your Mission," and sent up a written request (which I now have in my possession, and regard as a rare relic) to have it repeated.

Since then I have given services in all parts of the capital, for churches of different denominations, and have always had good audiences. My last visit was in the winter of 1878, *en route* for Texas.

Before leaving I wished to pay my respects to President Hayes and his estimable lady. Accordingly I sought opportunity to do so through the public reception at the White House. These receptions are occasions of great interest. They occur twice each week, during a part of the year, and furnish strangers an easy opportunity of meeting the President and his wife. The elegant grounds of the mansion are usually crowded with carriages, while the eastroom is thronged with the *elite* of the city, and many miscellaneous travelers who are visiting the capital. The company is a brilliant one. Beauty and wealth dazzle on all sides. The elegance of the apartments is only exceeded by the rich dress of the distinguished visitors.

The President and his wife stand waiting to receive their guests, and extend to them the courtesies of the House. Although much of this seems ceremonious and formal, there is an under current of sympathy and kind feeling which makes the people feel one with their chief representative.

On Sabbath I attended the Metropolitan church, and heard words of searching power from the lips of Rev. Dr. Newman. Ex-President Grant's pew happened that day to be occupied by the modern apostle of temperance,—Mr. Francis Murphy, and some of his co-laborers—Miss Frances Willard, Mrs. Annie Whittenmeyer, and Mrs. Mary C.

HALL OF REPRESENTATIVES, WASHINGTON.

Johnson, of the "Women's Temperance Union." In the afternoon, Lincoln Hall was crowded to overflowing to hear Mr. Murphy. It was his first appearance in the capital; and, as his fame had preceded him, and wonders of his great work in Pittsburg had become known abroad, many anxious eyes awaited his *debut* before the people of Washington.

This was made in his usual modest manner, and before five minutes he had carried his audience with him, till they breathed as he breathed, and thought as he thought. His personal magnetism is wonderful, and his eloquence as genuine as Gough's.

The meeting was one of marked success, and closed with a burst of song from the large choir, and a floral tribute to Mr. Murphy.

The following evening I held a service of song at the Metropolitan church. Through the good management of Mrs. Dr. Newman, I had an excellent audience. We continued the exercise for an hour and a half, when Francis Murphy, who happened to be present, was called out to "say a word." He arose and after kindly referring to the "feast of song" which they had all enjoyed, begged to be excused from speaking, saying he had but just so much capital, and wished to reserve his forces for his forthcoming temperance campaign, in their city. All were cordially invited, however, to attend his meetings. The service of the evening left an encouraging sum in the hands of the committee, towards discharging a debt upon the church. On Tuesday I reached the place of my next engagement,

ALEXANDRIA.

I almost forgot to state that I nearly always carried my own organ with me—one made especially for the purpose. When I entered the church here, with it, a Methodist class meeting was in progress. I sat down to rest, and enjoy the exercises with the class, and found them very interesting. But the night came on, and with it quite a small audience. We covered expenses, 'tis true, and the church had something left; but it was such a turn out as is always calculated to dampen ones ardor, somewhat. However we did not waste ourselves in grief, but pushed on, hoping for a better time in the next place.

At Alexandria, we were very hospitably entertained at the house of Mr. Harmon, a most estimable Virginia gentleman. Being compelled, however, to leave on the 3 a.m. train, I refused his kind invitation to remain for the night, and after adieus and well-wishes I bent my steps toward the depot. Is there any place much more comfortless than many of our railroad waiting rooms. If so, we have not found it. The very seats seems to be contrived for *discomfort*. There may be some advantage, some way, to some body, in having the benches divided off into square sections by iron arms, but we are quite certain it is not to the weary traveler, long detained, who otherwise could contrive a temporary bed on the seats. Future companies perhaps, may consider the comfort of the traveling public, somewhat more than our present railroad management sees fit now to do. It is high time there was improvement in the furniture, not only of depots, but of passenger coaches; but enough of this. We waited rather impatiently for the train, and had our weak attempts at rest continually rendered useless, from the coarse songs, and loud oaths of a band of ruffians, who hung around the place.

Young men who can only swear, tell vulgar stories, and contaminate the air with the breath of bad whisky, are fit subjects for the police force, and should not be inflicted upon decent people at railroad depots. For once I took great pleasure in a most unmusical sound—the shrill whistle of the locomotive—glad to escape my low company. Then off for

FREDRICKSBURG.

This is a place of about four thousand inhabitants. I arrived at a most unseasonable hour, but notwithstanding, was met at the depot, and conducted to a warm fireside in a Methodist parsonage.

Our host and hostess spared no pains to make us comfortable. Culture, refinement, simplicity, and unbounded hospitality characterized this household. Rev. Dr. Armstrong and his lady have exemplified to their neighbors what a model Christian home can be. Would there were many such examples! In Fredricksburg—unlike my last appointment—I was greeted with an excellent audience, but the acoustic properties of the church were so unfavorable, that it was a difficult matter to sing. I did as well as I could under the circumstances, and the patient audience kindly waited for the last song which *I* enjoyed most. Off again at four o'clock the next morning, I found myself soon seated in a railroad coach bound for the historic city of

RICHMOND,

Virginia. The "Old Dominion," has the honor of being the birthplace of seven of our Presidents. It is low and level toward the east, but gradually rises as the land grades westward, into the Blue Ridge Mountains. The history of Virginia is one full of interest, as she took such active part in the early colonial struggles.

No state in the Union has such universal reputation for whole-hearted hospitality as this one. Before the war, "an old Virginia planter's home," was the northern guest's paradise.

Richmond is a very old city, comprising a population of some 70,000 inhabitants. It is beautifully situated on the James river. During our late civil war, this city was rendered ever memorable, by the horrors of cruelty practiced upon Union prisoners at Libby prison, which is located here.

The fearful sufferings there endured by our patriotic braves, have sickened the world's memory of Richmond, and one passes through her busy marts, seeming to hear the cries of distress from those black walls, even when far away from them. Heaven only can atone to them, for those tragic days at Libby prison. While in Libby I thought of Chaplain McCabe, who, being a prisoner here during the war, managed to dig himself out, and bear to the outside world a true account of what was taking place inside these walls. Oh, how grandly he had sung the " Battle Hymn of the Republic," within its barriers, to cheer up the dispairing boys, and then let his brain and fingers contrive as grandly to find means for their escape or relief! No wonder, now, that people crowd houses to hear his story, sad as it is, for it has a heroic side, which is always attractive to patriotic hearts. But Libby is no more! The stranger may pass in and out the dark building, which has been converted to a business use, and never gather more than the faintest hint, within its precincts, of that terrible time.

But let us leave it, and wander in the subdued sunshine without, till we come to the beautiful home of Mr. Asa Snyder. It was in this cultured family that I found a most comfortable resting place during my singing in Richmond. A Sabbath here, especially, was a season of great refreshment, giving me an opportunity of hearing good Bishop Doggett, of the Methodist Episcopal Church, South. I also had the privilege of participating in the sacramental service, which followed the sermon. It was truly a feast of love and tears. My inner soul seemed utterly broken up at the memory of my Savior's sufferings for me. When urged to "sing a hymn," I could only let my tender emotions make excuse for me while I feasted in silence.

In the afternoon I gave my first song-sermon to a southern audience, and my own soul told me that it was a profitable service. It was well received. Before leaving the city I gave three more "evenings of song," to rather small but appreciative houses. My next engagement was but twenty miles away, at

PETERSBURG,

A city numbering about 20,000 in population. The chief commercial interest seems to be tobacco. I visited the large factories, where the weed is manufactured into the various trade articles, and heard 1,500 colored men sing together as they twisted the narcotic weed. Here I smelled, and smelled, and smelled, and smelled, until I felt like *eschewing* the abominable thing forever. The very air seemed contaminated with it.

I sang in the Baptist church, to a large audience. I liked the church, because the pulpit is baptized along with the candidates. The pastor has but to touch a spring, and the entire pulpit immediately immerses itself beneath the baptistry. This gives all in the congregation an opportunity of witnessing the baptismal scenes to better advantage. The church is a large, and very influential one, and our evening among its people passed quite pleasantly. From

RALEIGH

I received very urgent letters, asking me to come and give several services, but I was able then to give but one. However the cordiality of the letters, and their seeming interest in the matter, led me to project a special southern trip for the purpose. Imagine my astonishment, then, upon reaching the place, to find that it was decided not to open the church for me. No previous notice had been given, and there I was, with my organ (which had been purposely ordered on from Boston), forty dollars of traveling expenses, two hundred miles out of my way, and no engagement! I managed to restrain my "righteous indignation," settle my bills, and then shake off the dust of their city against them. Such unbusiness-like performance may be shrewd, but it is as dishonest as it is un-Methodistic. At the old Virginia port of

NORFOLK,

Whose population is twenty thousand, I met a crowd of most attentive listeners. They seemed spell-bound at the new rendering of gospel truth. My success here was attributable to the energies of Mr. J. R. Wilson, a Sunday-school superintendent. Many of the southern brethren were present and extended to me the kindly hand of Christian greeting at the close. "Stay another night," they said, "or come again, and we will give you a larger room than this and fill it with people for you." But our arrangements made it necessary for us to push on. Another long day's ride by train brought me to

GOLDSBORO,

A southern village of 3,000 inhabitants. Here my service seemed very dull to me. The place appeared so barren, the little old-fashioned Methodist church so forbidding, and the audience so small, that I was heartily glad when the programme had been completed. I did not feel in sympathy with my surroundings, somehow, and after thanking my audience for their attention went to my large, square, open hotel, and was off early next morning for

WILMINGTON,

North Carolina is the state from which we obtain much of our tar, pitch, and turpentine. Though on the sea-coast it has no commerce of its own, an account of the shallow, unnavigable nature of its inlets, and the presence of numerous low islands and sandbars along the shore. Its people, however, are practical and persevering, and have developed various other resources in their state,—mining, agricultural, lumbering, and commerce through other ports. Wilmington, the place of my appointment, is a city of 15,000 inhabitants, situated near the sea coast in the southeastern part of the state. A heavy rain prevented my audience from assembling in large numbers, and those who came found me with dampened ardor for singing. I missed too, the cordial greeting of Dr. Moran, which so much cheered me on my first visit to this city. But New York and Dr. Deems, perhaps, have made a wider sphere for his usefulness than he had here. Striking southward, an all day's car ride, brings me to

COLUMBIA,

The capital of South Carolina. This little state has long been noted as the first rice growing state in the Union. The coast is skirted with fertile islands, which produce the sea island cotton. Among the pleasant things of my visit to Columbia, was the new acquaintance and Christian sympathy of J. W. Wightman, D.D., whose hospitable "manse" sheltered the wandering pilgrim for a few days. I spent a most delightful Sabbath with him, heard the blessed gospel from his eloquent lips, and in the evening gave a song sermon service to a large and intelligent congregation. I labored to some disadvantage, however, for lack of singing books, twenty being all I had with me, yet, notwithstanding, the ready sympathy of the people enabled me to forget the embarrassment, and to have a very pleasant evening. At the close of the exercises, a collection was taken up to help pay for the church, which was new. The former building had been burned by the Union soldiers during the late war, under peculiar circumstances. It will be remembered that the first ordinance of secession, during the war of the Rebellion, was adopted in the Baptist church of that city. When the Federal soldiers passed through Columbia, they mistook the Methodist Episcopal building for the Baptist, and in their patriotic zeal burned it to the ground. It was a sad mistake, which the church of the same name north should endeavor to rectify. The organization is poor, notwithstanding it has made noble self-denial, and has built again. The building is consequently, not free from debt, but the little band of faithful ones are doing all that can be done to lift the burden. My song service did something in that direction, but much more is needed. A beautiful bouquet of southern flowers, handed me just at leaving, reminded me for weary miles, of the delightful Christian parsonage I had left. I sent them home—the beautiful messengers they ever are—as a January present to my dear wife in the North.

CHARLESTON, SOUTH CAROLINA,

Was also on my programme. It was here that the first gun was fired during our civil war. In the month of January, 1861, the steamer Star of the West, attempted to enter Charleston Harbor with supplies for the garrison stationed at Fort Sumter. In doing so, however, the vessel was fired upon and driven back by batteries which the South Carolinians had erected on the adjacent shores. Thus began one of the most lamentable wars on record. And now it was here, after all those terrible years of bloodshed and national disintegration, that I was called, in a time of peace, to sing to an audience of *freedmen!* There before me, with their ebon faces all aglow with enthusiasm, was the one grand result of that fearful struggle. Let us be thankful that it is over, and that we still have a united people in North and South!

My congregation was made up of colored people of all shades of complexion. There were many whose fairness made one doubt the taint of their blood, while others showed all the unmistakable features of the full-born African. They were very extravagant in their demonstrations of appreciation, and seemed, altogether, quite a refined class of their race. My next appointment was at

AUGUSTA,

A place of about 20,000 inhabitants, just on the state line between South Carolina and Georgia. I sang here under the auspices of the Young Men's Christian Association. There was a powerful revival of religion in progress when I came into the city, under the faithful labors of Dr. Menshall, of Indiana. Two hundred conversions were announced as having taken place within a few days.

Now this was exactly the kind of spiritual atmosphere that I liked to come into, for was not *my* work religious? Sacred song was the sweet evangel who carried the message of God's truth to human hearts in my method, but the message was just the same as fell from the anointed lips of the minister in the pulpit. Only let perishing humanity learn of the great salvation purchased for them, and it matters not how or by whom the glad news comes. Get the news into their ears and hearts, at all events.

Oh, how easy it was for me to sing in such an element as was there in that church at Augusta! I have frequently received letters from pastors asking me to postpone an engagement on account of a revival in the church. Such letters always cut me to the heart, for my chief desire is to awaken or help strengthen this very spirit among the people; but I must bear misunderstanding and be patient.

Well, where next? To a little city of about 6,000 population, called

ATHENS,

Out toward Northern Central Georgia. If my readers know what it is to go from a warm, blooming land, directly into one of wintry desolation, they can form some idea of how I felt up there at Athens. Everybody seemed shy of me. There was no hearty hand-grasp, no sympathetic " God bless your efforts," nothing to make me feel welcome, and at liberty

in my own soul. The first arrangement had been to have
the service in the church, but upon further consideration
a gay opera house was chosen. Whether my innocent
organ suggested *monkeys* and *monkey shines*, I do not
know; but I did my best with the support I had, and was
not unwilling to get out of the place when my engagement had been filled.

The great southeastern cotton market,

SAVANNAH,

Was my next point. This city numbers about 30,000 inhabitants. Here I had trouble again. The parties who
employed me did not recognize their obligations when I
came to hold my service, and I was reduced to the humiliation of renting my own hall, and announcing myself. I
could obtain nothing but the store-room of a music house,
and there a very slim attendance assembled to hear me sing
my hymns. Music and music books were piled all around
us, but I had no inspiration. I regret very much such misunderstandings as these, for they are detrimental in their effects upon the public mind in connection with Christian
effort. The capital of Georgia,

ATLANTA,

Was my next stopping place. The population here is 40,000.
My reception in this city was far different from that which
I received in the last. I had been in Atlanta for a song
service in March, 1871, and received this very flattering
notice from the leading newspaper of the place, the Atlanta *Constitution*.

"His power is marvelous, thrilling and subduing the entire audience into the deepest silence, and causing all to be
on the *qui vive* for fear that a single note may be missed.
There is not only the sweetest music but the purest gospel in Philip Phillips' singing."

This now prepared the way before me, and insured me

a hearty reception. My old friend, Rev. George Standing, had charge of the church where my service was conducted, and we had a most enjoyable evening. I was never in better voice and spirits, and my audience seemed well-entertained. It was composed mostly of colored people, with several teachers and members of the "Clark School Institute." I afterwards learned that the colored brethren were somewhat inclined to slight the press, and sent the newspapers no tickets for the service, which was quite contrary to custom. The brethren, also, did no advertising through the papers. This was a mistake, for it was resented by the press, and fell in unfavorable comment upon my defenseless head. Where before was fulsome praise, was now most unjust criticism.

Leaving quite early in the morning, I reached

OPELIKA,

A town of about 3,000 inhabitants, "away down in Alabama." While walking from the depot to the hotel, I was met by a half-drunken fellow, who professed to be acquainted with me. It may have been that he had attended some of my meetings, somewhere, but I did not recall his features. His good nature was consummate. He insisted upon walking with me, and introducing me to almost every one we met. It was ludicrous in the extreme. Perhaps he was one of my converts. I should look for no better result, either, if I did not depend upon God to do the converting in my work. After being presented to over a dozen persons by my jolly companion, we reached the hotel, and I managed to shake off the intruder.

My singing had been well advertised, and an excursion party from Albany had come on to be present at the service. Here I spent my first Sabbath in Alabama. In the afternoon I went to a large church—more like a barn with the windows out,—to hear a young colored preacher give his first sermon. I could hear nothing but his text, and that only about once in fifteen minutes. He halloed all the other parts in such a high, unnatural key, that I could make nothing whatever out of it. He frothed at the mouth and watered at the eyes, with his efforts. When completely exhausted, he let his voice sink down upon an ordinary tone, and repeated what he gave as his text : "I tell 'e what it is, ye must fear God." He had a congregation of at least one thousand people. During all his exercises, two old colored "mothers in Israel," were walking up and down through the audience, shouting, jumping, and clapping their hands. This evidenced religious joy, we suppose, but it was the most ludicrous thing imaginable. The din was incessant. Our ears were fairly singing with the strain upon the tympanum. This was another point from which we were glad to escape.

SELMA,

A place of about 10,000 population, near the center of the state, was the next point I visited. I found it a beautiful southern city. Through the excellent management of Mr. Hobbs, I had a good audience and a pleasant time. Jefferson Davis, ex-President of the Confederate States, sat in the assembly before me. What thoughts stirred in my mind as I gazed into his care-worn face, I shall not undertake to relate; but how thankful I was, that I, from the North, and he from the South, had no more need of embarrassment in meeting, but could rejoice in sweet fellowship over a simple gospel song!

From Alabama I went to

FLORIDA,

The land of flowers. What memories of old John Ponce de Leon here! We wondered why the grave looked so dark to him, and why he wished so much to prolong a life which had already became a burden. Ah! could he have indeed accepted the water of life, whose healing stream issues from Calvary, he would have sought no further for the fountain of perennial youth! But his heart was disappointed in its quest, and he went home only to tell of his failure, and of a land floating in perfumes, which he named Florida. Alas! poor Leon!

My first engagement in the state, called me to

JACKSONVILLE,

A beautiful city of 12,000, situated on the St. John's river. Here oranges hang temptingly above one's head on the trees, in January and February, flowers perfume the air, and birds circle about in the sunshine. This state is our Italy.

I had the great pleasure of singing to a large number of invalids, who had come here in search of health; oh, how many weary ones there are in this world, who spend the larger part of their lives in "looking for a climate!" and yet, where does the Great Healer dwell? faith, more faith, is what our poor humanity needs! The Good Physician can cure us in our homes, can He not? if we will but believe for healing.

From Jacksonville I struck due west for

TALLAHASSEE,

The capital of the state. It is a shady little city of about 2,000 inhabitants. I arrived just in time to appear before my waiting audience, which was a good one. I was compelled to use the organ provided me, which had been elevated to the top of the pulpit, on a level with the sides of the galleries. Between me and the audience was a great, burly negro, with a lever, pumping away with all his might, to give me wind for my organ, It was a very comical sight, and my sense of the ridiculous nearly overmastered me several times. How could one be expected to do one's best perched up in that style, as if some strange specimen to be examined; and that white-eyed, tugging, sweating creature just before one! It would be unreasonable certainly. But if a few notes were suspiciously *gay*, I trust my hearers attributed them to high art trills, they truly *were* trills! But to be serious, let no church ever try the experiment of putting a singer, preacher or lecturer, above the people's heads! They will give you no satisfactory performance with such embarrassing environments.

Every mile of my travel now is through delightfully green country, flooded with sunshine and the grateful odors of flowering trees. The pine, cedar, and live-oak forests, send into our open car-windows most pungent and refreshing draughts, as we whirl along on our way to

MONTGOMERY,

Alabama. We find here a beautiful city of some 15,000 population. It was once proposed during the late civil war, to make Montgomery the capital of the Confederate States; but upon further consultation, the idea was abandoned. The city shows taste and refinement in its buildings, decorations, and streets. The State House is so situated as to make a most imposing appearance, which can be said of very few capitols.

Here I heard a most excellent sermon by Dr. Wadsworth, which was the only thing I enjoyed in the city. My service was a failure. All my arrangements were made to sing in the Court Street Methodist Episcopal Church. Bills were out a day or two previous, announcing the meeting there, when the people took the liberty of changing the place to the United States Hall. I accepted the situation, but from such irregular announcements, I had a very small audience. Over head a company of "Greys" were drilling, and their incessant tramping, fifing, and shouting just above me, blended strangely with my quiet, religious songs. It was a most inappropriate and unfortunate change which was made, and the committee must have regretted it exceedingly. The few who came to listen to me were courteous enough to seem pleased, but *I* felt the service to be very unsatisfactory. After paying all my expenses myself, I left with the church employing me *one dollar and ten cents* as its share of the profits. Then I looked for the depot.

MOBILE

Is a fine commercial city of 40,000, situated on Mobile Bay, an arm of the Gulf of Mexico. Immense shipments of cotton are made from this place. Tobacco, rice, sugar and sweet potatoes are also largely exported. From its communication with so many water courses, Mobile has grown to be second only to New Orleans, in its commercial importance, as a southern seaport city.

I had an engagement here and met a very good audience. All listened very much better than I sang. The weather seemed intensely warm to me, which is probably because I am unused to such extreme heat as they have down here; for others did not appear to suffer so much as I. All professed themselves well pleased with the exercises, however, and I hurried on to my next appointment, which was at

MACON,

A place of 15,000 population. Here I was most heartily received, and sang at the Methodist Episcopal Church. Dr. Hicks, the pastor of the church, is a man of ability, and believes in "Christian progression," even in this life. The success of my service was much owing to his earnest efforts in exciting an interest in it. It seemed to do good.

At Macon I ticketed for

MERIDIAN,

In the eastern part of Mississippi. I had heard and read much of the people of this little town of 2,000 inhabitants, and was glad my pilgrimage happened to lie through it. My service was held in the Court House, which a few months before was the scene of bloodshed and murder. Previous to my coming the sheriff and my good friend, Mr. Brown, re-arranged the hall so as to banish any unpleasant suggestions which might arise in the people's minds. A small assembly came to hear the sacred songs advertised, and I was thankful to learn that they were from the very best families of the town. I sang an hour and a half, and what a privilege it was! How the exultant notes of gospel joy must have contrasted, in air, with the mad shouts of an infuriated mob! But we will not dwell on it here. Moving on I was soon at

JACKSON.

The capital of Mississippi, which has a population of 4,000 souls. My service was held in the Hall of Representatives, capitol building. It was most adroitly managed by the state secretary, James Lynch, Esq., who was fearless of public opinion when great principles were at stake. He was an eloquent minister of the gospel, as well as a politician. I was told that this was the first time that a *mixed* audience had ever assembled under the same roof in the town. Here were all classes, waiting to listen to my singing. His Excellency, the Governor of Mississippi, was one of my hearers. I felt very much in the spirit of song that evening, and so enjoyed it very much. An excellent notice of the service appeared in the daily papers the following morning.

I found my next city,

VICKSBURG

To be one of great natural beauty. It stands upon an eminence overlooking the grand " Father of Waters," and smiles in a wild luxuriance of tropical trees and flowers. The population is large, about 15,000. Its commerce is very considerable, though it is quite modest in its pretensions, with

New Orleans and Mobile close at hand. Everywhere you turn here, you are met by war memories. Old times flash up before the mind, and you seem to hear the tramp of soldiers just beside you. Buried scenes revive. You are again in Vicksburg with Grant or Pemberton, and it is 1863.

. . . .

But no! It was only a foolish dream; you are in the theater listening to hear Philip Phillips sing. The tread of armed men is thunder, for a fearful storm has come on, keeping nearly every one but you from the place. You are glad, no doubt, that it was a dream, and banish the troublous time from your thoughts, by humming over some remembered strain of the evening as you wend your way homeward.

And yet, since these days of my pilgrimage through this Southern land, a scourge, almost worse than war, has fallen upon its cities and well nigh depopulated them. The yellow fever reign of 1878 will long be remembered as the most fatal and wide spread known for many years. New Orleans, Memphis, Vicksburg, and many cities and villages of smaller size, were utterly desolated for many months. The fever claimed its victims by the thousand, and made great charnel houses of populous cities in a few days. The spirit of business was entirely quenched, and every one either sought refuge in some other place, or remained to minister to the sick and help bury the dead. Such a calamity had rarely been known in our country. Nothing seemed to arrest its ravages from early summer until late in November. The North was eager and bountiful in its expressions of sympathy and brotherhood, and sent its hundreds of helpful hands, and thousands of willing dollars to aid the numberless sufferers. Old grudges were not so much as thought of for the time; for, after all, our disputes are matters which usually arise in our *heads*, and leave our *hearts* true and united as the Master begged His followers to be. "That they all may be one," you remember He said.

And this summer's fell affliction on the South has brought much more of this spirit of real union to light than we ever dreamed could exist since the war. So let us be hopeful.

> "God moves in a mysterious way,
>   His wonders to perform!
> He plants his footsteps on the sea,
>   And rides upon the storm.
>
> . . . .
>
> His purposes will ripen fast,
>   Unfolding every hour;
> The bud may have a bitter taste,
>   But sweet will be the flower."

Leaving Vicksburg, I came to

NEW ORLEANS.

The great southern shipping port and metropolis. It contains a population of 200,000, and is one of the most quaint and ancient-looking cities in our country. Everywhere are evidences of its French and Spanish origin. The people themselves are not free from this foreign air, and indeed the old blood still courses in many of their veins. To go around the city slowly, in an open car or carriage, up and down its avenues of fragrant magnolias, is almost worth a trip south. Nearly every house is a study. There is a combination of the antique and modern styles of architecture, often in the same building, which would verily set our good friend John Ruskin daft were he over here in America to see. The oddities jut out at every angle, and leer comically at you from the black, tumbling walls. You almost fancy they have some appreciation of the funniness of the old town, for, leaning so confidentially toward you as you pass, you laugh outright at their rows of mysterious-looking, little French eyes—windows. Yes, the old city is alive yet, and mocks the new for a time; then sleeps again to dream.

But I have wandered far away from my subject. In New Orleans I gave several services of song, and in every case to full houses. My first engagement was at Ames Church, where I had an audience of about one thousand people; my second at the great Carondolet Street Methodist Episcopal Church South, and my third at the Union Colored Church. My second service was on behalf of Bishop Marvin's "Memorial Fund," and quite a satisfactory sum was realized. At the Union Colored Church I had arranged to give every one who purchased a full ticket a copy of my book. In this way several hundred were dispersed among the colored people.

A Northerner, or one unused to our characteristic "darky," can form but a poor estimate of the scene of that evening. The negro soul seems nine-tenths emotion, and nothing is so potent to arouse it as religious song. They actually bore me along on their own measures; for feet, heads, and often books were going at once, helping me keep time. Tears flowed, hands were clapped, and various pious ejaculations could be continually heard in the crowd. It was extremely laughable at times, but I could not but wish that all my *white* congregations would so readily catch and appreciate the religious tone of these services. The colored folks understand at once, and come *expecting* to be made good.

Getting on board one of Morgan's line of splendid steamers, I left New Orleans for

GALVESTON,

Texas. A delightful passage of twenty hours brought me to my place of destination at about nine o'clock in the morning.

The bus-drivers and porters from the hotels nearly deafen you as soon as you set foot upon the dock. Some of them make elegant speeches, recounting all the superior advantages of their house or carriage, and rattle them off in true parrot style. They have plenty of that species of bird down here, and they have learned its lessons well. If the fellows were not so exceedingly comical in all these airs, they would be a greater nuisance than good-natured travelers find them to be; as it is, one only has to do some first-class shoving, hold well on to one's carpet-bag, and push ahead to the bus-driver. Then all is peace as far as one passenger is concerned.

Galveston is a fine, growing city of about 45,000 inhabitants. It shares the fame peculiar to many of our larger western cities—that of being a very wicked city. The class of emigration which has been drawn to these border towns, explains at once how they have received this fame. The hope of large gains with small outlay of labor, at first attracted many idle and adventurous persons to the West. Those who had the courage to break off from all old associations in the eastern states, and try their fortunes in a new land, were certainly possessed of much spirit; and this same spirit finds outlet in a hundred different ways, when the country is new, and all the restrictions of a home-society are removed. No doubt they well deserve the name of "fast cities," but there is an immense amount of mental activity and power wasted here, just because the missionary, to turn it into better channels, has not come along. A superabundant energy, either of brain or body, must expend itself upon something, and the object upon which it is spent proves it vicious or holy. So Christians should bear into these western cities such objects of public interest as will be pure and elevating, if they would not have them still "fast cities."

Galveston is noted for its miles and miles of beautiful beach. A drive of eight miles along this surf-way, was to me, one of the grandest features of my southern travels. The carriage drive winds along over the clean sand, close by the water's edge. The salt spray sifts gently down into your face, but the salt breezes fan it quickly away, and refresh you with their invigorating breath. The city is rather low, which is a great disadvantage. A very disastrous flood happened here a few years ago, doing much damage.

The streets of Galveston are bordered with the most beautiful oleanders. In May these are in full bloom, presenting a fairy-like picture. Last, but not least among the city's attractions, is a wide-awake, fair-dealing newspaper, the Galveston *News*. It seems to be alive to all the interests of the state, and has an extensive circulation. This is very important. A daily or weekly newspaper, where it is regularly read, as it is in most families of the common people, has more to do in the shaping of moral and political issues than any other single force. A man naturally grows to have the opinion of his paper, unless previously prejudiced, and thus we see how great a number of followers the editor has, and how essential that his judgment should be sound and Heaven-directed. But to the singing: I gave here my first three services in the state. On the Sabbath I started out and found one of the most flourishing Sunday-schools I had ever seen. The superintendent, Mr. Edgerly, was one who seemed to be worthy of the name and position, which so many-called superintendents are not. He was awake to all that would improve and interest both teachers and children. We half suspected that he had "a Sunday-school conscience" down under his badge of office.

The attendance upon my services was much lessened by the celebration known through the South as the "Mardi Gras." On this occasion of festivity, the whole city seems to abandon itself to merriment, and to actually run mad in masquerade, and public procession. I also visited the great cotton markets and presses here, where they squeeze a bale of cotton five feet long by four deep and wide, down to four feet long, and one foot deep, in less time than a minute. To a resident of the North, this is very interesting.

From Galveston, *via* the Texas Central Railroad, I started for

HOUSTON,

About sixty miles distant. This is a handsome town of wide streets, white houses (mostly one-story), and shade trees. It claims a population of 32,000.

Mr. C. H. Cushing kindly met and cared for me here. He is one of the earliest settlers of the place, and is a man of culture, brought up in New England. He is one of the most progressive and enthusiastic Sunday-school workers in Texas, and his influence is felt throughout the state. Besides this, he does a heavy trade in the book line, as his private business. I gave two "evenings" at Houston. My audiences were not large, but appreciative ones, and this atoned very much for the lack in numbers.

From Houston, I went on to

AUSTIN,

The capital of the state. It is a thriving inland city of 19,000 inhabitants, beautifully located on elevated ground, and built up with handsome and substantial dwellings. I was more pleased with this, than with any of the cities I had visited in this great state.

Texas does a heavy trade in cattle;—indeed, it is the chief interest. This has drawn a class of population to the state, which has given it the name of being somewhat lawless. There is not that strict regard for "the proprieties" which we find in states farther east. The herder and trader are a "law unto themselves," as they pursue their free life on the plains.

But this cattle business is immense. Some men own as many as one hundred thousand head a piece. There is an aristocracy in the trade, too, it seems. A society has been formed, into which no one is allowed to enter as a member, unless owning one thousand head of cattle, at least. This society brands their stock, and, once a year, they go among the flocks and claim their calves in proportion to the number they own. These animals are perfectly wild, and often quite vicious. In going among them, the herders ride on horses or mules for safety. These cattle roam over the wide, grassy plains, and are no more valuable to their owners as milch cows, than a wild beast. Consequently, milk is almost as scarce in Texas as in Ceylon. The large drovers, or cattle dealers, have a stuffed ox with broad horns, mounted on the tops of their houses; so that when one sees this sign in passing through a Texan town, the conclusion may at once be arrived at that a cattle man lives there. But to our journey.

In going from Houston to Austin I was induced to stop over at the thriving little town of

BRENHAM,

And give an hour of song in the afternoon. About thirty miles from the place, my old Alabama friend, Dr. Pitts, came on board the train with some fifty of his young lady students from "Chapel Hill." This was quite flattering, I thought, and, as pious Frederick Faber would have said, "was the source of very profitable confusion to me." It did my soul good to see my friend's cheery face again, and to look into the dancing eyes of so many blooming girls. They were modest, intelligent and well-behaved. The good Dr. had given them a holiday, for the purpose of bringing them to hear me sing. Benham is only a smart young town of 3,000, but had just erected a neat Opera House. It was here that my service was held, at the solicitation of the Presbyterians of the community, who worshiped there temporarily. I had been refused encouragement and help by the Methodist minister at this point, but the Presbyterians gave me a cordial welcome. Having worked so much in connection with the Methodist Episcopal church, it grieved me to see my motives and the service I came to give, misunderstood by those whose sympathy I deserved, as a co-laborer in Christ's cause. However, it is often thus, and strangers give us the warm hand of brotherhood, while "our own" pass us coldly by. My visit was, after all, very satisfactory.

Leaving here, I took my train for the night *en route* for

WACO.

I found a crowded house awaiting me when I arrived next evening, and had time for only a hasty cup of tea before coming before the people. One cannot sing well on an empty stomach, and after so wearisome a ride as mine had been; so I fear it had not the spiritual or intellectual interest which it was designed to have. But I did my best, and Milton says that "angels could do no more." So I contented myself with the kind sympathies of the people, who listened to the full service very attentively. I sang in College Hall under the auspices of the president of the institution, Rev. Samuel P. Wight.

My next service was at

DENISON,

A place of 3,000 inhabitants. In making the trip I passed through the most fertile parts of the great state. I was shown fields where wheat, corn and cotton would grow thriftily side by side; and where is there another country such as that? This soil is almost entirely new, and its varied resources have not been exhausted by continual plantings, year after year. Young farmers would do well to consider Texas before settling down on a hill farm in crowded eastern districts.

The people of Denison are living in the fond hope of making their town the great railroad center of the southwest, just as Chicago is of the northwest. At the rapid progress it is making, they may realize their hope, and that in a near future. It is next door neighbor to the great Indian territory, where there is a civilized Indian government. Some of the Indians are accounted very intelligent, and many live in considerable style. They borrow most of their notions from the white people, and it is only to be regretted that they are not better ones sometimes.

SHERMAN

Is another thriving Texan city, claiming a population o 8,000. I think it evinces that spirit of progress peculiar to the West, more than any place I have visited. I stopped at the Brigley House, which is quite equal, in all of its appointments, to many an eastern hotel. Everybody one meets here seems to be in a hurry, yet most have that complaisant look upon their faces which makes one sure that they are being *successful* in something or other. A happy state, truly!

My service was held in an Opera House again—a circumstance which I always lament—yet I *did* enjoy this occasion, very much, despite the gay walls and hangings. The audience was large and responsive. Mrs. L. H. Carhart had managed the advertising so successfully, that, out of their share of the profits, the church people were able to pay for a fine Smith American organ.

Early next morning I left with a joyous heart for WACO, in which I had already given one service. This is the largest town, for its age, in Texas. It is but two years old and yet has a population of 12,000. Every school-boy in town, can give you its full history. It has a college, and some very fine buildings. Saloons, dance-houses, and other low places of amusement, however, have gone up side by side with the better class of improvements, and sin opposes an unblushing front all over the city

Just at the time of my visit, the comic lecturer, Josh Billings, was setting the people wild with his drolleries. Of course, my simple sing-song would have very little chance in such a place, and with such competition; so, after singing to a very small assembly, I left next morning for

DALLAS,

The central metropolis of Texas. Dallas is a city of considerable pretensions. It has a population of 10,000, and is full of energy and enterprise. It has adopted many of the improvements of larger cities, which often cause evident surprise to the "smart Easter," who comes out West with his carpet-bag, "just to look around."

My songs were sung in the opera house, to a fair audience. The people had looked for something simply entertaining. My hymns were not gay enough to suit their expectations. However, they endured patiently to the close of the service.

The editor of the *Commercial*, of this city, is doing a most excellent work for the community with his paper, and personal influence. I was glad to meet a man of such calibre down here.

My next service was at Shreveport, Louisiana, a long settled town of 5,000 inhabitants. Shreveport will be remembered as a locality in our country which has, year after year, suffered greatly from the ravages of yellow fever. The scourge seemed to rest upon it heavier than upon any of its sister towns, until the terrible summer and fall of 1878, when so many southern cities were visited with the destroyer. It is situated on the Red River, and, if the subject were scientifically studied, in this very fact might be found the cause of the yearly epidemic. The sanitary arrangements of most of these southern cities, will bear much improvement.

My service here was on Saturday night—always a poor time—yet I sang as usual to the few who came. Next day being invited to give a Song-Sermon, I complied, and the Lord richly blessed the effort. The hearts of the people were touched, and heaven seemed all about us.

The pastor of the church in which I sang, Dr. Daves, had been the first missionary to Mexico. It was most interesting and instructive to listen to his fine description of scenes and circumstances in that land. His cultured mind, however, charmed no less than his great sympathetic heart. He showed a nature whose bent it was to take upon itself all the joys and woes of his race. He longed for universal peace and fellowship. I learned to love the man for the great love wherewith he loved the world. During all my stay in the place, he showed me the most uniform kindness and courtesy. My next service was in

JEFFERSON

My last in Texas, and, I think, the least enjoyable of all. Though one of the oldest towns in the state, it has that fatal quality which an American expresses by *deadness*. The few persons who ventured out in the light of day, seemed, themselves, half fossilized, "So sleepy was the place." Most of the houses were unoccupied, however, and there may have been, after all, a very fair representation abroad. Jefferson was the place from which stages used to be despatched all over the state; but the railroads have now killed the trade and this town with it. My meeting here, despite its sacred nature, had some very comical features. It was held in Market Hall, which was kindly given by the people. I found a good old fruit-vender under the hall, who assisted me in carrying up my organ. So much done! Then the next thing which filled me with dismay, was the lack of a stool. What should I do for a stool? Nothing in that bare room sent me back any word of comfort. The matter began to look serious. All at once my odd new friend trotted from my side, without a word, and disappeared by some mysterious door at the farther end of the hall. Soon I heard his uncertain steps descending stairs. What now? My last friend had forsaken me! Had I said anything, done anything, to hurt the good soul's feelings? But just in the midst of these harrowing thoughts, the same step, with its little halt, is heard again on the stairs, and the old man comes triumphantly toward me with a great *half-bushel measure* in his arms! Do not smile, gentle reader, but rejoice with me. That simple measure, if you would review its public career, *may* not have been, it is true, as innocent as it looks; but rest assured, it never did more honest work than as a seat for the Pilgrim that night at Market Hall.

This ended my journeyings through Texas. I next went to Arkansas, and directly to the capital,

LITTLE ROCK.

This is a fine healthy city of 25,000 population and rapidly growing. Situated on the Arkansas river, which communicates with the great Mississippi somewhat farther down, it forms a popular shipping point for the agricultural and other productions of the interior. It adorns a state which has, thus far, not many attractions, for much of the Arkansas country is dreary in the extreme, to the traveler, and not very promising to the politician. Cattle raising, it is true, is quite a profitable business in many parts, but the whole state has yet to be developed in its resources. Railroad trains vex you with their slowness, and rough riding. You protest that you could make as good time in walking and have more comfort. Travelers are constitutional grumblers, of course, but there *is* much truth in what is said here. Time is going to do great things for Arkansas, and we must be patient. At Little Rock I had the pleasure of meeting Rev. Lewis, a most congenial spirit, and a fine speaker, who introduced me to a good audience.

MEMPHIS

Called me next. This is a city of 65,000 inhabitants. It is situated on the Mississippi river, just at the point where the Ohio makes its junction with the former. Memphis is consequently, the greatest commercial city in Tennessee. The state produces wheat, cotton, corn and tobacco, which with hogs, mules, and cattle,—largely raised in some counties,—find a ready market at Memphis. This city, also, was sadly depopulated by the yellow fever scourge of 1878.

When I reached Memphis, it was nearly time for my singing. If any of my readers have been over the M. K. & L. R. R. or the *best* of those southwestern lines, some idea can be formed of how I felt after that bouncing trip. But I was thankful to escape with unbroken limbs, and hurried away to my appointment, doing as well as the circumstances would permit. My next stop was at

BROWNSVILLE,

Somewhat of a rural town—with the old style forms and sentiments of the south. It contains 3,000 people, and enjoys a little aristocracy of its own. In this place I sang to a fair audience, and to the seeming satisfaction of all.

It was a great pleasure to pass on to the beautiful city of

NASHVILLE,

The capital of Tennessee, the pride of its people. It is very picturesquely situated on an eminence, which gives it a most imposing appearance. Indeed, the city rambles over the hills, and gives one a very delightful feeling of grace and freedom. The population is 30,000. Two institutions of learning, "Fisk University" and "Central College," add fame to the place, and bring in a class of cultured people, which nothing else would do so readily.

The "Fisk University," it will be remembered, was built

by the noted "Jubilee Singers," for the education of the colored class who aspired to a higher intellectual training, and admission to the professions. These "Jubilee Singers," a small company of gifted colored persons, determined upon a musical tour to raise funds. They possessed remarkably fine, rich voices,—as do almost all of their race. Their plan was to give religious concerts, using only the old plantation songs of their slavery. The attempt proving very successful in the United States, they were encouraged to go abroad, and here we have the result of their praiseworthy efforts.

Here we find the true aristocracy of the state, both colored and white. "Central College" is also for this class, and attracts a good attendance. It is presided over by the faithful Dr. John Bradden. It is worth a visit to Nashville to witness the "educated airs" which many of those people of color put on. They can not *help* but feel the difference in their position from what it used to be, and that knowledge *has* and *does* elevate them. Let them put on airs!

My "Evenings of Song" were at Masonic Hall. So well satisfied was my first audience, that I was requested to repeat the service on the following evening. To this I readily assented, though this necessitated me remaining in Nashville over the Sabbath.

On that day I had the opportunity of meeting our own Methodist Episcopal Sunday-school, and joining with them in the sweet songs of the gospel. I also sang some of my hymns, and spent a happy hour. In the afternoon I visited the College Sunday-school, and went through the same programme of singing. Then the Jubilee Singers gave me a rare treat in some of the slave melodies. I was particularly impressed with one entitled, "I've been Redeemed,"—so much so, indeed, that I went directly to the Church South, and gave a song sermon on redemption. The house was filled to overflowing. The service was so new and novel, that I fear it did not do all the good for which it was intended. People seemed vastly *pleased*, but *I* wished them *bettered*. Perhaps they were, for we can not read other hearts. I missed the ready response of congregational singing, which is such a great support to me North. However, I should not complain, for my stay here was very pleasant, on the whole.

From Nashville, I hurried on to

CHATTANOOGA,

A city of 20,000 inhabitants, near the famous Lookout Mountain. The place is historic. Most of it has been built since the war of 1861. The National Soldiers' Cemeteries here are a great credit to the South. Chattanooga impresses one as a very fast town. The people cared little, or nothing, for a service like mine, consequently I had a very indifferent audience. Nevertheless, I was glad to sing the gospel in sight of Lookout Mountain.

KNOXVILLE

Was my next objective point. I found here a city of 20,000 inhabitants, and good Dr. Spence awaiting me with a royal welcome. The church where my exercises were held was large and well filled. Everybody seemed enchanted with the new method, and I trust some real good was done for Christ. My next stopping place was at a small town in Tennessee, of about 2,000 inhabitants, called

GREENVILLE.

This was the former home, and is now the burial place of our ex-president, Andrew Johnson. The place has little interest to the traveler, but for this.

The greater part of Eastern Tennessee is mountainous, and a fine grazing country.

"OLD KENTUCKY"

Came next on my programme. I had an engagement at

Bowling Green, in that state, and found it to be a thriving town of 6,000 people, in a very fertile region. Here a large audience greeted me, and I was hospitably entertained by a good Michigan family, and the railroad agent. From this place I hurried on to

LOUISVILLE,

In the same state. This great mart has a population of 135,000, and is considered one of the most prosperous of southern cities. It is situated on the Ohio river, and forms a great center of trade for the surrounding country. Kentucky is a state of mild and healthful climate, most of it being mountainous. Strangers find an unfailing attraction in the magnificent Mammoth Cave, near Green river, which has been worthily classed among the "seven wonders of the world."

My service in Louisville, was under the direction of Mr. J. H. Wheat, in the Southern Methodist Episcopal church. In my audience was the venerable Bishop Kavenaugh and his estimable wife. The evening passed away pleasantly, the exercises being closed by the Bishop's benediction.

LEXINGTON,

A city of 16,000, was the next to hear from me. It is perhaps the most aristocratic city in Kentucky. Here our noble Henry Clay declared that he would "rather be right than be president,"—and he had his choice. In Lexington sacred song received a hearty welcome. I sang under the auspices of the Presbyterian church, headed by that excellent teacher, A. C. Hurst, who has since become a most efficient minister of the gospel.

FRANKFORT.

The capital of Kentucky, next claimed my attention. It is a new-fledged city, just now claiming its 6,000 inhabitants. Here I sang for the Methodists, and was most courteously introduced to my audience by Rev. Mr. Henderson, the pastor of this church, who gave me a far better name than I was aware I possessed. Glancing down my programme of appointments, I find several smaller places in Kentucky where I have filled engagements, Paris, Cynthiana and Marysville, one of the oldest towns in the state. In these I held my services, and found the people full of hospitality and kindly feeling to even a singing evangelist.

In due time I reached the fine old city of

COVINGTON.

It does not seem like a southern city, though accounted such. Situated on the southern bank of the Ohio river, just opposite Cincinnati, and with a population of 32,000 people, it forms one of the most important of trade centres. It is now connected with the great city just over the river by two most substantial and attractive bridges. These bridges make the two cities one. Singing in Covington was by no means a new thing to me. I had sung here many times previous to this, and always with good encouragement. This last service was not an exception to the rule. What a blessed thought it is, that the Lord knows and watches over His own, wherever they are; no good deed of theirs, though done with all the right and left hand secrecy, can escape His notice. I believe that Amos Shinkle is doing more for the city of Covington than any other man in it. He conducts a mammoth Sunday-school, and pays out a large sum annually to sustain it. During this year he has given away over one hundred Bagster Bibles, and two hundred of the teacher's Bibles, to his Sunday-school. Not only this, but various other benevolent causes, share his generous gifts. He has a soul all on fire with love for the Master, and is working accordingly. I commend his Sunday-school to the attention of all religious teachers passing through Covington. Crossing the Ohio river here, I arrived at my old home Cincinnati.

CHAPTER III.

SINGING IN THE CENTRAL STATES.

FROM 1860 to 1865 I was located at Cincinnati in business, and in no other place, save New York, have I done so much singing; almost every evening of the week was occupied in singing for some Church, Sunday-School, Conference, Convention or Hospital. And those were happy days, too.

Cincinnati is one of the largest and most wealthy cities in the United States. Its population is placed at 275,000. It is the metropolis of a state rich in agricultural resources, and far ahead of many older states in manufactures and commerce. The city does credit to the country by its numerous public works and handsome buildings. She is not only the greatest pork-packing point, but also the city of the famous Theodore Thomas concerts, and the new Temple of Music, with its mammoth organ. Cincinnati combines business and cultured pursuits in a most commendable manner. Ohio will always have a place of honor in my heart, for it was here I gathered strength beneath my fluttering wings, to cease trifling, and float out boldly on the pinions of sacred song, following my path of duty with faith and gladness, wherever His hand indicated the way; and in its modest little city of

MARION,

Having a population of 5,000, I found my dear wife, whose devoted companionship and love has been the chief comfort and solace of my life. Marion is located in the central portion of Ohio, in almost all of whose towns and cities I have given services, and in many of the most principal, several times. While here is to be found the most fertile and productive lands in the state, the prominent citizens, for the most part, are men of wealth and refinement, and bank and business failures are comparatively locally unknown. With such men as Abram Monnett, John Haine, T. P. Wallace, J. S. Reed, Henry Johnson, Amos Kling, and many others, steady, industrious and successful, having commercial honor for their watchword, the bright doors of prosperity have ever been ajar for Marion.

The city also is deeply indebted for its prosperity to James H. Godman and his wife, the quiet and genial T. J. Magruder, and to Jacob Fribley, ever an acknowledged power in the church, with voice as ready to condemn the wrong, as hand swift to battle for the right.

In this connection, too, how well do I remember the fine voice of Mrs. Osborn, which has given her the reputation of the sweetest lady singer in our country, and who so vitally aided me in my early work, once personating "Queen Esther" in that beautiful Cantata which was at that time so popular. Since then she has spent several years in the East, pursuing the study of her favorite art; but never can she become so proficient therein as to lead me to forget the tour from the headwaters of the Mississippi to the restless waves of the Atlantic, when herself and husband, and myself and wife, sang the songs of our old time quartette.

Beside my public services of song, I have taught music in the following towns of Ohio: Bellefontaine, Sydney, Chillicothe, Delaware, Mt. Gilead, Upper Sandusky, Bucyrus, Galion, Findlay and Kenton, in which latter place in the year 1859, during the session of the "Central Ohio Conference" of the Methodist Episcopal Church, the late

Rev. L. B. Gurley moved the adoption of the following resolution:

Resolved, That besides the local choristers and teachers, we name Philip Phillips as one who has manifested deep interest in our congregational singing, and recommend him as a teacher of music, well qualified to give instruction in churches and Sabbath-schools.

Every memory of my work in Ohio is pleasant, and it is not much wonder that I regard it the "Banner State."

NEW YORK STATE.

From Ohio I go on singing eastward, through the great state of New York, with its population of 4,500,000 souls, giving services at Buffalo, the immense wheat granary of the lower lakes; Lockport, the charming little city of canal locks; and at Niagara, where the hoarse thunders of the largest cataract in the world are often heard as far as thirty miles away from the chasm over which the mighty waters of the great western lakes roll in resistless and terrible grandeur. Thence I go forward to Rochester, where in a large hall, at the age of eighteen I made my debut as a singer of sacred song; to Auburn, the famous prison city, where the criminals of the western half of the state are confined; and to Syracuse, where that most successful young college is located, which was founded and organized by our good Dr. Peck, and which afterwards proved the influence in making him one of the bishops of our noble church. Thence I take rail to Rome, where dwells the famous Dr. Kingsley, whose skill in curing cancers and tumors of all descriptions is in constant employ, and whose great success in his great specialty is universally acknowledged and appreciated; to Utica, so noted for its great State Asylum for the insane, and whose officers are thoroughly awake to the alleviation and cure of this terrible infliction upon poor humanity; and thence to the flourishing city of Schenectady, where the old Dutchmen of Holland first drove the stakes of settlement. Up to the famed medicinal waters of Saratoga I take my way, the oldest, most noted and thoroughly frequented watering-place of our country, and from thence to the head of navigation on the noble Hudson, where stands the city of Troy, the cosiest for its size within the New York state borders. Just six miles further down this river, and nestled on its western bank, is Albany, the state's capital, as also the Knickerbocker city of America, from which I sail down the broad avenue of water to my home in New York city, the crowded metropolis of the western hemisphere. In all of these prominent centres I have given my services more than once, or even twice, and which have always been appreciated as well as I deserved. From this, my native state, I start out on the wings of song through the great length and breadth of

PENNSYLVANIA, THE KEY STONE STATE,

Which was founded by William Penn, has a population of 4,000,000, and which has filled so important a part in the country's history. Giving services in what is commonly known as the Dutch portion of the state, I stopped at Reading, Harrisburg, York, Lebanon, Allentown, Bethlehem, Lancaster and Columbia. Here the rich farms are under excellent tillage and very productive. Whatever be the size or condition of a farmer's house in this locality, he is certain to have an extraordinary good barn, always convenient and always painted, and oftentimes highly decorated. I found the people in all these cities and towns, not so demonstrative over my singing as in some others, but always candid, sober and attentive.

From these agricultural districts I proceeded to the coalfields in the Juniata valley, receiving a hearty reception from the citizens of Altoona, which seems to be a mountain railroad centre; at Mauch Chunk, the Switzerland of America, where the railway cars are carried over the mountain by the force of gravity; at Scranton, Wilkes-barre, Williamsport and Pittston, in which latter place a mountain of coal has been burning for the last three years, and almost threatening to undermine the city itself. All these localities are the centres of immense coal interests, and beneath the soil on which they are built and with which they are surrounded lie great beds of anthracite coal sufficient to furnish fuel for the whole world for centuries to come. Everywhere in this section of the state my services were largely attended and well received.

From thence I went on to Chambersburg and then on to Gettysburg, where the great and decisive battle of the rebellion was successfully fought under Gen. Meade. After a lengthy visit to the great battle-field where so many of my countrymen yielded up their lives, I returned to the city and gave my evening's service of song, but during its exercises I could almost imagine I could hear the sounds of the carnage which so lately filled the air where now I was singing the hymns of peace and love.

Going on to Pittsburg, which I suppose my friend J. C. Jolly, of Wolverhampton, England, would denominate the "black regions of America," but which we proudly designate the great metropolis of iron, the busy sounds of the manufacture of this important mineral into myriad implements, utensils and articles seems to be a key-note of our trans-Atlantic industry and enterprise. Yet after all, this busy city is as it were a black forest of high smoking and flaming chimneys reared upon and amid the grand old Alleghany mountains, and whose wharves are washed by both the Monongahela and Alleghany rivers just as they merge their waters with the broad Ohio. Pittsburg has always been a favorite city with me, with its enterprising and sensible people, who always attend my services in goodly numbers and listen to my songs with patience. In fact I have sung five or six nights in succession in this city at one visit, and always with success. Here was the home and field of labor of my friend, the late Dr. Alexander Clark, and I have not visited it since his decease, always feeling that it can never be the Pittsburg it has ever been to me. When there I may not hear his kindly voice and look again upon his dear familiar face, although the city has itself most tenderly expressed its bereavement at his loss.

My course from this point was on to Newcastle, to sing on the kind invitation of Ira D. Sankey, who is of late years, doing his own singing and with blessed results, and who, in a recent letter to me, says: " I shall ever look upon you as one of the biggest factors in my life, for it was you who opened up to me the wondrous power there is in singing the blessed gospel of our Lord and Savior, Jesus Christ." Thus my time and talent has ever been given to sing for those who, in their turn, may sing again for others. At this time Mr. Sankey was engaged in the revenue department, and was the efficient superintendent of the Newcastle Methodist Sunday-school. Subsequently he became associated with me in singing and in a business capacity for a few years, and, in this position, come in contact with Mr. Moody, the dual services of whom, in sermon and in song, the Christian world to-day delights to honor. In the next stage of my journey, I struck

OIL CITY.

Where I was met with an uncharitable editorial in a very questionable newspaper, whose editor, at that time, evidently held a sort of spite against my methods of singing. Although I never saw or knew him, he animadverted me with all the power of journalistic pen and ink, and probably to his temper's, if not to his heart's content. As a result, my house was quite thin, and I failed to strike oil, yet I gave the few who did come out to hear me, oil well refined in the shape of gospel in song. Wiping my feet of the oil, instead of dust of this locality, and proceeding to Erie, I there made up for all loss of time.

The vast quantities of pertroleum or kerosene oil which were at first discovered and obtained by driving and drilling artesian wells into the earth, from which this wonderful fluid deposit, flowed out for many months, and was afterward pumped by steam power, have become, in a great measure, exhausted, and the world is now supplied with three-fourths of all the oil consumed from the mountain basin in which the city of Bradford, in this same state, is situated, which fields are immediately reached by narrow gauge railroads running up the steep grades of the hills and crossing the great chasms between them on skeleton bridges of timber and spiles. Four years ago this agricultural hamlet, nestling among these old hills, was almost isolated from the outer world by the huge battlements of nature and barely contained one thousand inhabitants. But as if by magic wand it has sprung up into the proportions of a large city of 13,000 inhabitants by the discovery of its rich oil deposits, and in an area of thirty miles in length by from two and one-half to seven miles in width, six thousand wells have been sunk at an average cost of $3,000 each, whose skeleton derricks upreared against the sky, dot all the hills and valleys like so many sentinels, even the streets, yards and gardens of the city proper, having these not strictly ornamental structures planted therein as thickly as shade trees in many less fortunate but more aristocratic localities. The product or yield of these wells are all conducted to vast wooden tanks, and from thence forced by steam power through several main lines of large iron pipe which extend one hundred miles or more under ground, over hills, mountains and plains, and through valleys, gorges and rivers, to Olean, Williamsport, Salamanca and other points of railroad centre, where the oil is conducted therefrom into huge oil tanks built upon platform cars, and thence taken to the refineries in different sections of the country. These oil wells flow spontaneously for about

two years, and are pumped for two more, by which time
the supply is generally exhausted. The paying wells average a yield of two hundred and forty barrels every twenty-
four hours, while the aggregate supply of petroleum from
this great subterranean vat or reservoir at Bradford, is forty-
five thousand barrels each day. Here are gathered specu-
lative and money-seeking characters from not only all
portions of my own, but from many foreign countries, but
among whom there are enough Christian men of piety,
influence and wealth, to give promise that in the process of
time, this leaven of righteousness in the midst of so much
lust for gain and its usual concomitants, will, through the
grace and power of the Savior, raise up at Bradford fresh
triumphs to His holy name.

I have in my several song pilgrimages through this great
state, visited many of its towns and cities, and always with
success, leaving a margin in every case in favor of some
local Christian interest. From this section I shall jump
my readers to New England, and alight on the Pilgrim
soil of Massachusetts, the Old Bay State.

CHAPTER IV.

SINGING IN NEW ENGLAND.

THE city of Boston bears the name of the "Hub" from the original laying out of the streets in the form of a wheel, all having a common center or termination, but some of which "spokes" were of amazing crookedness, but more lately retaining the appellation because of its being the New England entrepot for wealth, learning, enterprise and intelligence. My first service here was in Tremont Temple, which has an almost national reputation from having been the scene of many of the most stirring and memorable events which have called the people of this commonwealth and section together, and in which the most eloquent voices of both hemispheres have often been heard in religious, secular and political speech. My second service in this city was held in Music Hall, which containing the big organ, has ever been to the musical public what the temple has been to the oratorical. Both of these services, bearing the impress of a new departure in song, were largely attended, the audiences giving me their patient and undivided attention until their close.

I suppose the Englishman would find a home likeness to the mother-land in Boston and New England as in no other portion of our great republic. Boston does really resemble, with its uneven architecture, irregular and narrow streets and lanes, its street names, chop-houses and many little shops, an English city of 310,000 inhabitants, though in its newer avenues and in the business portions rebuilt since the great fire, it has in late years grown rich in massive business and public structures and elegant in palatial residences, fronted with brown stone, marble and granite.

New Englanders, by common consent, compose the more cultured portion of our citizenship, yet I believe there are more shrewd people in the West than in the East; in the East, while the people are very dignified, conservative and slow to action, those of the West are keen, pushing and full of life. In fact, the West knows and fully understands both the East and the West, while the East stays at home and too often only knows there is a West as it consults the map.

Onward I go singing through the leading counties of the "Old Bay State," with its 1,500,000 inhabitants, pitching my key-note at Worcester, Gloucester, Waltham, Cambridge, Chelsea, Lynn, Northampton, Pittsfield, Holyoke, Greenfield, Northfield, Fall River, North Adams, Lawrence, Lowell and other cities and towns. At Lowell and Lawrence my audiences were very large as well as enthusiastic. In these two cities, are, without doubt, located the largest factories or mills in the world. I can imagine I hear some of my friends in Manchester, England, laugh at this assertion, but if they could stand with me on the banks of the Merrimac, they would award the palm for manufacture to these great mills, covering acres of ground, numbering their operatives by thousands each, and their spindles by the millions. Really, New England seems to be the great workshop of America, while the great West is not only the mighty granary of the country, but of the world. My services in all these Massachusetts towns and cities were well received, for notwithstanding New England seems to give birth to all the "isms" and to have its principal cities for their grand centres, yet its people like the simple gospel even when sung with unpretentious melody.

MAINE, THE PINE TREE STATE,

And also the banner temperance state of the Union, has a population of 700,000 and was my next field of song. I held my first service at Portland, which seemed very pleasant and home-like, and although my audience was not a large one, so evidently pleased were they with the exercises that I was invited to sing again in the large Music Hall. Portland, I found to be a charming city and sea port, and although it was nearly burned in the great fire of 1866, it has been elegantly rebuilt, now having a population of 40,000.

I next visited Lewiston, where, as in Lowell, I looked upon one of the largest mills in the world. My services were held in a church, and a good audience did me the honor of their closest attention for nearly two hours. Leaving here is went forward to old Brunswick, Bath, Belfast, and Augusta, my several services being well attended and received. Augusta, the capital of Maine, is a beautiful little metropolis of 8,000 inhabitants. Here I accepted an invitation to sing to the inmates of the Lunatic Asylum, which is finely located and managed, and where it brought my soul good to cheer for a moment the souls of "even one of the least of these." It was a strange scene in which it was of intense interest to witness how these poor unfortunates were swerved to and fro by the power of simple song, as the waves of their emotion surged and jostled them even as the waves of the ocean the rudderless ship. While some of them sang, others bowed their heads, beat the time, uttered words of delight and admiration, while a few hid under the benches or desks.

Taking a steamer, I sailed up the noble Penobscot river to the noted city of Bangor, having a population of 15,000 souls, and one of the most spirited and enterprising in the Pine Tree State. Here the New England Methodist Conference was in session, and I gave a service in behalf of

the worn out preachers' fund. Either the object, or some
other cause, drew out a crowded house. I was filled with
the spirit of song, and all seemed gladdened and exhilarated
by the exercises, which netted a handsome sum in aid of
these Christian ministers who had become enfeebled in body
in the service of the Master. It is always so pleasant to
sing before a body of Methodist ministers, who, more than
all others, give me heart in the rendering of sacred songs
with their liturgic "Amens" and "Bless the Lord," uttered
with all the fervency of throne-reaching appeal. From
Maine I crossed the border into

NEW HAMPSHIRE, THE GRANITE STATE,
Having a population of 320,000, giving my first service in
Concert Hall, Concord, its capital city, which boasts nearly
20,000 inhabitants. I was pleased to meet in my audience
quite a number of Shakers, ..ad in their peculiar garb, who
at the close of the exercises congratulated me on my success
in giving Christian sentiment so sweetly to their hearts in
song, showing that human nature is alike the world over,
no matter under what color of skin it is hidden or what cut
or texture of garment may cover the body. These
Shakers were members of a family residing in a town near
the city, and the sect has ten distinct settlements or communities in the several states of New England, besides six
located in different parts of Ohio and Kentucky. They are
dissenters from the Quakers, or Society of Friends, and
though there is nominally five thousand of the persuasion in
the United States, their number is rapidly on the decrease.
These American Shaker families were originally constituted
or planted by Mother Ann Lee, who emigrated from England to New Lebanon, N.Y., and whose disciples believed
was inspired by, and dual with, Christ. After her death,
these communities were fostered and perpetuated by the
skillful management and leadership of John Meacham, a

former Baptist minister. Added to other tenets of their faith, differing from that of the Quakers, is that of celibacy, their numbers being recruited from the poor children of the "world's people," who fall into their hands to bring up, and by disheartened men and women who have been unfortunate in providing themselves with homes, or have lost them through adversity.

From this place I proceeded to Manchester, Dover, Keene, Portsmouth and Nashua, singing to good audiences all the way. In my service at the latter city, just as I had finished singing "Scatter Seeds of Kindness," I was terribly embarrassed in the fine church and before the elite of the Christian public, to have my organ-pedal give out. I very happily thought to say to my audience in my emergency that "I should be under the necessity of asking them to make a practical application of the song then and there," at the same time turning my organ upwards and repairing the mischief.

From this point I took my family to old Orchard Beach, where we were most pleasantly joined by our dear friends Mrs. V. M. Bucklin, of Maine, and Mr. and Mrs. Fribley, of Ohio. Here I gave a series of "song-sermons" beneath the boughs of the pine grove auditorium, after which we went to the White Mountains for recreation. Here we found ourselves amid the most delightful mountain scenery, and beneath the cooling shadows of the grand old hills, we bade the hot sun of August defiance. The charming walks and drives, taking in as they did cascades, lakes, gorges, the flume, the rock-outlined countenance of the old man of the mountain, and a myriad other scenes of wild scenery and grandeur, would fill a whole volume in their description. Here at the commodious hotels we found guests from all parts of our land, enjoying the health-inspiring breezes, and gathering fresh strength for the battles of life when they should descend from these proud heights to the towns, and cities of the valley and the plain.

VERMONT, THE GREEN MOUNTAIN STATE,

I take my way, which has a population of 340,000 inhabitants, and where the Yankee blood is to be found in its native purity. Singing at Rutland, so famous for its excellent quarries of marble, I passed on, giving services at Montpelier, the state capital, as also at Middlebury, Bennington, Burlington, Brattleboro, Putney and in other smaller towns. The people seemed, as a general thing, to enjoy my services as in other states, yet there was a sort of coldness and lack of demonstration which did not impress me with the feeling that I reached their hearts and sympathies as I wished to do.

From this state I passed down into Central Massachusetts stopping off at Northfield to spend the Sabbath with my old friend D. L. Moody, whom I had not seen since his great success in England. He met me with his carriage at the depot, and we were soon on the way to his home, having met on the road thither a man whom Mr. Moody told me, as we approached, was an infidel, and to whom, as we passed, he spoke a word for Christ, inviting him to a meeting on the morrow. I was glad to find Bro. Moody so comfortably situated in his pleasant residence, in which was a fine library, piano and organ, together with many of those intellectual and domestic surroundings which make home the dearest spot on earth. In the evening, enough were in attendance upon his Bible reading service to completely fill his parlors and sitting room, and for the time I became his Sankey, interspersing the exercises with my songs of gospel truth. In the three services which he conducted on the Sabbath, he seemed to be still more than ever in earnest in the work of winning souls to Christ, while his preaching fell upon me like the rich dews of Hermon and refreshed my soul as of old. As I again sang my hymns at his request, I felt like accepting his kind offer of a lot if I would come and live near him, and were

I sure of his companionship when not on duty, I should decide on pitching my tent awhile at Northfield. But no, for both he and I are chained to the gospel oar—he to preach Christ's saving grace and word, and I to sing it wherever duty calls. Therefore I go forward to what is facetiously called the land of steady habits, or

CONNECTICUT, THE NUTMEG STATE.

Which has a thriving and industrious population of 540,000. I gave my first service in the Academy of Music at New Haven, which is charmingly located on Long Island Sound, has a population of 60,000, is noted for its Yale College and campus, its fine churches and its grateful shade of lordly elms. There were two thousand people in my audience, but whether their attendance was the result of the earnest labor of J. S. Searles, who had the exercises in charge, or through the influence of the Methodist ministers of the New York East Conference, which was there in session, I do not know. Suffice it to say that I mounted the rostrum with a very severe headache which I entirely sang myself clear of, and left a substantial benefit to the object for which the service had been given.

I next visited Hartford, the present state capital, and famous as the headquarters of life, fire and accident insurance in the United States. In this city I sang to a large audience in aid of the Women's Christian Union, a band of earnest workers in the cause of the Master. Winsted being my next objective point, I took the cars to Bridgeport, and upon arriving there found that an accident had occurred on the railroad leading thereto, which necessitated my riding fifty miles in a sleigh to fill the appointment, but which I fortunately succeeded in doing. Another sleigh-ride of twenty miles before five o'clock the next morning enabled me to connect with another railroad train and reach my service at Norwich the same evening, which trips, to use a familiar phrase, " nearly played me out."

Next in order I visited Waterbury, famed for its great manufactories of articles of brass and for other extensive industries. In this city I think there is the finest and most complete M. E. church, for the amount of money used in its construction, that I ever looked upon, and I would advise all who are proposing to construct a church edifice, whose cost will not exceed $30,000, to be sure and see this and pattern after it. There was a full attendance upon my service, and as I was packing up my organ at its close, whose external appearance had been somewhat marred by baggage-smashers, Mr. Gloss, one of the most prominent manufacturers of the city, told me he thought I needed a little brass metal to protect my peripatetic instrument. Therefore, taking its dimensions, he afterwards sent me enough brass sheeting to completely cover it, which saved it much wear and tear in my future journeyings.

Connecticut has always appeared to me to be the busiest state in the Union, her people being thoroughly awake to invention and manufacture, from the most costly and useful articles of daily commercial and domestic use, which everybody must have to be comfortable, down to the most elaborate as well as insignificant toy for the pleasure of babyhood and youth. As thoroughly busy as bees were the citizens of Ansonia, Bridgeport, Stafford, New London, and the cities and towns which I have visited throughout the length and breadth of the state, not excepting Middletown, which is denominated the Oxford of our Methodism, and I shall ever hold in grateful recollection the kind greetings and receptions I have always received in the "land of steady habits."

RHODE ISLAND, THE LITTLE SISTER,

So humorously nick-named as "Little Rhodie," though last in the enumeration of New England States, and the smallest in size of any in the Union, has a population of 220,000.

While to her sisters in the family of states has been accorded such greater breadth and width of start, unlike her they have no enterprising Providence, with a lively, active, pushing, commercial population of 100,000 souls. In this world-known and important metropolis, the head-centre and capital of the state, I have always met a hearty welcome with my services, as well as in Woonsocket, Pawtucket and other localities within its borders. My visit to Newport, the great New England sea-side resort, was during the bathing season, and I gave my service of song in its Academy of Music. But here I found the people so thoroughly absorbed with the sea and the pleasures of the surf and shore, added to the social and fashionable festivities held nightly in the spacious hotels, as to be quite unmindful of the rendering of the gospel in song, and therefore giving my best efforts to a small audience, I proceeded on my way rejoicing to my home in Gotham.

CHAPTER V.

SERVICES IN THE BRITISH AMERICAN PROVINCES

ESUMING my especial work, I visit the British provinces of Canada, East and West, prefacing the same with a tour of song in the smaller colonies bordering on the Atlantic Ocean, and coming inland from thence to those adjacent to the great western lakes.

At St, Johns, New Brunswick, I was very fortunate in having Mr. W. C. Wetmore, an influential banker and an indefatigable Christian worker, in charge of my services, who carried them forward to eminent success. This city, which is the largest in the provinces, is situated on the St. John's River, at the point of its entrance into the Bay of Fundy, and has a population of 32,000. Proceeding thence to Halifax, the principal city and capital of Nova Scotia, situated on an inlet of the extreme south-eastern coast of the Atlantic Ocean, the principal naval and commercial station of the North American colonies, and having a population of 30,000, I gave my first service in the Brunswick Wesleyan Church, to an audience which seemed thoroughly gratified and delighted, from its opening to its close. I also received a hearty welcome at Pictou, Truro, Moncton, Windsor, Fredericton, Woodstock, and as far down as Charlottstown, the beautiful capital of Prince Edward's Island, at which latter place I met that good Christian worker and banker, Mr. Heard, whose Bible class is one of the most efficient in this portion of the Queen's American dominions.

The country along the railway lines, where the forests are not dense, is very rocky and barren, giving the impression that one is passing through a new and undeveloped territory, while the principal business of the provinces, which could now and then be seen in progress, is that of lumbering and boat-building. Returning from my trip inland to St. Johns, I gave a service of song and Bible reading in the Brunswick Street Church, to a thousand bright-eyed, interesting Sunday-school children, whose voices were in fine accord as they accompanied me in song, the occasion being to me, and very evidently to them, one of great pleasure and gratification. At the close of the service these children gave me a small sum for my Mission Hall fund, which "little brick" is out on interest, waiting for companions of the same sort.

THE PROVINCES OF QUEBEC AND ONTARIO.

From St. Johns I journeyed to Montreal, the largest and most important city in British America, and which, for the sake of my many English friends, I shall give more than a passing mention. Montreal has a population of 130,000, is situated on an island of the St. Lawrence River, at the mouth of the Ottawa, being built at the base of Mont Real, or royal mountain, from which it derives its name. Its public and business buildings are generally constructed of a fine gray stone, while its people are for the most part of French origin or descent. The Roman Catholic element is greatly in the ascendency here, having one of the largest and most costly cathedrals on this continent, and only exceeded in size and magnificence by that of New York. Yet notwithstanding the prevailing religion is Papist, there are several large and influential Wesleyan and Presbyterian Churches, and a very flourishing Young Men's Christian Association, occupying a beautiful building of its own.

I find myself the nicely and comfortably-quartered guest of James S. Matthewson, the great tea merchant, in a home which, though luxurious, is rendered doubly pleasant by the piety of its inmates. My services here commenced at the great St. James Street Church, where I was greeted by a large audience, who seemed to be greatly pleased with my style of singing, and although, as I commenced my exercises, I felt somewhat embarrassed at seeing the eloquent Dr. Punshon just in front of me, yet I finished my programme without failure.

The next morning witnessed the opening of the Wesleyan Missionary Anniversary for a session of several days, at which our eloquent divines, Dr. O. H. Tiffany, Dr Punshon, Dr. Douglass, and Dr. Sutherland were the principal speakers, whose addresses I interspersed with gospel song. It was a season of great spiritual and intellectual Christian enjoyment, at which I sang for the first time the following lines written for me by Dr. Wm. Morley Punshon, and for which I had composed a new tune:

THE PILGRIM'S MISSION.

1 Listen! the Master beseecheth,
  Calling each one by his name,
 His voice to each loving heart reacheth,
  Its cheerfulest service to claim.
 Go where the vineyard demandeth
  Vine-dresser's nurture and care;
 Or go where the white harvest standeth,
  The joy of the reaper to share.

2 Work for the good that is nighest;
  Dream not of greatness afar;
 That glory is ever the highest
  Which shines upon men as they are.
 Work, though the world would defeat you;
  Heed not its slander and scorn;
 Nor weary till angels shall greet you
  With smiles through the gates of the morn.

3 Work, though the enemies' laughter
  Over the valleys may sweep;
 For God's patient workers hereafter
  Shall laugh when the enemies weep.
 Ever on Jesus reliant,
  Press on your chivalrous way;
 The mightiest Philistine giant
  His Davids are chartered to slay.

4 Offer thy life on the altar:
   In the high purpose be strong.
And if the tired spirit should falter,
   Then sweeten thy labor with song.
What if the poor heart complaineth?
   Soon shall its wailing be o'er;
For there, in the rest that remaineth,
   It shall grieve and be weary no more.

From Montreal I proceed one hundred and sixty-eight miles by rail, through a beautiful country, to the quaint old city of Quebec, which is shadowed by Cape Diamond, the strongest fortified citadel on the Western hemisphere. On the brow of a precipice rising abruptly three hundred feet from the waters of the St. Lawrence, and protected by massive fortifications on its land sides or slopes, this stronghold stands out like a grim sentinel overlooking a landscape of ideal beauty, hardly equaled in either the old or new world, and certainly not surpassed. Quebec has a population of 100,000, the foreign element being predominant, while its ancient features and its narrow streets give it the appearance of an old European city, not unlike that of Bologne, France.

My services here were under the auspices of the Young Men's Christian Association, and although not largely attended, were greatly appreciated, netting quite a respectable sum for the Society. On this trip I made several interesting visits to the surrounding country, taking delightful drives, that over seven miles of excellent road, profusely lined with charming natural views and scenery, to the Falls of Montmorenci, which even surpass those of Niagara in wild beauty, being especially enjoyed.

From Quebec I proceeded to West Ontario, giving my services at Brockville, Preston, Kingston, Bellville, Cornwall, St. Catherines, New Market, Brompton, St. Thomas, Woodstock, Paris, Ingersoll, Strasburg, Petrolia, London, Hamilton, Toronto, Ottawa and the Thousand Islands. In all these cities and towns in Canada, with a single exception, in the several visits I have made them., I have always had a cordial welcome. The people of these Provinces appear in their manners, customs and habits, almost like the English, and sometimes we Yankees think them to be an improvement on the real Britain, having about them more of the air of home-like America. Besides this, they seem to possess a sort of dignified sentiment which we of the States are too apt to treat lightly rather than imitate in our own demeanor.

Of these towns and cities of Ontario, several deserve more than cursory notice. Petrolia, the oil metropolis of the Dominion, hastily built up and greasy in the extreme, has a cozy population of 4,000, whose principal employment is bringing this rich liquid deposit to the surface of the earth with an army of wells and derricks as numerous as themselves. London, a city of 20,000 inhabitants, is laid out after the same plan as its great namesake, having also its river Thames, and many streets named after those so famous in the mother-land. Hamilton, with a population of 40,000, to me the Queen City of Canada, with its wealth of churches, colleges and schools, and abounding in the highest Christian intelligence and culture. Here I was most hospitally entertained at the residence of J. E. Sanford, Esq., one of the Canadian merchant princes and a noble Christian philanthropist as well, who is at the head of quite a number of flourishing charitable and benevolent enterprises, and who is nobly seconded in his labors by his wife, a thoroughly cultured and devoted Christian lady. In their company I visited the Branch Children's Home, originated by that ardent Christian gentleman, Rev. T. Bowman Stephenson, of London; heard the little ones sing sweet hymns of praise, and gave them a word of kind encouragement, many of them having but lately arrived from England.

I next visited Ottawa, the capital and seat of government of Ontario, having a population of 30,000, and situated on the Ottawa River and Rideau Canal. With its Parliament buildings and spacious residences, and being the favorite resort of royalty, it can be appropriately termed the aristocratic city of the Canadian Provinces. My services here were in aid of the Young Men's Christian Association, and I had large and appreciative audiences on two evenings.

Going forward I come to Toronto, also a principal Canadian city, built on the shores of a fine harbor on the northern shore of Lake Ontario, and having a population of 80,000. The name Toronto is an Indian one, signifying in that language, "a meeting place," and while it is of great importance to the Dominion as a lake-seaport, it is especially noted for it its beautiful Queen's College and Park, which are approached by one of the stateliest tree-lined avenues in the world. This was not my first visit to this metropolis, for I have sung many times here, and always to full houses. My present appearance here was of more than usual importance, as I came especially to conduct the service of song for the session of the Provincial Sabbath-school Association, which was to continue several days. This great gathering was held in the Wesleyan Metropolitan Church of Canada, which can appropriately be termed the model church building on the Western Continent. It was constructed from plans drawn and perfected by that prince of eloquent preachers, Rev. Dr. Punshon, who left it after four years of earnest, successful labor in the Canadian field, to return to his home in England. In its perfectness and beauty, it stands a memorial monument to his faithful Christian work in this Western world and the great service he rendered to Methodism in the British American Provinces, the fruits of which are multiplying as year follows year since his departure, signally bringing to mind the words of scripture, " Truly their works do follow them."

Our great meeting was attended by fully one thousand delegates from the ministry and laity, while the entire seating capacity of the church, which would conveniently accommodate twenty-five hundred persons, was fully occupied at each session. These audiences seemed to receive my songs of Jesus and His love with much more enthusiasm than common at my evenings of song, and some of my friends tell me that nowhere am I so effective with my gospel singing as in a religious convention where I am in charge of this portion of the exercises. It is a fact that I never listen to a sermon or Christian remarks, but that an appropriate verse or hymn, all set to melody, comes whispering to my mind, which seems to apply exactly to the subject in hand and to give it the freshness and fervor of convincing power. In these meetings, where all were infused with religious fervor and spirit, I was thoroughly at home, and my talent was at its superlative height. During my stay here I was made most comfortable by the ever to be remembered hospitality extended to me in the home of Daniel McLean, Esq. From Toronto I sped on my way still farther westward to Michigan, the Wolverine State.

CHAPTER VI.

SINGING IN THE WEST.

MICHIGAN has a population of 1,200,000, and Detroit for its principal city, where I made my first halt. This great central metropolis, with a citizenship of 80,000 people, is of great commercial importance, being charmingly situated on the Detroit river, the great water avenue connecting the northwestern lakes of Michigan, Huron and Superior with that of Erie, and thence by the Welland canal with Ontario, the St. Lawrence and the Atlantic seaboard, and being finely built and the seat of great wealth, it is pre-eminently the pride of all Michiganders. Here I was the guest of the noble Christian banker, David Preston, Esq., in whose home I was most handsomely entertained. Holding my services in the central M. E. Church, one of the finest edifices west of the Alleghanies. I was greeted with a full house and by a warm-hearted people who seemed to drink in enjoyment from the same source and the same fountain.

I next visited Ann Arbor, situated on the Huron river and having a population of 10,000, where my service was well attended and gave great satisfaction, being given almost within the shadow of the structures of the State University. Adrian, a young city of 10,000 population, was the next point reached, where I sang to a small but appreciative assembly, and which being the home of my old friend Major Cole, his cheerful spirit and presence greatly

Beaver Brook, U. P. Ry.

cheered me. Thence I proceeded to Jackson, having 20,000 population, where I sang in the M. E. Church, being introduced to my large audience by Rev. J. S. Smart, D.D., whose intrinsic Christian worth and manliness of character make him much more than an ordinary doctor of divinity.

Lansing, the capital of the state, situated at the confluence of Grand and Cedar Rivers, with a population of 8,000, and Saginaw City, having a citizenship of 10,000 souls, were the scenes of my next services, both being young cities of wonderful recent growth. I sang two evenings in the latter in aid of the Methodist church, which was then largely in debt, both services proving very successful under the management of Rev. Dr. J. H. McCarthy. While this excellent minister and his wife were listening to my songs, thieves entered the parsonage, which they stripped of several hundred dollars' worth of clothing and furniture. But the misfortune was not long grieved over, for these good people had laid up their priceless treasures "where moth and rust doth not corrupt, nor thieves break through and steal."

I next gave services at Grand Rapids and Grand Haven, both havens of great enterprise and natural beauty, and moving forward to Kalamazoo, with its 10,000 population, and which is to me the gem city of Michigan, I found the the M. E. Conference in session. A large audience greeted me here, and although I did not feel in the best of moods, my services were received with apparent satisfaction, and netted quite a considerable sum in aid of the worn-out ministers of that conference. After singing in Niles, Hillsdale, Jonesville, and other smaller towns, with my dear family I started on a trip to the Lake Superior districts, in the extreme northwestern portion of the state. Through all these immense mining and lumbering sections, in which are the towns of Sheboygan, Marinette, Pere, Nagauna, and Ishpeming, I gave my services to most enthusiastic audiences, where I met many Cornish people, proverbial for their love of sacred song. From these regions I crossed over into the

STATE OF WISCONSIN,

To the west of Lake Michigan, bounded by the great waters of Lake Superior on the north, and having a population of 1,100,000. I gave my first service in Milwaukee, which has 130,000 inhabitants, fully two-thirds of whom are Germans, and besides being the most populous city in the state, is one of the greatest primary wheat markets and ports in the Union. This beautiful metropolis is a favorite resort for both pleasure seekers and invalids, on account of the purity of its atmosphere, while its cream-colored brick, with which its public and business buildings and residences are mostly constructed, are of world-wide fame. These brick are made in great quantities for exportation to all parts of the United States, being much sought for the construction of the fronts of public edifices, business blocks, and elegant mansions. My evening of song was held in the Summerfield M. E. Church, which was crowded with attentive listeners, and which was so thoroughly pleasing as to ever afterward bespeak me a full house in subsequent visits to the city.

Passing westward to Madison, the state's capital, having a population of 10,000, and one of the most beautiful cities within its borders, I found it planted on an isthmus between two charming inland lakes, for which isolated bodies of water Wisconsin is peculiarly famous. I sang here in a hall to a few people, who received my songs with unmistakable pleasure and heartiness. Passing along, I gave very well-attended services at Janesville, Monroe, Racine, Kenosha, Green Bay, Menasha, Portage City, Appleton, Oshkosh, Eau Claire, Chippewa Falls, Baraboo, La Crosse, Waunakee, Waukesha, Mineral Point, Brodhead, Plattville, Waupun and other well-known towns. At Waupun

I visited the state penitentiary, where I gave a service of song in the presence of nearly a thousand convicts incarcerated therein, for to such I always like to sing, as I can never forget the passage: " I was sick and in prison, and ye visited me." Crossing the Mississippi, I entered the great wheat fields of the West, the

STATE OF MINNESOTA,

Which has a population of 500,000, and whose principal cities are St. Paul and Minneapolis, each being peopled with about 45,000 inhabitants. Here one is thoroughly impressed with western thrift and progress, and if he is accustomed only to small things, the enterprising people and fertile country at the head of the great waters of the Mississippi will be sure to expand him. St. Paul is a finely built and located city, while Minneapolis, with its great flour and lumber mills, and St. Anthony, with its unequaled water power, teem with the hum of busy industry. Not forgetful of the Falls of Minnehaha, whose "laughing waters" have been so beautifully described in verse by our poet, Longfellow, I go thither, to find them laughing still, as they playfully leap from that beautiful cascade.

Fine hotels, good audiences, appreciative listeners, were mine to enjoy in this state, from whose centres I made several expeditions, giving services at Stillwater, Austin, Rochester, Faribault, Northfield, Mankato and other smaller towns. Taking steamer, I visited Red Wing and Winona, two charming localities on the Mississippi's banks, in both of which I met most hearty welcome. These upper waters of this great river, are full of beauty and sublimity, bordered as it is on both banks with miles of high bluffs and rocks through which the stream seems to have been for ages wearing down from and receding to its present channel. For immense distances these bluffs rise in unbroken and often precipitous front on both banks of the river with great uniformity of height, shape and feature, though often with great stretches of low land, marsh and prairie between them and the stream, to which they occasionally return to frown at and overshadow with their grim battlements, again to recede to a distance of from one to five miles away.

In the four visits I have made to this great and fertile state, the last one impressed me most thoroughly with the vastness and richness of its lands and the capabilities of their wonderful development in the future. Here educational culture, religious labor, and agricultural and business enterprises go hand in hand with mighty strides, and the blessings of our republican form of government are to be seen in every centre and on every side. Hurriedly passing down through Iowa and Illinois I come to

INDIANA, THE HOOSIER STATE,

With its great population of 1,700,000, rich soil, plentitude of mud, black walnut lumber, porcine wealth and any quantity of good hospitable-minded and handed people. My first service in this state, on this visit, was at South Bend, which has a population of 13,000, and whose fine qualities and immense quantities of hard wood timber give it great advantages for the manufacture of wagons, ploughs and other agricultural implements. Here, in addition to the celebrated works of Studebaker Bros., who turn out their millions of carriages and wagons every year, are other great industries which have a world-wide fame. This is also the home of Hon. Schuyler Colfax, associated in the presidency with the lamented Lincoln, and whose public life so singularly terminated with that of his illustrious associate, with whose inner life and thoughts no one in this land was so well acquainted as he. I was most appropriately and eloquently introduced to my audience by ex-President Colfax, and although it was not so large as it was appreciative my singing was most pleasantly received for a full hour and a half.

From here I went on singing to good audiences in Michigan City, Logansport, Warsaw, Lafayette, Fort Wayne, Columbus, Muncie and other smaller towns, to Greencastle, the Athens of Western Methodism, in which is situated the most thriving University in the West, whose presidency our dear Bishop Bowman left to assume the Episcopacy. In this town I have sung many times, as also in Terre Haute, Madison, Vincennes, Richmond and Indianapolis, having always been welcomed by good houses. In Indianapolis, with its population of 70,000 inhabitants and the state capital, in which there is a strong Methodist element, and in Richmond, having a population of 25,000, the headquarters of that noble class of citizens, the Western Quakers, I have ever been made especially welcome. Proceeding to New Albany and Evansville, the two leading cities in southern Indiana, I give pleasant services in each, meeting in the latter, his residence, that well-known Christian philanthropist, Mr. De Paw, who shines in every centre, nook and corner of this region by his Christian activity and princely gifts to promote and promulgate the gospel. From Indiana I cross into the

STATE OF ILLINOIS.

With its enterprising and wide-awake population of 3,000,000, and which the Chicago people will tell you is the banner state of both hemispheres. Well, we must give Chicago the palm after all; for, in almost any way you may view it, it has not its equal, as a city, on the face of the globe. It is the largest of its age, having a population of more than 500,000; it is the finest built and truest American type of indomitable pluck and perseverance; it is the king grain depository and market of the world, and the greatest railroad center in the states, besides being the largest shipping port of cattle and swine known in any land. It can also boast the biggest fires, their setting by the most homely accident, their quickest extinguishment and the rebuilding of flame-swept districts with more rapidity than known in any metropolis of the earth.

I have sung in Chicago many times, both in song service and religious convention, before the largest audiences and always with eminent success; and, while it may properly be termed the wickedest city of America, it has been the home of some of the most earnest and faithful ministers of the gospel, and Christian workers and evangelists, known to both the eastern and western continents. Here was the residence of D. L. Moody, and here he began his great Christian work in earnest. Here lives B. F. Jacobs, the inventor of the uniform National Sunday-school Lessons. Here Dr. Edward Eggleston arose in might of mental strength and eloquence, and shot out like a new star, into the evangelical firmament, and, here our Dr. Vincent commenced his great and successful mission in Sabbath-school work by starting and publishing the National Sunday-school Teacher. Here also our good, true worker, S. A. Kean, commenced his great Missionary Sabbath-school, which has grown up into the full stature of a noble church of Christ. This, too, is the city which gave the world the lamented song-evangelist, P. P. Bliss, whose translated soul, with that of his dear wife, in one disastrous mid-winter night, ascended to glory in a chariot of fire, but whose sweet songs go circling through and singing over the earth, while their author sings the praises of the redeemed standing among the harpers "Around about the Throne." Here, too, is the home of George F. Root, who always seemed to me to be the parent of our American song-poets, as also of the princely John V. Farwell, whose modest ways and unassuming charities have made him well known to the Christian world.

Having so proud a record even in its infancy, and having given so many good things to the world, from or near

Chicago is a good place to hail, be you in whatever portion of the Christianized or civilized globe. When visiting this energetic state, so eminently the Harvard and Yale of business brains, and, remembering the contributions of such a patriotic President as Abraham Lincoln, and successful a warrior as Gen. Grant, to both of whom, in these later days, our Republic is so signally indebted, for services, wisdom and courage, we ever feel to accord to it all the honor which to it belongs.

I have visited this great state many times, singing through its length and breadth, and in all its principal towns and cities, meeting with the most cordial reception, and, among many others, have to personally thank such men of influence as Wm. Reynolds, Alexander Tynge and Philip S. Gillet, for many courtesies and kindnesses extended to me on these occasions.

Among some of the most prominent cities and towns are Galena, Freeport, Peoria, Rockford, Joliet, Bloomington, Ottawa, Sterling, Jacksonville, Springfield, Decatur, Alton, Pana, Mattoon, Bellville, Centralia, Cairo, and others too numerous to designate. From this I turn to what I call "my pet commonwealth," the

STATE OF IOWA,

Having a population of 1,300,000, which always elicits my admiration for the evenness with which nature has supplied its rich soil and beautiful prairies with pure waters, and for an entire land surface of such similarity and ease of access as to dot it all over with large cities and towns, railroads, schools, colleges and manufactories, thus effectually preventing one section from being envious of another, as in some of the older states, because of superior beauty, privileges and advantages. In this state I have made several tours of song and never without attracting good audiences and successfully aiding the cause for which my services have been given. Among the principal towns and cities thus visited are Davenport, McGregor, Iowa City, Marshalltown, Mt. Vernon, Mt. Pleasant, Cedar Rapids, Des Moines (its beautiful capital of 25,000 inhabitants), Dubuque, Burlington, Keokuk, Knoxville, Ottumwa, Muscatine, Fort Dodge, Sioux City, Forest City, Spencer, Independence, Mason City, Waterloo and very many others. From this point I go southward to the

GREAT STATE OF MISSOURI,

Which, although of magnificent area, having a population of 2,000,000, and rich in fertility of soil and mineral wealth, has always seemed to remain at a stand-still until the close of the war of the rebellion. Here is located Kansas City, having a population of 50,000, and which appears to be grandly struggling to become the gate city to the great Southwest, whose high bluffs are gradually being leveled by the great washings of the Missouri River, on whose banks it is located. Thence I go on to Sedalia, a live city of 8,000, and to St. Joseph, with its 20,000 people, which latter is perhaps the wealthiest metropolis in this portion of the state, and which is quite jealous of its rival, Kansas City. In turn, I also visit Hannibal, Lexington, Mexico, Louisiana and Jefferson City (the state capital), which has a population of only 4,000.

Missouri can boast one of the largest, and perhaps, for its size, the wealthiest city in America, having a population of 400,000 souls, and of vast commercial importance to the Southwest and the world. St. Louis is finely situated on the west bank of the great Mississippi River, and had its citizens been possessed of the driving spirit of enterprise of those of Chicago it could not have failed to have become pre-eminently above all others the great commercial center of export and import of our western world. Here the Mississippi is spanned by the longest and finest bridge in the United States, connecting the Illinois and Missouri shores, over which passes an almost constant stream of railway passenger and freight cars, as well as vehicles and foot passengers, while the city proper is so tunneled that passengers and freight pass under it in transit to and from the far West, without change or transfer.

Although quite Romanish in its forms of worship, yet there are many large and flourishing Christian churches in this city, by whom I have always been welcomed, although the southern element and northern sentiment about equally divide the opinions of the people on the several topics on which they essentially differ. Crossing the celebrated old Mason and Dixon line of the past, I came into the

STATE OF KANSAS,

The first northern territorial border land on which the settlers, backed by the foes of the institution, refused to have the curse of American slavery planted. Born in the great throes and struggles of our body politic to successfully remove that dark stain from the face of our free republic, under wise and economical government, Kansas has grown to be one of the model states of the Union in its financial, educational and agricultural management, and to be thoroughly illustrative of the wisdom of our constitution in its priceless guaranty of "life, liberty and the pursuit of happiness."

Kansas has a population of 500,000, and my first services were held in those sections where its pioneers spilled their blood to preserve it to the sisterhood of the then free states, and where old John Brown, afterward martyred in Virginia, the cradle of our older presidents, shed his first blood to keep our northwestern territories sacred to freedom. Here in Lawrence, one of its foremost cities, Quantrell, the cruel tool of this wicked institution, murdered two hundred male citizens in cold blood before the very eyes of their wives and children, which, instead of crushing out the spirit of liberty, watered and nurtured it until it culminated in the penning of the proclamation of emancipation by the backwoodsman president from this very West, the noble Abraham Lincoln, who not only, by that sublime action, banished slavery from this continent, but indirectly caused its abolishment in all republics, kingdoms, empires and lands. Here, as also at Topeka, Atchison, Manhattan and Leavenworth, at which latter place I received a telegram one morning that I had lost all my earthly possessions by a city fire, I sang to good audiences and with good results. Thence onward I go forward to the

STATE OF NEBRASKA.

Which, like the gourd of Jonah, has grown up into national importance, as it were, in a night, and which, in a few short years, has attained a population of 400,000, its settlement having been greatly accelerated by the discovery of gold and other rich minerals. Here I gave two services at its principal city, Omaha, which in a dozen years has increased to a citizenship of 40,000, and which is evidently the extreme southwestern gateway to the Pacific coast; singing also at Lincoln, its capital, all of which services were very fully attended.

Here I was joined by my dear little family, by Dr. and Mrs. Vincent, Mr. Moody and quite a number of other dear Christian friends, and, providing ourselves with food and other necessaries for the trip to California, we took our places in a palace car, tarrying by the way for a few days in the great mining state of Colorado.

My breth-ren, these set-tings ought not so to be.

MORMON TABERNACLE, SALT LAKE CITY.

Salt Lake City—Mormon Tabernacle on the right.

CHAPTER VII.

COLORADO AND THE PACIFIC COAST.

COLORADO has a population of 100,000. Here I gave song services at Georgetown, Cheyenne, Greeley, and Denver, which are its most important cities and towns and which are situated on the great Union Pacific Railroad, constructed at such immense expense by our government to connect our Atlantic and Pacific coasts by a great artery of transit and commerce. Departing thence our next stop was in the

TERRITORY OF UTAH,

Having a population of 100,000, and Ogden, for the halfway city on the overland route to the Golden Gate.

Bro. Moody feeling a strong desire to preach to the Mormons of Salt Lake City, preceded us thither to make arrangements, and secure the use of the old Mormon Tabernacle, the new one being refused for all Gentile purposes. Dr. Vincent and myself joined him on Saturday evening, but although the building had been secured there seemed no possible way of advertising the occasion; but the Lord made all things easy in the following manner: On Sunday morning we three friends visited the Mormon schools, where we found one of my music books in use, and my presence being announced, I was asked to sing, which I promised to do after Mr. Moody had spoken. Going from thence we attended service in the new Tabernacle, where, after a two hours' address by Orson Pratt, the

Mormon Apostle, one of the elders said: "Brother Pratt, you've preached long enough," and the superintendent of the school we had just left added, "We've got Philip Phillips here from New York, and many of us would like to hear him sing." Upon this I was invited forward, but there being no instrument, I merely told the people that if they wanted to hear me they must attend the service to be held afterward at the old Tabernacle. This was the only announcement that was possible, but as there were 10,000 people present, it was more than enough. Upon hearing the name of the old Tabernacle, several people called out, "Why not the new? the old one is too small," and it was immediately arranged that the service should be held in the very place that had been previously refused for it, and an audience of 8,000 was secured in the only possible way. Such was an early result of Mr. Moody's faith, which afterward accomplished so much both in England and America.

Again we are seated in a comfortable palace car and are speeding over the broad plains and prairies en route for the great states of Idaho, California and Oregon. Through tunnels and gulches, and along the brow of ravines and precipices, our iron pathway takes us until we reach the grade and descend the slopes of the Rocky Mountains to go forward, and still rushing upward to the summit on the Sierra Nevadas. Halting at Virginia City, in the territory of Nevada, having a population of 10,000, and at an altitude so plentifully supplied with oxygen that I could hardly sing a note, it was a pleasant relief to pass down into the soft, balmy air of the valleys below and beyond into

CALIFORNIA, THE GOLDEN STATE,

Which has a population of 600,000, and my introduction to whose Christian people was very auspicious, in company as I was with Brothers Moody and Vincent, and associated with them in the conduct of the first California State Sabbath-school Convention at San Jose. Here we were welcomed by a great company of the ardent and earnest Christian workers of the Golden State, and at the close of the deeply interesting exercises of the convention, Bro. Moody and myself remained in the city for several days, in which we held a protracted meeting, which resulted in the conversion of quite a number of souls to Christ. In response to invitation to sing in different parts of the state, I gave services in its capital, Sacramento, Stockton, Colfax, Grass Valley, Nevada, Marysville, Petulama, Calestoga, Napa, Hollister, Santa Clara, Gilroy, Helena and Chilco, where resides the noble Gen. Bidwell and his most charming wife, who entertained us for several days in his fine home, in the centre of a giant farm of 22,000 acres. In all of these cities and towns, as also in Oakland, the veritable Brooklyn of San Francisco, and more than all to me and mine, the home of our dear friends, Dr. R. E. Cole and family, I was most cordially received.

Leaving San Francisco with its population of 300,000, Dr. Vincent and myself embarked on the steamer "Oraflame," for a three days sail up the Pacific coast to attend the first state Sabbath-school Convention in the

STATE OF OREGON,

Having a population of 130,000, with Portland for its chief city, from whose streets five snow-capped peaks of the Cascade Mountains are visible in mid-summer. We assisted in the exercises of the convention for three days, when we took train for Salem and Halsey, at both of which places I gave song services.

At the latter point we took stage overland for California, riding for seven hundred miles over the worst roads or "trails" ever traversed with vehicle, many times being at the complete mercy of drunken drivers, and on one occasion being overturned in a roaring creek at midnight, covered with mud and drenched with water, and so soaked and bedraggled as to be compelled to build a "tramp" fire to dry our clothing. Our vehicle being unfit from the results of this accident for further present and probable future use, we were transferred, with our soiled baggage, to a lumber cart, in which sorry plight we made the balance of our journey, stopping at rough hovels for our meals or "grub," as they term it here, and learning through both fear and hunger to devour almost anything, palatable or unpalatable, in the semblance of food which was set before us, knowing that if we attempted any criticism on our bill of fare, or made manifest any dislike at the preparation of our dishes, that we should be violently ejected from the table de hote, or be treated to a shower of profanity fully up to the powers of old Beelzebub himself. Thus we rode forward for nine days and nights on the very worst trip I was ever called upon to experience, and never were two travelers more glad to exchange the mud wagon for a railway carriage than were we as we arrived at Tama City, and from thence to San Francisco.

Remaining in this city for a period of five months, I gave services of song in the country each week, returning to sing every Sunday morning at the meetings held by the late Dr. Cunningham in the Presbyterian tabernacle, at the Sabbath-school services at noon, at the prayer meetings in the afternoon, as also at the preaching services on Sabbath evenings. These meetings were truly blessed of God, and were the most happy in which I have participated in the course of my life-long services in sacred song.

Returning directly to the city of New York I there commenced immediate preparations for a still further and prolonged absence upon the eastern continent.

View of San Francisco, Cal.

Come and hear the grand old sto - ry.

CRYSTAL PALACE, LONDON.

CHAPTER VIII.

"OVER THE SEA.

AND ahead! shouted the man from the "lookout," and, as if at the potent word of a magician, a dozen telescopes immediately sprang into position and swept the distant horizon.

On and on sped the good ship Baltic, and larger and larger grew the speck beyond the sea. Minutes grew to hours, and hours filled out the day, and by nightfall we had clearly sighted the cliffs of the "Emerald Isle."

Any port is welcome after miles and miles of sea, and to one who is so bad a sailor as myself, the sight of one's destination, after days of nausea and nights of sleeplessness, is a sensation that well-nigh compensates for the discomforts of an Atlantic passage.

Ireland, however, was not my immediate destination, and though, of course, we stopped at Queenstown for letters, we were soon under way again, and having steamed up the Irish Channel, anchored in the Mersey on Thursday, July the 18th. Thus commenced my second visit to the old country.

Impatient to disembark, Dr. Vincent and myself soon found our way on shore where we were not long in securing that hotel accommodation which Liverpool is so well able to afford.

This northern part of Great Britain has been visited by so many of my countrymen, and described by so many travelers, that it is needless for me to enter largely into details here. Suffice it, therefore, to say now that Liverpool is the second city of the United Kingdom, very large, very busy, and in wet weather very dirty. Liverpool may be said to have grown with the United States, as it has little or no history anterior to the creation of the great republic; and it is as the port for communication between England and America that it has sprung into importance and becomes the centre of gigantic industries.

But we have no business to detain us here; we are already due in the metropolis of the old world, and so within a few hours of our arrival at the Liverpool landing stage we are whirling along the iron road to London.

This was not my first visit to England, but if I visited it a hundred times, I think I should always be impressed with the leading characteristics in which the old country differs from my native land. At the very outset, instead of the broad avenues that characterize the cities of the United States, where land is plentiful and cheap, we find the narrow thoroughfares and crowded streets, that indicate a desire on the part of the authorities to make the most of the space at their disposal, rather than of their opportunities for city adornment. And again when seated with Dr. Vincent in a first-class railway car, which the exclusiveness of the Englishman causes him to make as small as possible, how strongly is the contrast forced upon me, when I think of the palaces on wheels that afford locomotion to our citizens at home, and then as to the country through which we were passing. Not the wild tracts of unpopulated prairie, so familiar to the American traveler; not the colossal scenery of the Pacific Coast, nor the gigantic foliage of the forest whose trees have not yet bowed their heads to the enterprise of man, but acre after acre, mile after mile, league after league of cultivated and productive soil, every spot being apparently under the care of experienced husbandry; and the whole landscape, and indeed the whole country, being like one large and well kept garden.

But on and on we went, and with such reflections as these were mingled not unnaturally feelings of thankfulness for the protecting mercies of a long sea voyage, and grateful acknowledgments of the "goodness and mercy" which "have followed me all the days of my life." Here I was dashing on at the rate of sixty miles an hour, through shire after shire of the country in which I was to labor for the next six months. As I looked at the long list of the cities I had undertaken to visit, as I thought of the one hundred successive nights that lay before me in which I had promised to pursue my ministry of song, when I contemplated the thousands upon thousands of people whom I should be called upon to address, and realized at once the object of the burden of my singing, how could a heart conscious of its own weakness refrain from crying "who is sufficient for these things." And yet, when I looked back upon the way I had come, as I thought of the countless mercies that had attended me in all my work, at my successes which had always exceeded my deserts, and my failures which had always been better than my fears, how could that same heart help recognizing the true source of all sufficiency, raising its Ebenezer, thanking God and taking courage.

But English roads are not so long as many with which we are familiar at home, and though the road from Liverpool to London is not a short one, it did not take long for our express train to carry us from the banks of the Mersey to the center of English life and action.

Here we met Brother Moody, whose name has since become as a "household word," and "whose praise is in all the churches," and truly pleasant was it thus to meet in a strange city, one whom both Dr. Vincent and myself had been often happily associated. Accompanied by Dr. Vincent I proceeded to the Jubilee Building of the Sunday-school Union, which is situated in the Old Bailey, immediately confronting the ancient jail of Newgate.

Upon our arrival we found that the Continential Committee of the Society was in session, and as it was under the direction of this committee that my present journey had been arranged, we were at once invited to enter. Here I renewed acquaintance with good friends whom I had learned to love during my short stay in England in the summer of 1868; and here, too, I made acquaintances which were destined to ripen into friendships no less strong.

It was at this meeting that I was introduced to Mr. Matthew W. Richards, whose guest I became in the interim from that evening to the commencement of my English pilgrimage. Mr. Richards had been charged with the superintendence of my visit generally, had conducted all the correspondence, completed all the local arrangements, and prepared traveling directions to facilitate my movements from day to day. It was felt to be convenient therefore, as it certainly was congenial, for me to accept the hospitality so courteously offered, and the result was the growth of an intimacy which I shall always cherish with fond regard.

My first engagement was fixed for August 3, and as this was only the 19th of July, I had nearly a fortnight's interval at my disposal. Those who know me best, will, I think, do me the justice of saying that I am by no means disposed to be an idle man, and even if I had desired to rest awhile prior to commencing my engagements, with such active friends about me as Mr. Moody and Dr. Vincent, I really think it would have been impossible.

Mr. Moody was at this time about to visit Dublin, in response to an invitation from Henry Bewley, Esq., of that city, and as he very much desired it I consented to accompany him. Mr. Moody spent the night previous to our journey with me, at the house of Mr. Richards, and early the following morning we were "en route" for the capital of Ireland.

Mr. T. B. Smithies, (editor of the *British Workman*) was also one of our company, and a more delightful railroad ride we never experienced. Having the carriage to ourselves we prepared to spend the eight hours' travel in the most agreeable manner suited to our tastes.

As we came to the stations, we distributed some of those beautiful papers of Mr. Smithies, and during the journey we held a social prayer meeting about sixty miles long, and while crossing the English Channel to Kingston, the writer beat out of his brain the song "Prodigal Child, Come Home." Soon after we landed we were most hospitably domiciled at Henry Bewley's, Esq., in whose spacious parlors we had come to attend a three days' meeting of Bible study and consecration; at this place there were earnest workers not only from many parts of Britain, but even the good Mr. Wall from Rome; others from Spain were present. It was a season of holy refreshing, never to be forgotten by either Mr. Moody, Vincent or myself.

O, that the wealthy homes of our own dear country were more often the scenes of such blissful entertainments.

In Dublin we spent a brief but pleasant time, holding a few services, doing I hope some little good, and enjoying the princely and Christian hospitality of one of the wealthiest men in the country. Our good friend and host, Mr. Bewley, has now gone to his reward and of a truth " his works do follow him." How very many with whom I held sweet counsel during this journey have passed into the better land! It was truly pleasant to grasp their hands as we journeyed together awhile; but thrice happy will be the reunion when partings shall be no more.

AN ENGLISH WELCOME.

Whatever diversity of opinion may exist as to the various traits of English character, there can be no doubt as to its heartness. The Englishman undoubtedly is more reserved than the American, and less polite than the Frenchman, but he atones for these defects, if defects they be, by a heartiness which, when once excited, is real, thorough, and enduring. This characteristic was amply proved in my experience by a thousand hearty welcomes received at different times in different parts of the country, of which the first was a public one, arranged for by the Committee of the Sunday-school Union, for Thursday evening, Aug. 2, and which took place in the Lecture Hall of the Society's Jubilee Building.

The first of my long series of evenings of song was to be held at Torquay, on Friday, August 3, and it was thought well, previous to my starting, to hold a meeting as indicated above to bid me welcome, and to wish me "God speed."

I was not the only lion, however, that this festival was designed to honor. My good friend, Dr. Vincent, who had come with me across the water, and who was charged with the mission of entwning another cord of union round the two great English speaking countries, was also to share the reception, and truly the welcome was large enough for both.

The rooms of the society's premises presented an animated spectacle on the occasion of this truly happy meeting. Refreshments were provided in the library at six o'clock, and a large number of the *elite* of the Sunday-school Society assembled at that hour to commence the engagements of the evening with an hour's social intercourse over "the cup that cheers but not inebriates."

At the conclusion of an elegant and bountiful repast, the company were invited to withdraw to the lecture hall, where the more important engagements of the evening were to be fulfilled.

Here, according to English custom, a Chairman was appointed, and Daniel Pratt, Esq., the Chairman of the Sunday-school Union Committee, was made President for the evening. The beautiful hall was well filled, and on the platform there were those whose fame is world wide, and who are honored for their work's sake.

Van Meter was there from Rome; Pastor Paul Cook, from France; Dr. Vincent and myself from America, and Henry Varley from "everywhere."

Mr. Fountain J. Hartley, whose visit to the United States some time since is well remembered by Sunday-school folks at home, was the first speaker. As one of the secretaries of the society, he, in his own felicitous manner, first in the name of the Sunday-school teachers of England welcomed all, and then introduced each to the other. In the course of a happy speech he was kind enough to say that as I had a long course of hard work before me, which would extend over several months, it was desirable that I should rest as much as possible that evening, and with a view to giving the meeting a practical turn, he suggested that the speeches should be directed to pointing out ways in which the Sunday-school teachers of both countries (England and America,) could best unite to promote the common end they have in view.

At the close of Mr. Hartley's speech I sang "Scatter Seeds of Kindness," which, at that time was a comparatively new song, and which was received with unmistakable manifestations of favor.

Dr. Vincent then took possession of the meeting, and spoke at some length on the advantages of unity of action. He described the growth of the uniform lesson system in America, and urged the arrangement of an international scheme which would bring the whole Christian world into the systematic and contemporaneous study of Scripture truth.

What a catholic idea was this! And how has it prospered! Looking back from the present time one can hardly realize the fact that that which then was no more than " a thought," has now become a recognized system, under which millions of people in all quarters of the globe are simultaneously brought face to face with the perfect law of God.

Dr. Vincent went on to urge the necessity of paying greater attention to the training of our teachers in the art of teaching, and concluded his pleasant speech by calling upon all to show greater earnestness and more dependence on the divine Spirit.

Here followed some more singing, and then the Rev. Paul Cook gave some exceedingly interesting information concerning the progress of Sunday-school work in the south of France, where, for the first time in the history of the world, a Sunday-school Convention had just been held. A great revival had been taking place in certain districts, and the children were coming forward in tens and twenties to testify their simple faith in Christ. Happy the day for *la belle* France when Sunday-schools first started in her midst.

Some more singing followed Paul Cook's pleasing testimony, after which Van Meter took up the thread of Dr. Vincent's speech and spoke on unity of action. We had, he said, only to realize the oneness of our aim in order to forget many of our minor differences. How united we become in times of persecution, or when the influence of great lives prompts us to charitable dealing. When the disciples quarreled as to pre-eminence, Christ placed a little child in their midst. We, too, had children in our midst, and if we united for the purpose of saving them, our differences would hide themselves or fly.

After some reference to the work now going on in Italy, Van Meter concluded by asserting that never was there such an opportunity as then presented itself for both sowing and reaping in that country.

Henry Varley (who has done so much since that day), was the next speaker, and his earnest words will always linger in my memory. He took for his subject, "Definiteness of Aim," and having enlarged upon that, urged the necessity for the stimulating influences of the love of Christ as a motive power.

Another hymn having been sung, my good friend, Mr. Richards, made some announcements concerning my journey, and gave a brief epitome of the circumstances which had led to my undertaking to sing through the country on behalf of the Continental Sunday-school Mission.

Then came the closing devotional exercises, and the numberless hand shakings, that proved the welcome to be individual as well as general. Then the departure for the house of my friend and host, and then the countless reflections which always crowd the brain on such occasions, and which revive again in dreams when the night is far spent.

Truly, the opportunities and the responsibilities of the present age are enormous. France is opening up to gospel influence and her children are breaking from the blind leadership of priestcraft. Italy, the long enslaved, is panting to be free; and even Spain, perhaps the darkest of all the nations of Christendom, has its Sunday-schools already at work. And it was to aid in this work that on the morrow I was to commence my pilgrimage of song. Of a truth the harvest was great, but the laborers were few.

CHAPTER IX.

SINGING IN ENGLAND.

WITH the echoes of my welcome still ringing in my ear, I started early on the following morning to commence the real business of my visit. My first journey, which for England was a rather long one (220 miles), lay through some of the most picturesque districts of the old country, and as this month, August, is perhaps the finest in the English summer, I was fully prepared for the full enjoyment of the scenery. English railways, however, afford the traveler but little opportunity to inspect the country through which he passes, as the pace is too great to allow him other than a most rapid glance at scenes among which he must linger awhile if he would fully enjoy their beauty.

TORQUAY.

Was the town at which I was to commence my one hundred evenings of songs. This town is situated on the southern coast of England, in the county of Devonshire, and is one of the most beautiful of English watering places. It is sheltered on three sides by lofty hills, on the sides of which, stand elegantly built villas and terraces, interspersed with foliage and winding paths. From the extreme salubrity of its climate, Torquay has become one of the most popular places in England for winter residence. It was late in the afternoon when I reached this charming spot, and I had only time to take a hasty meal, and start for the building in which I was to conduct my service of song. The length of the journey however, together with the excitement of the previous evening had not strengthened me for the effort I was now called upon to make, and truly it was not in the highest spirits that I commenced the first of my long series of engagements. Looking back upon it as I now do from some considerable distance of date, I am strongly impressed with the way in which I have been at all times upheld by the sustaining grace of Him whose sufficiency is at all times equal to the necessities of His children. The service passed off well, the people were pleased, and I trust some little good was done; but I must confess that looking to the future as I then did, with all the responsibilities of my long engagements before me, I felt somewhat dispirited. But singing is the best cure for dullness; praise is the straightest faith from the valley of despondency to the mountain top of joy, and so I kept on singing, and as I sung from time to time I saw fresh evidence of the divine favor, and with the Father's smile to cheer me I have continued even until now. My next journey was a short one. I had several engagements for the county of Devonshire, and my traveling for a few days, only being that of short distances, I had good opportunities of rest. On Monday, August 6, I was due to sing at

PLYMOUTH,

Which is in many respects the most important town on England's southern coast; the extent of its anchorage, marking it out from an early period, as the chief station of the British navy. Elihu Burritt after a visit to this celebrated town wrote as follows: " Plymouth! old Plymouth! mother of full forty Plymouths, up and down the wide world, that wear her memory in their names, write it in baptismal records of all their children.

" This is the mother Plymouth sitting by the sea. * *

* * Across the bay is Mount Edgcombe, a baronial park and residence, which for varied and vivid scenery, can hardly be surpassed by any other nobleman's establishment in England. Here are some of the grandest cedars in the kingdom, and trees of every order of architecture, and leafage. The house is a veritable palace of several centuries' growth and adornment. In the front view, from the facade of the house, you see Plymouth, Stonehouse and Devonport spread out before you, in one continuous city, divided into three blocks by arms of the sea. On the left looking northward is Devonport, the great naval arsenal, where the mighty men of sea are put to practice and for service. In the winding river, lie the wasteless hulks of giant ships that will walk the waves no more. On the right are huge forts and batteries, high and low, on island, cliff and beach, with broadsides pointed in every direction to raise a thousand streams of shot and shell upon advancing foes. It is estimated that the government has $500,000,000 worth of public property, including ships of war under the protection of these guns. As you raise your eyes from these busy, solid towns, they rest upon the slopes of Dartmoor with its trees standing like giant sentinels of nature to keep watch and ward over its solitudes. The dockyard alone covers a space of ninety-six acres, and in time of peace employs twenty-six thousand hands." Perhaps, however, the most remarkable feature of Plymouth is the breakwater, which is certainly the greatest artificial sea wall ever built. It is upwards of a mile in length, and cost nearly eight million dollars. In width at the top forty-five feet; its depth varies from fifty-six to eighty, and the total weight of stone deposited to form this gigantic structure exceeds four millions of tons. Inside this barrier, is anchorage for hundreds of ships safe from the tempests of the wild Atlantic.

But my visit to Plymouth was not that of a surveyor, but

that of a messenger of peace and good tidings, and I was, naturally, more interested in such religious life and history as the town possessed. It was from here that the "Mayflower" started across the bounding ocean with its faithful band of voluntary exiles who sought a free soil whereon to worship God. It was here, too, that good old John Kitto was born in the earlier part of the century; here that he endured the hardships of his early years, and here in Plymouth workhouse, called at that time the "Hospital of the poor portion," that he began to show his literary taste by keeping a diary. I have often stood upon spots sanctified by noble character, and it has been my joy to feel that in my own humble way, I have been working for the same great Master, who raised in days gone by "so great a cloud of witnesses." At Plymouth a large congregation assembled to hear my simple gospel songs.

My next service was at Devonport, which is so contiguous to Plymouth as to seem in company with Stonehouse, to be but a subdivision of one large and populous whole. On the day following I crossed the borders of the country and passed into Somersetshire, to visit the town of Frome, and to go from thence to Stoke. Both of these towns are quiet country places compared with some of the cities I afterward had occasion to visit; but I have always found that human nature the same everywhere has always been ready to welcome simple gospel teaching concerning Him who is "the same yesterday, to-day, and forever," when associated, as it has always been in my efforts, with unpretentious melody. On Monday, August 12, I found myself once more in Devonshire, and this time for the purpose of visiting its chief city,

EXETER,

And, although I had not much time to spare for sight-seeing, I could not but spend an hour in its magnificent cathedral. This splendid edifice which is the principal building of an ancient city, has neither the picturesque nor the lofty majesty of the cathedrals of Durham or Lincoln, but its high embowered stone roofs display a boldness of design and a consistency of symmetry, equal if not superior to any architecture in the kingdom. Its stained windows, clustered columns, spacious aisles, and numerous statues, produce an impression upon minds imbued with a true taste for architectural beauty. The earliest buildings on this site date back a thousand years, and during the intervening time the city of Exeter has passed through the vicissitudes of a fortified town, at one time besieged by insurrectionists in civil war; thus there now cluster around it a hundred romantic traditions which hang upon its history like the ivy upon the ruins of its walls.

During this hour or so of sight-seeing, I carried with me a package of tracts, distributing them as judiciously as I knew how. Some seemed pleased to receive them, and some would tear them in my presence, yet I went on silently scattering the seed, with the prayer that it might bear fruit to Him "who went about doing good."

Here I found the hall a difficult place to sing in, pronounced so by Jenny Lind. I was shown great kindness while in this city, by Mr. Wilson, secretary of the Sunday-school Union.

Passing from Exeter, I was soon on my way to another Cathedral town of scarcely less interesting character, for, on the evening following my appearance at Exeter, I was to sing in the ancient city of

BATH.

It is not always easy to discern a reason for the name given to a place one visits; but the reason is not far to seek in Bath. The fact is the city is rich in the possession of some remarkable medicinal springs which have been used

for many centuries for drinking and bathing purposes.
Tradition says that Bladud, a son of Lud, who was king
of Britain a thousand years ago, was cured of leprosy in
these waters, and that he founded the city, when in due
course he became king. Be this as it may, it is certain that
this spot soon became a favorite resort of the Romans after
their conquest, and it was the site of one of the earliest
monastic institutions founded in England after the introduction of Christianity. At the present day Bath is one of
the handsomest cities in the country, and, apparently
throughout its history, has enjoyed a large share of public
favor as a fashionable watering place. Taking a last look
at Bath from the railway station, from which, by the way,
an excellent view of the city may be had, I passed on to
the next scene of my labors,

YEOVIL.

This is as picturesque a country town as any one could
wish to see, but, like all the country towns and villages of
England, so different to the outlying townships of America.
There is no appearance of the wild, uncultivated luxuriance so familiar on the outskirts of American cities. All
here bears the unmistakable impress of careful husbandry
and scientific farming, in which the utmost use seems to be
made of even the smallest plots of ground. From Yeovil,
I proceeded to

SWANSEA,

And in so doing entered the principality of Wales. It is a
matter of curious interest to the traveler to note the diversities of dialect, habit and fashion which may be seen in the
different quarters of this one "United Kingdom." I suppose
it would be impossible to find within so small an area elsewhere, races so distinct and different as those of England,
Ireland, Wales and Scotland. The vernacular of the
Welsh people, which, however, is only spoken by the

poorer classes in the country districts, is, though somewhat musical of sound, most strange of appearance in manuscript or print, the double f's, y's and w's, which abound in its etymology, making the words appear peculiar in the extreme. The appearance of the old market women, too, who speak this language, and who wear short skirts, and high-crowned hats with enormous broad brims like great extinguishers, is very novel to eyes accustomed to "the latest fashion."

There I sang in the music hall to at least two thousand people. It was a hearty audience, and one that loved simple, sacred song; and one, too, that could sing well, for near the close I gave the audience an opportunity of joining me; and they gave me the most lusty congregational singing I have ever heard. I at once said the Welch know how to sing. My next engagement was fixed for the center of one of the largest industries in the world, and in due course I found myself at

MERTHYR TYDVIL.

The mineral resources of this district have for many years been a source of immense wealth to those who have cultivated them. Iron and coal is found here in large quantities, and to such an extent are these resources employed, that the Dowlais iron works, situated here, provide work for upwards of nine thousand men. One would scarcely imagine the difference in character existing between my audience in such a place as this, and that of a city like Bath In the one place the refined and quiet influences, always more or less evident in a cathedral city, showed themselves in the more subdued, if no less genuine reception accorded me; in the other, the rugged enthusiasm of more boisterous if no more hearty feelings found vent in rounds of applause, more befitting a concert room than a church. But in either case, as far as I was able to judge, the charms of simple gospel song only needed to be shown in order to be appreciated. From Merthyr Tydvil I went to Thornbury, and from thence to Newport, after which I visited the ancient city of

WORCESTER.

This place, as all the world knows, is celebrated for its china, in the manufacture of which it has attained to a high state of excellence.

A journey of about fifteen miles brought me, next morning, to

KIDDERMINSTER,

A manufacturing town of considerable importance, and where the best English carpets are made. In England it is a very common practice for those who pursue the same branch of trade, to congregate in close proximity, hence Lombard street, London, is known universally as a street full of banks, and Paternoster Row has attained an equally extensive fame as a district monopolized by publishers. Thus too Kidderminster has become noted for carpets and Watsall, the scene of my next engagement for the manufacture of saddler's iron-mongery. After visiting Stafford and conducting a service there I went on to

CHESTER

A city in which I have been most heartily received on several occasions. It is an ancient place. The older houses are singularly constructed. They have porticos running along the front, affording a covered walk to pedestrians. Beneath these are shops and warehouses on a level with the street. Chester abounds with antiquities, having once been a Roman station. Its ancient walls are still standing, and are about two miles in circumference, and form a delightful promenade. With my wife, and a gentleman who kindly proffered his service as "friend, philosopher and guide," we traversed the circle of these walls by moonlight, gazing upon the softened, fine views, and listening to the historic reminiscences of this, and that, with intense interest. For the next three days I moved amidst the vast manufacturing centres of England, giving my songs in all these places to large audiences, first going to Oldham, where the largest machine works of England are situated, passing thence to Dewsbury, an interesting spot being one of the earliest places to receive Christianity, in England; an old inscription declares that "Paulinus, the first Archbishop of York preached here in the year 627, nearly thirteen hundred years ago." Then on to

MANCHESTER,

A most interesting place, being the "manufacturing metropolis of England," and the chief consumer of American and other cottons. If to Liverpool be conceded the title of "second city of the Empire," there can be no doubt but that Manchester can claim the third position unchallenged. It has a large number of public buildings, including magnificent town halls, exchanges, infirmaries, libraries and colleges, as well as a cathedral and numerous churches and chapels. It is surrounded on every side with vast factories, and its spacious streets are the scenes of that continued bustle and noise, incident to the prosecution of great commercial undertakings. With my Manchester engagement, I concluded the first month of my journeyings in the United Kingdom, a month which was to me a season of many happy experiences. Everywhere I went I found hospitality open-handed and Christianity open-hearted. It mattered not whether I visited the mansion or the cottage, I met with uniform kindness and Christian courtesy, such as surely "a pilgrim" never experienced before. The pursuit of any common object of interest, will always engender a degree of sympathy between those who unite in the pursuit. In nothing is this so fully proved as in the sympathy everywhere to be met with among the true followers of Him who only needs to be uplifted, "to draw all men unto Him." It has been my pleasure and privilege to enjoy this sympathy in almost every part of the world, and whether it be in the north, in the south, in the east, or in the west, communion is very sweet with those who form the great " household of faith."

"STILL I AM SINGING."

On leaving Manchester I turned my face towards Chesterfield, where my heart was greatly cheered by the arrival, from London, of my good friend, Mr. M. W. Richards, to whom I am indebted for so many kindnesses. Every person who has traveled much knows what an exquisite pleasure it is to meet an old friend in a strange land. Such a pleasure was mine, when I met Mr. Richards at Chesterfield. In company with him I started next day to

HUDDERSFIELD,

Where, as everywhere else in the manufacturing districts an enormous congregation assembled to hear my simple gospel songs. It seems strange to me, as I look back from this distance of date, to think that such gigantic audiences should have gathered in a foreign country night after night to hear an unpretentious stranger sing the simple ballads of the cross. Perhaps, however, in this I undervalue the influence of the "Sunday-school Union," under whose auspices I was singing, or greater still, the influence of Him who has said that wherever his word is faithfully proclaimed (and He himself has attested its proclamation in song), it shall accomplish his own great purpose, and in due time draw all men unto him.

> "The tongue may weary in an hour,
> The voice move harsh along,
> But who shall tell the music's power
> If Christ is in the song."

My evening of song in Huddersfield passed off with more than usual *eclat*, but with the dawning of the following day I was obliged to part company with my friend, Mr. Richards. His business called him back to the great metropolis, and mine called me forward to the town of Leeds, thence to Bradford—to Glossop, Halifax, Brunley and Clithreo; and after singing at Stackshead, Blackburn, Bury, Wigin, Berkenhead and Liverpool, crossed over the narrow stream which divides Britain from Hibernia, and spent some time in Ireland. When my friend Mr. Richards returned to London, he wrote an article entitled " Personal recollections of a short pilgrimage with Philip Phillips," which was published in a forthcoming number of the London " Sunday-school Teacher." In this article Mr. Richard describes with so much truth and impartiality the characteristics of my experience, that I feel I cannot do better than quote at least some of his words. Alluding to the circumstances under which I commenced my work Mr. Richard's said:—" The knowledge that Mr. Philip Phillips was about to visit England was sufficient to cause a furor of excitement amongst the Sunday-schools of the United Kingdom. The popularity of his works, especially the " American Sacred Songster," which is now so universally used, is so great, that it was no matter of surprise that all Sunday-school teachers and scholars should have a craving desire, to hear and to see the composer of that greatly admired work. It was therefore only what might be expected, that after filling up the one hundred nights for which Mr. Phillips engaged to sing there should still be upwards of one hundred applications doomed to disappointment." After further reference to these details, Mr. Richards went on to say:—" And who is there, who having heard Mr. Phillips once, does not desire to hear him again, and still hear him—and who is there that having heard him ' singing for Jesus,' is not inspired with an holy inspiration to go and do likewise. I commiserate the man or woman, the boy or girl, who has no soul for music, or not sufficient soul to desire to sing like Phillips. The power that Mr. Phillips throws into his singing is marvelous; the expression is touching, and the effect upon the audience is electrical. A profound, yea, breathless silence is observed during the singing, a look of intense wonder is noticeable on the countenances of the audience, until, when the piece is finished, it appears as if the people felt it a relief to breathe freely. Then comes the close, and everybody is surprised that it is time to go home; they won't believe they have been sitting so long, the time has passed so quickly. They rise to go home—but no, they cannot leave the place, and they flock 'round the platform; they must shake hands with the singer who has so enchanted them. One claims kindred with him for having been to New York; another has a dear son in America somewhere and wants to know if he has ever seen him; a father wants to send money to a son who, alas, has been a prodigal, and wants Mr. Phillips to take it to him. Then comes the invitations to supper and 'we have a spare bed.' What lots of spare beds to be sure, there are in some towns! But Mr. Phillips won't leave his friend; then his friend must come too. This causes late suppers and still later hours, which quite unfits him for his next day's work, and almost brings about that awful tragedy of being 'killed by kindness.' Nor is this all; at one place when we came down to breakfast, a gentleman who had walked three miles that morning was waiting to shake shands with him, and in another town the audience was so enthusiastic that one person got up and said he thought everybody ought and would be pleased to shake hands with the singer. This suggestion was to a great extent carried out, until Mr. Phillips became almost weary of the shakers. These are no fancy pictures but realities, illustrations of which might be multiplied."

The foregoing account written by an eye-witness, will give a very fair idea of the daily experience of this my first journey through England. Plenty of welcome everywhere, and as much of personal kindness as one could well desire, but not so much of that retirement and quiet, which is so necessary to those who are called upon continually to put forth exhaustive efforts. As already stated, my next appointments were in "ould Ireland," and during my several stops in Dublin, where I disembarked, I was most hospitably entertained by Henry Bewley and Samuel McComas, Esqs., both of whom have since deceased, but whose names are widely and honorably remembered in connection with many good works. American readers may think that they do not need to be introduced to the typical Irish character, as they have met with many Irishmen in New York and other parts of the United States; but I am able to say that but scant justice will be done to the Irish character if it is judged by what we are generally familiar with at home. The real curse of Ireland is, of course, the priestcraft with which it is fettered. That system of so-called religion which everywhere and in all ages of time, in proportion as it has flourished as a system, has always debased and humiliated the people. In few places, perhaps, is the contrast more apparent, of the influence of Protestantism on the one hand, and of Romanism on the other. In the north where Protestant Presbyterianism is strong, we find towns comparable with those of England, in which commerce flourishes, order prevails and charity and cleanliness abound. In the south where Romanism is in the ascendant, we find squallor, ignorance, misery, outrage and almost rebellion. To judge of Ireland by the south, would be to apply to it terms which the most indignant might select; but to judge it by the north would be to give it an honored place among the nations of the earth. The society of the educated Irish is charming in the extreme, being characterized by a union of the politeness of the French with the sincerity of the English, and it is greatly to be regretted that so fine a race of people should be to so large an extent degraded by so false a system of religion. After a somewhat extended and pleasant tour of Ireland, my closing service for that time, was given in Belfast, where I was privileged to be the guest of Rev. Dr. Knox. From his pleasant home, I turned my face and thoughts to "the land of cakes," and took ship for Scotland. On arriving at Arbroth, I found that my good friend, Mr. Richards, had provided for me and sent down from London a traveling companion in the person of Mr. Alfred H. Miles, of the London Sunday-school Union staff, who from that time traveled with me, during my stay in Great Britain.

CHAPTER X.

SINGING IN SCOTLAND.

I SUPPOSE there is scarcely a land in all the earth, to which the feet of Scotchmen are unfamiliar. All the world knows how a brave son of Scotland, Dr. Livingstone, labored for the civilization of Africa, and how our American Stanley, ministered to him in the trackless region where he found him, and this is by no means a solitary instance of Scotch devotion any more than it is an isolated case of American enterprise. Born in a country calculated to develop hardihood of character, the natives of Scotland have showed themselves capable of great endurance, perseverance and enterprise in almost every quarter of the earth.

Such were the people among whom I was to spend a few days now, and, after quitting Arbroth, I took the train for

ABERDEEN.

Aberdeen is a very fine city, built of granite, and, it is said of it, "the more it rains the cleaner it is." However this may be there can be no doubt but that the material of which the city is built, gives it a very massive and cleanly appearance.

THE INTERDICTED ORGAN.

From Aberdeen I proceeded on my journey, and, upon my arrival at Glasgow, at once had my peripatetic organ landed at the Gothic Church in Hope street, where, to my

surprise, I was informed by the sexton that the use of such
instruments was not allowed in the Scottish churches, and
that even in this instance if he suffered my organ to be
placed inside the edifice he was fearful that he should lose
his position. Certainly not wishing by any act of mine to
rob him of his situation as a "door-keeper in the house of
the Lord," and at the same time being conscious that I could
not sing without the accompaniment of my little reed or-
chestra, I left it on the steps of the structure and made my
way to my hotel, fully resolved not to attempt my service
without it, my thoughts reverting back to far away years
in my own country, when the sound of anything but a
tuning-fork and the human voice, even down to the big
bass-viol, was looked upon as church sacrilege. But presently I was waited upon by three of the brethren, who
urged me to yield my point and leave my organ out of the
service, to whom I replied that to do so would prove its
failure and thus do great injury to the cause of the Sunday-
school Union. After some consultation, one of these remarked that "we had better permit him to use his instrument," to which I immediately replied that I did not relish
the spirit with which this concession was made, especially
as I was to receive no remuneration for the service, for
which, I had learned, they had sold over two thousand
tickets, and that it would seem more fitting, under the circumstances, that they should be to me a Horr and Aaron,
and do all that was possible to give me aid and sympathy
in the exercises, rather than to coolly and simply *permit* me,
a comparative stranger, to use an instrument which was a
vital aid and necessity to me in the conduct of my service
of gospel song. "Well," said one of the triumvirate, "I
like that kind of spirit, now what shall we do?" I replied
that I should like to conduct my service after my own fashion and to have it opened by Rev. Dr. Bonar with prayer.
They cordially and readily assented, and a more hearty

service and accompaniment of congregational singing I
never enjoyed than on this occasion, all seeming delighted
with the exercises, while the "interdicted" organ fully divided the honors with the singer, and thoroughly cleared
its reputation of being a "mischievous music-box," unworthy of being an accompanist in sacred song worship. Since
then my brother Sankey has used the organ in singing in
Scotland until it has now grown to be a thorough adjunct
instead of an innovation in the song services in most of its
churches. How appropriate in this connection is the Scriptural passage:

"Praise God with the psaltery and harp; praise Him with
stringed instruments and organs; let everything that hath
breath praise the Lord."

At the close of my service, resolutions commendatory of
the same, were adopted, and ten pounds presented me for
conducting it. Proceeding to

CAUPER ANGUS,

I was most kindly received and entertained by Rev. Mr.
Bane, whose Christian hospitality has been a dear memory
to me ever since. While here I paid a visit to an aged
aunt of the noted Dr. Burns, the first missionary to China,
and who, although ninety-six years of age, with her extraordinary Christian culture and devout piety had been for
years a fruitful source of sunshine in this community. As
I left the home of this aged lady, who was also a relation
of the poet Robert Burns, she handed me as a memento of
my visit, a copy of Dr. Duff's "Minds and Words of
Christ," which proved a new blessing to me as I perused it
day by day, while on my tours of song. Here I spent a
still, quiet Scotch Sabbath, listening to an excellent sermon
by Mr. Bane, and quite enjoyed the psalm singing on the
occasion. During the afternoon, in company with this
good pastor, I visited the home of a blind woman, who had

attained the great age of one hundred and four years, and
who was calmly awaiting her release from this earthly
tenement of clay and summons into the eternal life of glory
which lies beyond. We had a refreshing season of prayer
and song with this dear aged disciple, whom I learned had
never during her lifetime been beyond the limits of this her
native town, and then returned to the church for the
evening service. On Monday evening I gave a song
service to a very large and enthusiastic audience, and
although the Scotch people are not noted for singing
hymns, they seemed to very thoroughly enjoy the exercises
on this occasion.

JOHNNY GROAT'S LAND.

Thence I journeyed on to Perth, Inverness, Dundee, and
Wick, to the very edge of Johnny Groat's land, where boys
so suddenly become men, and where the inhabitants have
hardly two hours of night, it being in my memory while
in this locality that I was able to read without lamp, candle,
or gas, at midnight, and to have arisen at two o'clock in
the morning, it then being early dawn.

In all of these old Scotch towns and cities my services
were gratifyingly received; and such was the charming
scenery in these grand old highlands, and the hospitality of
its people, that I sincerely regretted that my stay was
necessarily so short. June is the most delightful of all the
months for a visit to these noble northern hills, with their
bracing and healthful breezes, their beautiful heather,
dancing cascades, and pure atmosphere, upon which even
the Scotch mists conspire with the rest to make the change
from the lowlands sweet in present enjoyment, and dear to
after memory. My next visit was to

EDINBURGH,

The charming capital city of Scotland, where a large
congregation assembled to listen to my simple songs. The

meeting was kindly presided over by Rev. Dr. Horatius Bonar, whose sweet Christian poesy has found its way to so many responsive hearts, in both England and America.

It is difficult to say for which Edinburgh is the most famous—its historic associations, its literary annals, or its natural beauty. The crumbling walls of Holyrood remind us of the unhappy Mary, Queen of Scots, and the palmy days of the kings of Scotland; the castle in the centre of the old town of the birth of James the First, under whose dynasty the kingdom of Scotland became united with that of England, and to whom the authorized version of the English Bible was dedicated.

The beautiful memorial, peeping out from its surroundings of shrubs and flowers, remind us of the great Scotch novelist, Sir Walter Scott, whose works produced such a profound sensation fifty years ago; and the position of the town reminds us of that passage of Scripture, which speaks of a city that is set upon a hill and which cannot be hid. John Knox lived and died here in a house which still stands; besides whom, Dr. Chalmers, Dr. Livingstone, Dr. Guthrie, and many others, continue to live in the hearts of their countrymen as truly as they once inhabited the precincts of the town.

My next stopping place was

DUMFRIES,

A town celebrated for its recollections of Robert Burns, the Scotch poet, whose remains lie entombed in the grave-yard of the town. After singing at Dumfries I once more crossed the borders into English soil, and after giving one night to North Sheilds, turned to

NEW CASTLE UPON TYNE

Here I arrived on a Saturday, and became the guest of Mr. Thomas Bainbridge, with whom I stayed until the following Wednesday morning. About this time I commenced the preparation of my "Song Ministry," which I afterwards used at all my meetings. This work, however, was not completed in a day, and many a weary hour of railway travel was beguiled with preparing copy and reading proofs, before I was able to use it in my evenings of song. South Sheilds and Sunderland were the next places I visited,

SCARBOROUGH AND HULL

Following. These latter towns present a striking contrast. Scarborough is one of the most fashionable of watering places; Hull, one of the busiest of ports; Scarborough, the resort of recreation and amusement; Hull, the abiding place of trade and work. In each place, however, I found the charms of simple gospel song quite sufficient to draw assemblies together, and both at the Claremount chapel, Scarborough, and the artillery barracks, Hull, large congregations gathered to give me audience. From Hull I went to

LINCOLN

The city of the famous cathedral which, situated on the summit of a hill, may be seen for many miles around. Lincoln is one of the many old towns which are closely associated with the country's history. At the time of the Norman conquest it was already one of the richest parts of the empire, and for centuries it has maintained a leading position among the provincial towns. The interior of the cathedral is said to be only surpassed in beauty by that of Yorkminster; and the exterior, as it appeared on the night of my visit to the town, standing out in the full moonlight, head and and shoulders taller than all the town besides, presented an imposing spectacle as it shot its many spires far into the night. My evening of song was held in the Corn Exchange, and, I believe, was felt by all to be a great success. From the quiet which always seems, more or less, to reign in cathedral towns, I passed, the next morning, to the noise of furnace-burning, hammer-welding, scissors-grinding

SHEFFIELD.

From the times of Chaucer, Sheffield has been celebrated for its cutlery; and now its hundreds of factories turn out, week by week, enormous quantities of cutlery of various kinds. It is here that many of the guns are cast, which are at all times ready to pour their tons of missiles upon the foes of Britain, or to engage in the more peaceful, and happily the more frequent occupation, of firing a royal salute. At Sheffield I met Mr. Thomas Newton, brother of Rev. Isaac Newton, of our Central Ohio Conference, and with whom I had formed acquaintance upon the occasion of my first visit to England. I was very glad to avail myself of the shelter of his hospitable home. While here I had the opportunity of visiting one of the great foundries and witnessing the moulders at work. In the soot and grime which clings, more or less, to all its public buildings, Sheffield bears an indication on its face of the kind of work it does; and in this characteristic it presents the strongest contrast to the country by which it is surrounded, and where may be seen some of the finest scenery the country of Yorkshire can boast; but the town itself, especially in hot weather, such as I experienced, from a picturesque point of view, has very little charm. Here my hymn singing was most enthusiastically received. My next meeting was at Manchester, from whence I went to

NOTTINGHAM,

The centre of the great lace industries of England. Here I spent two successive "evenings," on both of which occasions the Castle Gate chapel was filled to overflowing. On the outskirts of Nottingham is Sherwood forest, celebrated for its connection with the bold outlaw, of whom the song says:

> "Bold Robin Hood
> Was a forester good
> As ever drew bow in the merry green-wood.

Many an old legend is still extant among the local peasantry concerning this wonderful individual. Next came Derby, a town in which the first English silk mill was erected, and where Spa and marble ornaments are largely manufactured. From Derby to Loughborough, and on to Leicester, one of the oldest and most flourishing towns in England. In all my journeyings I have made it a point to be at the places where I have engaged to sing, as early as possible on the day fixed; and this rule observed at all times, and in all countries, has enabled me to fill my engagements with a promptness which I could not otherwise have done.

BANBURY.

Was my next destination, a town which has more than one title to fame. In the first place its name is associated with "Banbury cakes," which are familiar to every pastry cook and of which most persons, who possess a sweet tooth, are very fond. Secondly, it is celebrated in the old nursery rhyme,

> "Ride a fast horse
> To Banbury cross
> To see a young lady get on a white horse;
> With rings on her fingers
> And bells on her toes,
> She shall have music, wherever she goes.

Further titles to fame might be alluded too, but I prefer to honor her for these simple nursery associations. My next halting place was

BEDFORD,

And few towns that I have ever visited have afforded me greater pleasure than this—the scene of Bunyan's inimitable dream. I could not help but be intensely interested in all that could be seen in any way connected with the author of the "Pilgrim's Progress," and I can well remember the thrill of pleasure I experienced when, standing up to commence my evening of song in "Bunyan's Meeting House," I realized the thought that it was in connection with this same church that the glorious "Dreamer" ministered and suffered persecution. Of course there are many spots in and around Bedford, connected closely with the history of Bunyan's remarkable career. The old prison consecrated by his incarceration, has given place to a more modern and commodious building, but the spot still remains to prove that the greatest achievments may sometimes be accomplished by the humblest means, and under circumstances of the utmost disadvantage. In the afternoon of the day I sang at Bedford, under the guidance of my good friend Mr. Curruthers, I visited the pastor of the old meeting house, and there saw a number of relics, kept in memory of the great man who has made the name of Bedford famous the whole world over. Among these were the old church books, with their numerous quaint entries, and many other objects cherished with loving care as memorials of the Bedford tinker. Since my visit, however, public honors have been paid to his memory by some of the most illustrious of his countrymen. The Duke of Bedford, a peer of the realm of which he was but a humble peasant, and the Hon. A. P. Stanley, a dean of the church which persecuted him, united to do honor to his marvelous genius. A handsome statue of Bunyan now ornaments the town and a pair of magnificent bronze gates, designed to illustrate portions of the "Pilgrim's Progress" have been erected in front of his old chapel. From the city of the unlettered preacher, I turned my steps towards the ecclesiastical and university city of

CAMBRIDGE,

And passed from thence to Ipswich and Chelmsford. Of the latter place I will merely say that I was favored with large audiences, and enjoyed happy seasons, but Cambridge demands more than passing mention. As it is interesting to stand at the source of mighty rivers and contemplate the influences and uses of the many streams that flow toward the sea, so is it interesting to stand in a city like Cambridge, a noble seat of learning, and think of the vast influence it has exercised upon the world century after century, for a thousand years. The University of Cambridge is said to have been founded in the seventh century, so that it has actually been in existence for twelve hundred years. The number of students that have passed through its degrees during that time, is of course beyond conjecture, and it is almost as difficult to realize that this spot was the resort of the thoughtful and the studious nearly a thousand years before America was rescued from the wild beast, and the bramble. We arrived at Cambridge early in the day and determined to spend the afternoon in visiting the various buildings of the university, and where we were greatly interested in what we saw and heard. There are seventeen colleges in connection with the university, each of which is governed by its own statutes, and supported by its own endowments, and each of which has been rendered famous by the illustrious men who have passed from its sphere of preparation to the scenes of activity and honor in the outside world. It would be easy to fill many volumes with interesting matter concerning many of the spots I have visited during my tours of song, but as the places are so numerous, I must necessarily make but the briefest reference to the most important of them, and at the risk of being thought unmindful of the kindnesses received, pass by with but a mention, many places in which happy hours were spent. In two more days I was back in London, having been absent for several weeks, during which I had traveled many hundreds of miles, renewed acquaintances with many old friends, and formed new associations which I now look back upon as among the brightest memories of my life.

CHAPTER XI.

THE ENGLISH SUNDAY-SCHOOL UNION.

S my visit to England was made under the auspices of the English Sunday-school Union, and, as that society differs very much in constitution from the kindred society of America, it cannot be out of place, and it may not be uninteresting to give here some account of this the oldest and the largest Sunday-school organization in the world.

Established in the year 1803, within a very few years of the founding of Sunday-schools by Robert Raikes, the Sunday-school Union had, at the time of which I write, nearly attained to the 71st year of its age. Although organized in an imperial country, it is thoroughly republican in its character. It is governed by a representative committee of about sixty gentlemen, who are elected annually by the representatives of the subscribing schools of the metropolis. Twenty of these gentlemen are elected at the annual meeting of the society, and the remaining forty attend as representatives of the various auxiliary committees, who watch over the local interests of the various schools in the different districts which they in turn are elected to represent.

Each subscribing school sends a representative to the local committee, and each local committee sends one or more representatives, (in proportion to the number of teachers represented by the local committee), to assist in forming the committee of the present society.

In addition to the above, there is a President, a number of Vice-Presidents, all of whom have served the office of President; a treasurer, a chairman and four honorary secretaries; all of whom hold office by virtue of the annual elections of the society.

Throughout the length and breadth of the land, there are numerous local Sunday-school Unions, affiliated with the parent society, subscribing to its funds, furnishing it with statistics for its annual report, and dispensing its benefits among local associated schools. Every officer and teacher belonging to a connected school, is a member of the Sunday-school Union, and in this way an army of 100,000 teachers is banded together to "overcome evil with good," to inculcate religious principle, to build up in Biblical knowledge and to promote the spiritual welfare of Britain's rising race.

For the systematic discharge of the functions of the society, the committee of the parent institution is divided into a number of sub-committees, bearing such titles as "Continental," "Finance," "Trade," "Publication," "Exhibition," "Library," "Extension," "Visitation," etc., etc., the work undertaken by these several committees being, of course, indicated by their various titles.

Under the direction of the Continental committee, numerous missionaries are at work in different parts of Europe, France, Germany, Spain, Italy, and other countries being the scenes of constant Sunday-school enterprise. The duty of the Finance Committee is that of watching and contributing the funds of the society, and that of the Trade Committee the arrangement of all matters concerning the operations of the trade department. The publication committee is responsible for the publications of the society, which are both numerous and divers. The exhibition committee consists of a number of gentlemen who hold themselves in readiness to visit any part of the metropolitan schools with the panoramas, a dissolving view apparatus of the society, for the purpose of giving explanatory lectures on the same. The library committee superintend the fine collection of books known as the Sunday-school Union Library, which, with the spacious reading room of the society, is open to all teachers of the metropolitan schools at a nominal yearly subscription. The executive committee as its name implies, is charged with promoting Sunday-school extension, while the members of the visitation committee devote a large amount of their time to visiting the different local societies in various parts of the kingdom, stirring them up to renewed effort, if energy be lacking, in learning from them such lessons as their prosperity may teach.

In addition to the foregoing, moreover, there are committees for the management of training classes for teachers, normal classes for intending teachers, week evening entertainments for senior scholars, besides special committees, which are appointed from time to time as special circumstances may require.

At the monthly meeting of the general committee, reports are received from these various sub-committees as well as from the representatives of the several auxiliary committees as to the progress of the work in their respective spheres of labor.

For the carrying out of the honorary work of the committee, a large staff of paid officials is necessary. This includes a trade manager, a publication superintendent, several editors and sub-editors, a number of clerks, shopmen, warehousemen and porters, the whole forming a corps of fifty officers engaged exclusively in the trading department of the society.

The extent of the society's operations may be judged by the fact, that the trade returns of the society amount to nearly $250,000 per annum.

The society's publications embrace every department of Sunday-school necessity. From the Union press there issues, in one continuous stream, Sunday-school literature of all kinds for scholars, teachers and parents; a weekly newspaper, a number of monthly magazines and several annual volumes, from the Union contributions to periodical literature.

In addition to these there are issued from time to time large numbers of elegantly bound books suitable for Sunday-school rewards, private gifts, or day school prizes; thousands of small picture reward books for little people; literally, millions of pictorial and other leaflets, handbills, &c., suitable for broadcast distribution; large varieties of ornamental texts for house and school decoration, as well as illuminations, certificates and motto cards; scripture prints plain and colored, illustrative of both Old and New Testament history; music in books and sheets for public worship, the home circle, school festivals and anniversary gatherings. Books for the teachers' use, works of reference; works illustrative of scripture; works on school management, and the principle and art of teaching; school stationery; learning books and general educational requisites; scripture maps of all sizes, as well as hymn books to suit all ages, and miscellaneous publications too numerous to mention.

Who can calculate the influence of this vast machinery! as wide as civilization is its area and as long as eternity will its effects endure.

One of the main objects of the society as determined by its constitution, is thus to provide, in cheap form, suitable Sunday-school literature for teachers and scholars, and naturally from the first its committee has paid great attention to the preparation and issue of lesson helps of various kinds. This work at a very early stage of the society's career necessitated the opening of premises for the sale of the publications so prepared, and commencing in the day of small things with a single room, these premises grew with the Sunday-school movement until the year 1855, when the institution celebrated its jubilee and erected a memorial building?

This building, as already intimated, is situated in the Old Bailey, contiguous to Newgate prison. It is a large and handsome structure, and is devoted entirely to the furtherance of the various objects of the society.

The ground floor and extensive cellarage is used for the storing and selling of the thousands upon thousands of books which issue from the society's press. Several large apartments in the front of the building are devoted to the retail trade, while equally commodious offices in the rear afford accommodation for the foreign and country departments. On the first floor are several committee rooms and other offices, as well as the magnificent library and reading room of the institution, which is open daily for the accommodation of teachers, and with its more than 5,000 volumes for reference and circulation. On the second floor is the Biblical Museum, in which is stored a valuable collection of articles obtained from various sources, illustrative of Biblical truth and the manners and costumes of oriental life. Here too is a beautiful model of the tabernacle, made at great expense, upon a scale given in the books of Leviticus and Numbers, and adjoining is the lecture hall, a truly beautiful apartment, in which almost every evening a Sunday-school meeting of some kind is carried on.

This then, in brief outline, is a description of the society under whose auspices I had undertaken to sing throughout the length and breadth of the land, but I cannot conclude this chapter without paying a passing tribute to the self-denying labors of the sixty gentlemen, who at so much sacrifice of time and money conduct this society without fee or reward.

All of them men of business, with their own daily avocations to pursue, it might reasonably be supposed that their attendance would not be very numerous, and yet there are often three committees meeting at one time in different rooms, and the attendance of many members averages three committees per week.

Truly may these gentlemen say, "the love of Christ constraineth us," and just as truly may others say of them, "He that seeth in secret" shall one day reward openly.

The London *Christian World* contained the following notice of Mr. Phillips' departure from England:

"Mr. Philip Phillips has taken leave of his English friends, having completed the work which he came here in the summer to do. It is not often that one sees such a gathering in the Old Bailey as came together to what was called a farewell soiree. People were there from all parts of the land, who had come to see the last of one who had sung to them of Jesus. I believe the visit now closing is Mr. Phillips' second one to this country, and, according to all human probability, we may see him here again. He is on his way to California, *via* New York, where he is under an engagement to do what he has done so successfully here.

From the proceeds of his meetings, after all expenses have been paid, there is a profit to be devoted to the Continental Sunday-school Fund of nearly £900. It is worth crossing the Atlantic and traveling up and down the country for this. Mr. Phillips has done good, and it is to be hoped he has received good. It is to be believed he will take back with him to his native land, pleasant memories of England and her people. At any rate, he must feel that, whatever politicians on either side the water may say, the churches of America and England are one—one in aim, in heart, in creed, and life. It is a common language they speak, a common song they sing, whether that song be

TOWER OF LONDON.

raised on the banks of the Thames, on the rushing waters of the Mississippi, or on the golden slopes where a city gay and luxurious as San Francisco, has all at once started into vigorous life.

The rooms of the Old Bailey, as was to be expected, presented an unusually cheerful appearance. Tea and coffee were served in the library, but the centre of attraction was the lecture-hall, which was filled long before the time had come for Charles Reed, Esq., M. P., to take the chair. One or two absentees were specially alluded to. There was no Mr. Pratt, who was, alas! unable to be present, on account of illness. There was no Mr. Smithers, who had done so much to introduce into the country the name and fame of Mr. Phillips. In this latter case, absence was peculiarly painful. That very day a beloved sister had passed away, with, for her last words, one of Mr. Phillips' songs on her dying lips; and thus pleasure and pain, as usual in this world of ours, stood side by side. On the platform were blended the flags of England and America; behind the chair was a farewell blessing inscribed. As was natural, pleasure predominated. Every one seemed pleased— Mr. Phillips, because he had done his work and was going home; the Committee, because their plan had succeeded; the friends of the Continental Sunday-school Mission, like Mr. Shrimpton, because they had what they wanted—cash for more extended operations; and the general public because they had come to look upon Mr. Phillips as a friend, and wished to see his face once more. The interest of the proceedings was heightened by the presence of Mrs. Phillips; and by the presentation of an address, beautifully inscribed and magnificently framed, and of a handsome ormolu timepiece, expressive of grateful appreciation on the part of the Sunday-school Union, of Mr. Phillips' labors in this country.

The public meeting commenced at half-past seven with

an appropriate prayer, offered by Dr. Underhill. Mr. Reed then spoke of the pleasure that it gave him to be once more with his friends in the Old Bailey, and to the character of the meeting—one of social intercourse and deep religious feeling. He then referred to Mr. Phillips as a Christian brother from another land, who had performed a special work with great assiduity. Mr. Phillips then sang, and Mr. Richards, the secretary, into whose hands the business arrangements with regard to Mr. Phillips' services had been placed, read a report. From the report it appeared that correspondence on the subject began in 1871; that in July, 1872, Mr. Phillips landed on our shores; and that in August he commenced his first services in the West of England. His audiences were at first 300, then 600, then 900. At Liverpool the numbers were 2,000. They were more at Birmingham, and at Bristol they had reached 2,730; and at Mr. Pennefather's the numbers present were 3,000; and at the East London Tabernacle 3,300. As many as 92,296 had heard Mr. Phillips sing, and many reports were read showing how much spiritual good had been accomplished. To give an idea of the work connected with making the arrangements, Mr. Richards said 836 letters connected with the country and London had been written, and 1,092 received. It was noted that no accident had occurred. *In no case had Mr. Phillips been unable to keep an engagement*, and it was evident that the work was blessed and owned of God. Mr. Groser, senior, in moving the adoption of the report, spoke of Mr. Phillips's modesty—a modesty, as he playfully termed it, marvelous in a Yankee. Mr. Cooper, from Birmingham, said they would long cherish the memory of Mr. Phillip's in that town, and expressed a hope, in which most of the speakers joined, that he would be spared to return to them again. Mr. Reed, in rising to offer the testimonial to Mr. Phillips and his beloved wife, referred to the many distin-

guished Americans they had been privileged to receive—
such as Ward Beecher, Dr. Todd, Dr. Tyng, Dr. Vincent,
etc. Such visits formed a bond of Christian friendship.
They had been enabled to send Mr. Phillips through the
country, where he had met most of the best men in it; and
he had done them good service. He had an hereditary
pleasure in meeting Mr. Phillips. It was his father who
was the first minister sent out by any denomination in
America, and he himself had long been connected with
Mr. Peabody, who had done so much for the poor of
England and America. He then read the address, and
presented it and the timepiece to Mr. Phillips, who, in
acknowledging the gift, expressed himself as greatly
gratified. Mr. Reed then testified to the earnestness and
zeal of Mr. Phillips; of the work which he had done for
their continental mission. He observed, too, his songs were
now being sung in Germany and France, in Waldensian
valleys, in Swiss chalets, even in the seven-hilled city itself
—Rome. In few, but feeling words, Mr. Phillips returned
thanks. It would remind him of old friends. His one
regret whilst on his singing tour was, that he was unable
to make the acquaintance of the Christian men and women
with whom he came in contact. He would be glad to meet
them all, and to declare what a glorious work theirs was.
After he had sung,
"Blest be the tie that binds
Our hearts in Christian love."
Mr. Hartley presently began complimenting everybody—
Mr. Reed for being in the chair; the ladies for being
present; Mr. Phillips for his services; the Continental
Committee for taking the matter up, and placing it in the
hands of Mr. Richards; and Mr. Richards for the labor he
had endured as extra secretary. Another song from Mr.
Phillips followed, and then Mr. Reed called upon Mr.
Shrimpton, who, as treasurer to the Continental Mission

held the money raised, and Mr. Richards, who had made the arrangements by means of which the money was raised. Mr. Shrimpton was jubilant in the extreme. He referred to Mr. Hartley's going to America as the representative of thousands of Sunday-school teachers and 3,000,000 Sunday scholars. He then spoke of himself as representing the Sunday-schools of Europe, and gave one or two illustrations of the fact that in Germany Sunday-schools were attracting the attention of royal personages. Mr. Richards said he never entered on a work of such interest, and spoke of the plesant intercourse he had with Mr. Phillips, who, in order to fulfil his mission, had sacrificed much ease and comfort. Mr. Tressider, as one of the Trade Committee of the Sunday-school Union, thanked Mr. Phillips for the impulse he had given to the sale of their publications. Mr. W. H. Groser was glad to see so many country friends present. Mr. Hall, from Derby, exulted in the fact that he had cleared £30 in that town by Mr. Phillips' visit. And then came the end—a new piece composed by Mr. Phillips, while Mr. Richards at intervals read appropriate texts from Scripture, and all joined in a chorus of sacred song; and thus closed a night long to be remembered, or we are much mistaken, in the annals of the Old Bailey."

CHAPTER XII.

THE START FOR AUSTRALIA.

IN the year 1872, while singing in London, England, for the first time I met that earnest, indomitable and successful evangelist, Matthew Burnett, of Australia, who then said that I must visit that island. Subsequently meeting him at Scarboro, he warmly repeated the previous invitation, but without awakening in me more than a mere cursory thought of the possibility or probability of such a trip.

A year later a letter inviting me to come to that far-off big sea land was received, which was soon followed by the formation of a committee consisting of several noble ministers and laymen of the Wesleyan Church at Melbourne, with Rev. J. C. Simmons acting as its secretary, and a proposition to pay me £500, together with one-half the proceeds, for one hundred services throughout the different colonies, with instructions to draw on them for £200 as an acceptance of the invitation.

Had I more thoroughly realized what it would be to break up and leave home with my family for such a long and hazardous trip, I should not have attempted its accomplishment, yet the thought that my services, under Divine guidance, might do good to some who might hear me, and bring spiritual strength to myself, added to a desire of seeing that portion of the great world, proved a temptation which I did not resist, and therefore I accepted and went, singing all the way westward until my feet again crossed the threshold of " Home, sweet Home."

My furniture and personal effects nicely stored and packed away, and good-by said to my city home and neighbors, I'm off for Australia, 14,000 miles away, with my dear ones by my side. The hack conveys our family quartette and our luggage to the Erie railway station, and seventeen hours of broad-gauge ride in a palace sleeping car takes us to my birthplace, where the great Chautauqua Assembly is holding its sessions, so successfully planned and continued by that prince of Sabbath-school men, Dr. J. H. Vincent.

Ten days of song service at *such* a meeting and among *such* friends, was enough to waft one on the wings of song around the world.

WESTWARD TO THE GOLDEN GATE

Westward I go on, singing in the principal cities, and towns of the great states of Ohio, Indiana, Michigan, Illinois, Iowa, Nebraska, toward the Pacific coast, it being my second service of song among the Mormons at Salt Lake City, and also my second on the Pacific slope. They have a custom in the far west of reporting in advance at San Francisco the names of overland passengers, which brought several friends of mine from the Central Tabernacle to the dock to meet us (foremost among whom was Mr. A. Hemme), who received us with kindly greetings and open arms, and conveyed us in carriages to our resting place, where we were glad to cleanse ourselves of the dust of the journey and refresh ourselves with the rich bounties and luxurious fruits which always adorn a San Francisco table.

The welcome greetings of my California friends, on this occasion will ever be kindly remembered, for they confirmed the sincerity of the sorrowful good-byes which were said to me at my departure on my first visit to them two years previously. If I desired to make a home in any other part of the world other than New York my choice would certainly fall upon California, with its even climate, delightful valleys, its thrifty wheat fields, its delicious fruits, its beautiful flowers, its wonderful vegetation and its richness in minerals, surpassing as it does, in these, almost every other country in the world. Here I remained a sufficient time to give some fifty evenings of song, many of which were held in the same places which I had sung in two years before.

It is hardly possible that there is any locality in the world where more radical changes could take place in the space of twenty-four months than in California. Since my previous visit hydraulic mining had torn down the mountains and new rivers and streams had been provided with channels for the purpose of irrigation, which had caused the desert places to spring up and blossom like a rose. In fields where wild oats grew indigenously, stood beautiful wheat producing seventy bushels to the acre, waiting the coming of the reapers, while the wild canons were becoming prolific vineyards and overheads of fruit, in one of which latter I was shown 38,000 cherry trees all of which were in bearing. Towns were becoming cities, railroads taking the place of stage-routes, little Sabbath-school missions were becoming large and influential churches, and improvement in society correspondingly advancing.

EMBARKED FOR A FOREIGN SHORE

On the 8th of March, 1875, we bade our California friends adieu, and being nicely located on board the staunch steamer "Cyphrenes," we set sail for the largest island in the world —Australia. From childhood a charm had associated with the name Australia. The word is from the Latin *australis*, signifying "southern." A strangeness and a far-offness had always lingered in the meaning of the word; and no books on the subject, nor any of the occasional newspaper accounts—although I had latterly perused not a few—ever fully dispelled the sense of isolation and weirdness represented by the musical syllables—Australia.

The anchor weighed, the ropes cast from the moorings and hauled in, the gangway drawn which separates us from friends and native land, slowly we glide away from the wharf, past Alketras Island and Seal Rock, down through the Golden Gate, while the waving handkerchiefs of our dear friends grow fainter and fainter to our sight, now appear as tiny white specks upon the horizon of our vision, and finally make us alive to the reality of crossing the great Pacific as all at once they disappear altogether.

Our steamer was a good, strong ship, which was built on the River Clyde for the eastern tea trade, was owned in Liverpool, and was well manned by English sailors. Its captain, Mr. Wood, was an excellent mariner, was quite wonderful in athletic feats, having under him a retinue of officers, among whom was the chief engineer, a teetotaler, who was a world of comfort to us during the entire passage on account of his freedom from a vice to which so many who follow the high seas are addicted. The ship's surgeon, however, was directly the opposite of this gentleman, being profane in language, prolific in abuse, brutal in habit, and had not the captain placed him under guard on several occasions during the voyage, we fear serious consequences would have resulted. As to his medical skill, evidently some special providence gave little or no opportunity of putting it to the test.

Imagine yourself and family confined within the narrow limits of a ship, with some twenty-six passengers, having nationality in almost every part of the world, whose principal pastime was gambling and drinking, on a thirty-eight day passage on the pathless ocean, bound for the farthest land of which we all know too little. There was a complete sense of isolation from mankind in this voyage, as with my dear little family, we occupied our time in reading, conversation, playing at quoits and in other simple pastimes which served to relieve the monotony of sea life.

Our steamer, although of staunch build, was not noted for speed, its average being about two hundred miles in twenty-four hours. On pleasant days we spent much time upon the deck, where from time to time we made the acquaintance of fellow passengers. Here we watched the hundreds of sea gulls who circled round and round the ship on graceful wing in quest of bits of food that might be thrown to them, while they wildly screamed in their attempts to preserve their maritime rights, one against the other, in gaining possession of the same. But the sailors say we are to soon loose sight of even these ærial companions of our trip, as these birds will cease to follow us when our prow begins to part the waters of mid ocean.

The habits of the flying-fish also afforded us much amusement as they would suddenly start up from the waves in schools and alight again about two hundred yards away. It is said that the larger fish eat them, and that when closely pursued by their implacable enemies, the good Creator has bestowed on them this wonderful power for escape. I would that humanity were possessed of such a gracious gift, wherewith to baffle and fly away from the clutches of temptation. These singular fish are from four to eight inches in length, and glisten like pieces of burnished silver as they dart through the air, about ten feet above the water. It often happens that these fish fall upon the decks of vessels, and they are accounted most delicious food.

With beautiful moonlit nights and wooing breezes, we begin to feel the warmer breath of the tropics fanning our cheeks. The sea gull has been left behind, and that large, brown bird, the "Albatross," measuring several feet from tip to tip of wing, has taken his place as ocean mendicant. It is our first Sabbath on the Pacific. At eleven o'clock in the morning the captain reads the service on deck, but it seems so cold and heartless. How the Christian heart does love to whisper into the Infinite ear its present necessities, framing its own prayer from personal wants, and expecting present answers to its personal needs. How thankful I feel on board this good ship, that we are not dependent on surroundings for communion with our dear Savior.

CHAPTER XIII.

THE HAWAIIAN OR SANDWICH ISLANDS.

FTER a smooth passage of ten days, at two o'clock in the morning, we were safely moored in the peaceful harbor of Honolulu. Late in the afternoon we had passed Maui to our extreme left, but were too far distant to behold her luxuriant tropical growth of fruit, flower and foliage. Soon after we were passing through the Molokai Channel, but it was so late that we could only see the volcanic cliffs of Oahu, of which Honolulu is the capital, faintly outlined by the moonlight. Rounding Diamond Head at about midnight, rockets were sent up to signal the pilots that they might come on board and take our ship safely through the hidden reefs and coral beds so plentiful in the beautiful bay of the metropolis of this famous island group.

Landing at the unseasonable hour of three o'clock in the morning, we proceeded to the only hotel on the island, and which is under the management of the government. Here we found every room occupied; but the clerk kindly vacated and prepared his own room for our accommodation that we might take a short rest, and for about two hours our little family quartette lay crosswise on the one bed and soundly slept. When we awakened in the early morning and looked out upon our surroundings, it seemed as though we had been suddenly transported into an earthly paradise of fresh fruits, beautiful flowers and rare exotics. At six o'clock we were agreeably surprised by a visit from the good Dr. Damon, the seaman's friend, one of the oldest missionaries upon the island, and known the world over by mariners as the spiritual father of the children of the seas. His gentle tap at the door and a response from his lips brought me quickly to my feet, and I found him all aglow with hospitality and anxious for a service of song before I should re-embark. Ascertaining that our ship would remain in port for twenty hours, a service was accordingly arranged and advertised at six o'clock that afternoon, to be held at the Congregational Church, of which Rev. Dr. Friers was pastor.

Now for a full day of sight-seeing in and about Honolulu, which then seemed to us the most enchanting spot our eyes had ever rested upon. But first of all we desired to see Mrs. Thurston and Mrs. Webb, the dear old missionaries, of more than thirty years' residence on these islands, the latter a sister of Dr. Thos. Hastings, of New York. Dr. Damon placed himself and his carriage at our disposal, and a kind stranger loaned a fine riding horse for my James to follow us from behind, but he followed us, as most boys do, on before, and secured to himself an amount of exercise in the saddle which nearly incapacitated him from keeping his feet when he dismounted. Never did we spend a more enjoyable day than here on this pioneer American missionary ground.

Honolulu is a city of about 20,000 inhabitants, 4,000 of whom are for the most part Americans, and the balance natives. The latter are a noble looking, large and well-proportioned people, of about the same complexion as the North American Indian, cleanly in habit and well dressed, and very little of the African type is visible in their features. The women are of large build and good looking, and wear long dresses hanging loose from neck to heels

It has often been said and written that the natives were once cannibals, but the more intelligent people here deny the charge, and assert such as incapable of proof. It is true, however, that fifty years ago this people were uncivilized and sitting in heathenish darkness, and we cannot but be grateful that God ever put it into the hearts of some of New England's sons and daughters to try and do them good, and that He blessed their efforts so signally.

During the forty years that the Hawaiian language has been invented, written and printed, school-houses and churches have sprung up as plentifully, according to the population, as in the United States, and I was informed that an equal proportion of the people can read and write as in either England or America. It is estimated that there are about 60,000 inhabitants on all the islands of the group, but it is authoritatively stated that for the last twenty years the native population thereon has steadily decreased.

THE PRODUCTS AND THE KING.

The principal product of these islands is sugar, and it is believed that in no part of the world so large a crop can be raised to the acre as here. Up to the time of my visit, the planters had labored under great disadvantages in not having a market for this crop near home, while expense of transportation to distant parts had left the grower but little or no profit whatever. In the year 1875 the king, Kalakaua, made an extensive visit to the United States, and by his genial and winning manner and diplomatic skill, so managed his suit as to induce our government to pass the Hawaiian sugars through our customs free, or nearly so, from duty. Now the islands are more prosperous than ever before, and this great triumph of the king in the interests of his subjects, has made him exceedingly popular.

As we were driving past the king's palace we observed quite a collection of natives in front of the main entrance, when upon alighting from our carriage and going near, we learned were singing the king's welcome home again, he having returned only a day or two previous, from his visit to America. Several hundred of them had also come bearing little tokens of regard to their king, such as eggs, potatoes, cabbage, money and any thing by which they might express their loyalty to their sovereign and their joy and gladness at his return. We were much interested in witnessing this devotion of the people to their ruler and in gazing upon his great piles of vegetable gifts, as well as listening to the Hawaiian festivities partaking so thoroughly as they did of the aboriginal custom of celebrating this event.

The king having observed us near his palace came to the front door and invited us to enter, which courtesy we gladly accepted. I had a very enjoyable chat with his majesty, in the course of which he expressed himself as having been very much pleased with everything which came to his notice during his recent visit to America. He speaks the English language very fluently, is a good conversationalist, and is seemingly as thoroughly polite and intelligent as any one of our members of Congress.

From the palace we went to the House of Parliament, a fine structure, whose walls were tastefully adorned with pictures, having for their subject the history of the island. We also visited one of the native churches having seating capacity for at least twenty-five hundred people, where the gospel is preached in the Hawaiian language. Without doubt there has been no field of labor which has shown a greater success in answer to missionary effort than this, and all in the short space of forty years.

The tropical fruits are of the finest quality, are in great abundance, while the oranges and bananas are luscious and beautiful. The chief food of the natives is poie, a vegetable somewhat resembling our potato, which is prepared for eating in the form of a batter, and sold on the public streets. The hospitality of the people is unbounded and one of their most striking characteristics, and it is not unusual for them to vacate their own apartments for the accommodation and entertainment of even strangers.

Some of the residences here are equal in beauty and elegance to many found in Europe or America, and are embellished with fine grounds and ornamentation of shrubbery and flowers. Of these we particularly noticed the palatial homes of several wealthy Chinese merchants. We dined with H. M. Whitney, the editor and publisher of the daily newspaper, a large bookseller, and one of the most influential citizens of the island, from whom we gathered much reliable information of the islands and their population. Perhaps Mr. John Waterhouse has the finest residence in Honolulu, to which we were invited after my service of song and partook of one of the most luxurious repasts ever spread for the refreshment of the body. During the hour which we spent at his table in the enjoyment of the good English cooking and rare delicacies of confection and fruit, he set his music boxes in play and his birds to singing, while he discoursed of his religious works and enterprises with his soul full of evangelistic ardor. Among other things of like character, he owns a mission hall, which he supports with his means, and in which he preaches and reads sermons when he is unable to obtain other talent to conduct these meetings. He is a rich merchant, and has earnest and faithful zeal in doing the Master's work. On my departure from his home he said, " now if you cannot stay here a month or two, do send some one who will." All manifested a strong desire that we might linger with them longer, while in one instance, we were offered the use of a whole house, with servants, horses and carriages free of charge if we would but tarry for a month.

Evening came on apace, and had I not been so weary in body I really should have felt myself in an earthly paradise, the people were so cordial, loving and kind, while these fair islands looked as beautiful and peaceful as the Gardens of the Lord. Then came to me an almost overmastering desire for resting for a time among the Sandwich Islanders, and singing the new songs of our Saviour-King to the curious inhabitants, who had been transformed from paganism by the power of the gospel, and of sharing the joys of salvation with the missionaries and Christanized multitude.

At my only service of song at Honolulu was a large audience of English speaking people to whom I sang as well as I could for an hour, with the soft tropical breezes fanning my cheeks, and the distant roar of the waves of old ocean falling upon my ears. The assemblage listened to my songs with deep attention, one of the natives expressing himself concerning them as being "so restful." The pecuniary result of the service was the leaving of $100 with Dr. Damon with which to prosecute his great and good work, while with a similar sum I sought my berth on the steamer which was to leave at eleven o'clock that evening.

Never have I spent a more intensely interesting and enjoyable day than the one just closed upon this island, so memorable for the killing of Capt. Cook, the great sea explorer, and for the blessing of God upon the pioneer American missionary work, now filled with intelligence and gospel liberty and without doubt the most quiet, peaceful spot on His great footstool where weary people can find *rest*.

YORK STREET CHURCH, SYDNEY.

Did He lan-guish and suf-fer for me?

CHAPTER XIV.

OFF FOR NEW ZEALAND.

OUR ship berths brought us the sweetest repose after this eventful day, and next morning when we arose the lovely Oahu was fully out of sight. At the breakfast table we missed four of our former fellow passengers, but in their place had gained another, a fine looking young man of about twenty-six years of age, genteeley dressed and of prepossessing appearance. So quiet and reticent in manner was this gentleman that for several days we thought that he might be a young clergyman seeking health, recreation or knowledge by foreign travel. A few days after my wife said to me, "Why does our friend look so wild and singular, evidently seeking to avoid every one upon the deck?" This strangeness soon became so noticeable that we made inquiries of the captain as to its cause, and learned to our great sorrow that he had been indulging in intoxicating drink and was suffering from an attack of delirium tremens, that fearful concomitant so sure to fall upon those who become a prey to this habit, so fatal to the highest interests of humanity, both in this world as well as that which is to come. We further learned that this unfortunate young man was the only child of a wealthy Catholic widow, who had fitted him out for a voyage from San Francisco to Australia, in order to separate him from the evil companionship with which he associated in the former city; that he had been put ashore at Honolulu from the vessel in which he originally embarked

on account of his inebrieties, and that he had taken our boat to complete his trip. Alas, if that mother could see him to-day, battling with wild hallucinations and struggling to escape the clutches of imaginary demons, all hope would die in her heart. The evil conduct of the ship's surgeon, urging him to drink when orders had been given to withhold it from him, and thoughts of that poor mother who loved him, drew us toward this poor man in kindly sympathy, who had finally become so delirious that a watch was placed over him.

One Sabbath evening, as we were singing hymns in the cabin, he suddenly jumped up from his chair, and exclaiming "I am not going down with this ship!" ran sprightly up the companion-way and leaped overboard into the sea. The women shrieked and swooned with fear, the great engines were brought to a stand still, the boat was lowered, and three sailors went out in the darkness of the night in search of him. In about thirty minutes, filled with anxious suspense to those in waiting, he was discovered and brought on board in an insensible condition, and the greater part of the night was spent in resuscitating him and saving his life.

When he came to his senses he said: "Well, I've been with the devil three months, and I did not like it and so came back." The dangerous sea bath had a good effect upon him, however, and he became more and more frightened at his narrow escape from drowning as his mind grew clearer, and entreated us to watch over him, which we did until we reached Australia, since which time we have neither seen or heard from him. How true it is that there is no bondage so galling and so degrading as that of intemperance, whose ways take hold on death. Dear reader, be wise in your day and generation, and taste not, touch not, and handle not the fatal cup.

The evenings on deck are lovely, and atone, in part, for the heat and for the severe blowing of the trade winds during the day. The sea is very quiet as we sail along with nothing to attract our attention but the appearance of a large, white bird called the Boatswain. The day after crossing the equator we observed a little brown land-bird, hovering about the ship, which had evidently followed some vessel out to sea and become lost, even like some individuals, who have been lured from duty and home by some object, which to their blinded imaginations promised profit and pleasure, but has proved the veriest will-o-the-wisp, and left them homeless and shelterless upon the ocean of life.

We had felt quite often in our history that we had lost a day, especially wherein we had failed to do some work for Jesus and our fellow-man. But now we have really experienced the loss of twenty-four hours out of the calendar of time. Yesterday was Friday, March 5th, when we crossed the 180th meridian; and to-day is not Saturday, but Sunday, March 7th. We are half way round the world, and the chronometer at Greenwich marks eight o'clock at night, the very hour in which our clock marks the hour of eight in the morning. Practically we have lost but just half a day; but should we continue on to Greenwich, making the same discrepancy of time, we should lose the other half; and the scientific world has decided that one full day be totally blotted out on the 180th meridian.

We are now sailing beneath new skies, having exchanged the North Star and the Big Dipper for what is to us a most beautiful constellation, the Southern Cross. It is composed of five fixed stars, in the shape of a cross, four of which shine with wonderful brilliancy in the southern heavens, and by it the mariners steer their course. The nights are most enchanting, the waters gleam with phosphorescent light in the wake of our ship, the moonlight touches the dark waves as with pencils of light and glory, and my heart keeps singing all the time:

> "The cross, the cross.
> The blood-stained cross,
> My Savior bore for me."

After seventeen days' voyaging we came in sight of New Zealand at three o'clock in the afternoon, and anchored at Auckland, an English looking city, of about 25,000 inhabitants. We were met at the wharf by Rev. Mr. Baker and two other prominent Christians; were shown the principal streets and buildings, and after we had spent a pleasant evening in song, prayer and conversation, we again took ship at 11 o'clock the same evening. Just before the anchor was weighed a party of friends came on board bearing a large basket of peaches, figs, fresh butter, and other delectables, for our comfort and refreshment, gave me an earnest invitation to come and give them fifty evenings of song-service on my return homeward, and bade us good-bye. Not being able to sing for them on my return, I however hope to do so sometime in the near future.

AUSTRALIA AS SEEN THROUGH OUR EYES.

Sailing over the calm, hot waste of waters, where the sun quivers in his direct beams upon the placid expanse, and where the air is sluggish in the oppressive noons, we slowly approach the shores of our present destination—the mysterious island-continent. Day by day the temperature changes, until the mornings become delightful, the torrid heats recede behind us as the appointed oppressions of the North, and we have solved the mystery known as the " Sunny South." We had penetrated through the very pulsing heart of that problem. The southerly skies now portended a cooler and pleasanter climate. The spirits of the weary voyagers took courage. Here and there along the level horizon appeared strange islands, rimmed with coral reefs and set in tufted palms. The color of the sea assumed a deeper hue, the heavens arched in clearer and ampler grandeur as we advanced, and at length our good steamship was anchored within sight of our long-expected haven. Here we were most kindly met by representatives of the committee—Rev. J. C. Symons, ex-Mayor Crouch and S. G. King, who escorted us to pleasant quarters in "Royal Terrace," Melbourne.

THE COLONY OF VICTORIA.

Victoria, of which Melbourne is the capital, and which is the most southern of the Australian colonies, was discovered in 1802 by Lieut. John Murray. Its geographical position gives it a much better title to the appellation of "South Australia," than its sister Colony, which bears that title, hardly any portion of the latter being as far south as the most northerly portion of Victoria.

THE CITY OF MELBOURNE.

Melbourne has a population of 265,000, and was named after Lord Melbourne, who was Premier of Great Britain when the city was founded, some forty years ago. It is a monument of what wealth and enterprise can do in so short a space of time, abounding as it does in costly public works and structures and magnificent edifices, which rival those of the older capitals of Europe. Its principal thoroughfares are a mile in length by ninety-nine feet in width, and run at right angles, being intersected by smaller streets, which also bear the names of the larger with the prefix of "little."

Elizabeth Street is laid out at the base of the two principal hills or eminences on which the city is built, and divides it into "East" and "West." This street is very low, and sometimes in rainy weather becomes the bed of an angry torrent, and quite impassable to foot passengers.

The city proper is situated on the banks of the Yarra-Yarra, or "ever flowing" river, eight miles from the sea by water, and two and one-half by land. It is connected by railroad with Sandridge, its seaport, which is at the head of Hobson's Bay, and where massive piers extend far out into the water, alongside of which vessels of almost any tonnage can lie with safety. The Yan-Yean reservoir supplies the inhabitants with abundant water of an excellent quality. The Free Library contains 60,326 volumes, and the Athenæum 12,356. The most noteworthy structures are the Houses of Parliament, Government buildings, the Post Office, Town Hall, the Exchange, the University, the Young Men's Christian Association building, Wesleyan Church, St. Patrick's Cathedral, the Independent Church and Baptist Chapel. It has a branch of the Royal Mint, a Royal Theatre and Opera House, well-appointed public markets, good hospitals and institutions for the care of the aged, infirm and unfortunate, many fine hotels, four daily newspapers, two religious weeklies, the "Spectator" and "Southern Cross," and quite a number of secular weeklies and monthly magazines.

A FEW SOLID FACTS.

Australia is the largest island in the world. In dimensions and resources it is almost a continent, its extent being, from east to west, 2,540, and from north to south 1,600 miles, compassing an area of 2,975,000 square miles. This vast domain lay unknown in the bosom of the ocean, untouched by the foot of civilization, for more than two hundred years after Columbus landed upon an island of the New World; but, like America, it was the prize awarded to the perseverance of a Spanish navigator; for Louis Vaez Torrez, commanding an expedition from Peru, was the original discoverer of Australia. He landed upon its coast in 1605, although the Dutch descried its northern borders from the ship *Duyfen* early the next year.

Australia is indeed a remarkable land. There are but few ocean indentures or bays; and for a thousand miles of its southern coast, there is not one permanent river. The streams are swollen and muddy in the rainy season, and run dry the rest of the year, the wind raising clouds of dust from their sandy beds. The trees are scattered in the forests, like the trees of an orchard or park; and such as bear leaves are evergreen. The foliage is leathery and less beautiful than that of our own country. There are but few tangled or compact forests such as abound in North and South America, while springs of sparkling cold water are of rare occurrence. The plants are abundant, varied, and often magnificent in their array of blossoms.

British convicts were sent to this remote frontier to serve their years of penalty for crime, in utter isolation and hardship. These outlaws were indeed rough pioneers to develop the possibilities of a new country; but Christian missionaries and teachers speedily followed the forced immigration, and were soon along side of the criminals, and the gospel made conquests over the stubborn hearts of the convicts as well as over the wandering and benighted souls of the natives. After groups of felons came colonies of honest settlers from Great Britain and from Holland. The cities of Sydney and Melbourne were planted, and now their splendid streets stretch for miles along the once desolate wastes of a pagan wilderness, and the stranger meets as many evidences of enlightenment here as in the older communities on the Thames, the Tweed or the Zuyder Zee. But the population of the towns is mostly British. The habits of the people are strikingly similar to those of England. Australia might be called another New England with the characteristic Yankee left out. There is no disposition to rebel against the Crown, or to change any of the peculiarities which everywhere in the British dominions stand for loyalty to the Queen.

The gold discoveries of 1851, in the southern midlands of Australia, gave a new impetus to the well-begun movements toward a better and permanent civilization, by bringing thousands of adventures to the country, many of whom remain to this day. The mines are not equal to those of California, and yet immense sums have been realized in the precious metal. The product is still considerable, adding greatly to the industries and commerce of the settlements.

WESLEYAN CHURCH, MELBOURNE.

CHAPTER XV.

SINGING IN AUSTRALIA.

BUT I set foot upon this land as an evangelist of sacred song, and not as a tourist, statistician, speculator, or adventurer. While I enjoy the scenery, study the history and geography, and read the current events with real interest, still my mission is to sing to those who, in turn, may sing again, and more sweetly, to others; and so I hope, by the divine blessing, to strike chords which shall vibrate with praise for ages to come.

The most difficult thing I had to contend with is, to get the public, even the Christian public, to feel that my evenings of song are not concerts, but services of worship. My purpose has ever been to present religious sentiment in unpretentious melody, by which the words can be definitely expressed, as in speech. But the people, not thinking carefully, seem prone to construe this exercise as an exhibition of musical talent, or a professional *fete*. I must say I met this peculiar form of obstruction on my arrival at Melbourne. I do not specially complain of it; it seems a natural conclusion, reasoning from fragments of facts; but the real design of the ministry of song soon becomes apparent in the earnestness of the service itself; and a few words of explanation usually make the purpose plain, and elicit a sincere sympathy in the hearts of the people.

Well, here I am, in this nethermost land, with all these peculiar surroundings, expected to give my first service to an audience of at least two thousand persons. I must not deviate from my chosen and conscientious forms of religious expression, and yet my anxiety to please, I must confess, was never quite so great. The press had announced me in generous words; and even the Mayor of Melbourne had given me a formal welcome in the great Town Hall. The committee of noble Christian men, under whose auspices I came from the United States, were all full of excitement, wondering whether the novel experiment would prove a success; or, perchance, fearing they might lose the £500 pledged as an offset against necessary expenses. It was but human nature to express anxiety under such circumstances. It was an hour of unusual concern to myself and family, as well as to the friends who had assumed the responsibility of introducing song sermons into Australia.

The preliminaries were all adjusted. Four large boxes, to contain the tickets, were located near the door; and there came enough people to take up tickets by the basketfull! The capacity of the large church was soon tested by an expectant congregation. With an earnest prayer, and my heart beating rather irregular time, I ascended the platform, fronting as attractive and intelligent an audience as ever assembled anywhere, to make my *debut*. I felt something like a Botany Bay convict, gauging my own resources by the evident demands of the hour. And yet I knew that divine grace makes liberty for heart and tongue and pen whenever and wherever faith takes hold upon the promises.

I was pleasantly introduced to the two thousand listeners by the Rev. John Harcourt, the President of the Wesleyan Conference, amid demonstrations of kindly greeting, which gave me courage to deliver my message here as I had often tried to do in distant lands. Little books containing the tunes and words of my songs were taken by the hundreds; and, the page announced, I began my initiatory service of song.

After the introductory exercises, my first song on the programme proper was "I will sing for Jesus." It was not my own choice to use this composition as my first solo in Melbourne, but through the urgency of a true friend I yielded my preference, and the song was heard with manifest feeling, as I am quite sure it was feelingly rendered; for I tried only to honor the blessed Master in the service. I took occasion at the close of this selection to impress the people with the fact that it was *worship*, and not a concert, and asked them to assist me in honoring the Savior by abstaining from any external manifestations of approval, as at mere entertainments—such as might be orderly elsewhere, but would mar the beauty of the service here. I was understood, and assured by the tender interest displayed in the faces of the people that my songs were sung as in the fear of God and love of souls.

Then followed my usual order of singing for an hour and a half, at the intervals between selections speaking a few words touching the special truth sought to be magnified by the song, and exhorting briefly, as the moments were precious, all who heard to take the lesson home. At the close of this, to me, memorable evening's exercises, the benediction was pronounced by the Rev. Dr. Dare, who will be remembered by many who read these pages by his eloquent sermons at the Union Methodist camp-meeting at Round Lake, N. Y., in the summer of 1874.

Thus ended my first service in Australia. I felt a reaction of relief when the pressure of responsibility was over, and yet I was more than ordinarily solicitous with reference to spiritual results.

For the cause's sake I was also anxious to see what the press might have to say on the morrow; for this was an evangelical venture without precedent, and in the Master's name I sincerely hoped for success. Two of the morning papers, the *Age* and the *Post*, spoke very favorably of the meeting, and one pronounced emphatically against it as an unwarrantable innovation. This criticism pained me, for, knowing my own heart, I felt it to be a sincere service, as much my duty as to speak or pray; and it was my trust that this purpose might have been apparent to all. I feared I had unconsciously provoked adverse comment. This thought prompted me to prayer, and taught me to lean more wholly upon Him for whom I sang and whose I am.

On a second reading of the unfavorable newspaper opinion, I thought I discovered the reason for this sinister criticism; and when I came to see the committee soon afterward, I was informed that this paper, the *Argus*, was not given to complimentary notices of any evangelistic movements whatever. It had indulged in severe editorials against Messrs. Moody and Sankey in their work in England and elsewhere, and was an iconoclast by instinct and habit. So I was in good company! This discovery brought peace of mind again, for the opposition of certain forces is more to be desired than their approbation; and, like Christian at the cross, I felt relieved, for the ice was broken.

The anxiety of a first service before a strange people, or before the friends of my youth, is always a different experience to me from that which attends ordinary exercises. If I get through without breaking down, I consider myself fortunate. In this important instance I conducted the service through without failure, but not without considerable trepidation.

Plans were matured for me to sing several evenings in different parts of the city. Melbourne, it should be remembered, is a group of municipalities, each having a mayor, city hall, etc.; a very different arrangement from that of American cities. Melbourne is a unit; but the distinct districts, each like a part in music, contribute to the harmony of the whole. The order corresponds somewhat to that of the several United States combined in one general Government, although each separate commonwealth is independent in local affairs. The great city stands as an illustration of the law of variety in unity—of "many in one." Each successive service I gave seemed to be better appreciated than the last; and by the time I was ready to go to the country, the people of the southern metropolis were in thorough sympathy with my work.

On Sunday evening, before going to "the bush" (as Melbourne people call the country), I was invited to the great Congregational Church, the pastor of which was the Rev. Dr. Henderson (since deceased), and here gave my first song sermon. The building will accommodate at least two thousand persons; and yet before the hour announced had arrived the spacious edifice was densely filled, and the aisles were packed to the utmost possibility of standing room by expectant people, and many were turned away.

The printed hymns and lessons were judiciously distributed through the audience, and the dear Lord helped me most wonderfully that memorable night. The people were in sympathetic accord with the service from the beginning. All souls were in tune for praise to God. It was a time of real joy. So great was the success of this effort, that the committee were besieged from many quarters for similar services. To answer the popular demand, I agreed to sing gratuitously whenever I felt able, taking up a collection at the close of each service in aid of the Home Wesleyan Missionary Society. The Rev. John Watsford had been appointed secretary of the Society, and a more devoted, competent, warm-hearted and eloquent Christian worker could not have been found in the colony. He was engaged to assist me, so that I was enabled to give a service nearly every evening during my sojourn of six months in Australia. These collections amounted to several hundred pounds, and, better than this, wherever we held an after-meeting, there was always earnest seekers for salvation.

Melbourne has some of the most consecrated Christians I ever knew, among whom are the Rev. H. B. McCartney, of the Church of England, full of evangelical zeal and moved by genuinely pious impulses; Mr. W. G. Marsh, Secretary of the Young Men's Christian Association, one of Mr. Moody's converts while he was an unknown toiler in Providence, Rhode Island, many years ago; the Rev. J. C. Symons, Editor and Book Steward for the Wesleyan Church; Mr. A. J. Smith, President of the Young Men's Christian Association, and an extensive bookseller, whose leisure hours are spent in soul-winning; Mr. S. G. King and Brother Crouch, the former a leading merchant, the latter, ex-Mayor and architect, as well as many others whose names are precious memories.

THE TRIP TO BALLARAT.

I must give some account of my first ride and service in the country. The trip was to Ballarat, one hundred miles by rail, from Melbourne, although the distance in an air line is but sixty-five miles. The route bears southwestward for half the distance, skirting the Bay of Port Philip, to Geelong on Corio Bay, a town of 25,000 inhabitants, and the centre of the Australian wool trade. The seven flourishing banks of Geelong indicate its thrift and wealth.

From this point the railway diverges from the coast, and extends almost due north toward the mountains. The range is sometimes called the Pyrenees, by others known as the Grampians, and further east, where the peaks are higher and the general contours more abrupt, the series are named the Australian Alps. The scenery between Geelong and Ballarat, being characteristic of vast regions of South Australia, may well occupy the eye and mind, and is worthy of portraiture on these pages, if only I had an artist's pencil. On the way are to be seen forests and gum-trees, many specimens reaching a height of 150 feet and more, and with a girth of from twenty-five to forty feet. Mingled with these lofty gums are groups of wattle-trees (*acacias*), with countless myriads of yellow-tufted flowers, like bean-pods in shape; wild figs of immense size, the ample food for birds, such as blue pigeons, magpies and swamp pheasants; rank weeds along the levels; now and then a stunted palm-tree, with strange vegetable growths of various forms and hues, the paradise of a botanist. Think of nettles fifteen feet high, multitudes of proteceous plants with hard, gristly, almost wooden leaves, hair-branched weeping casuarinas and myrtaceous herbs arrayed in white blossoms, studding the deep emerald of the wild meadows, or pendant tassels of yellow, purple and crimson stamens, combining to arrest attention and to challenge delay and delight at every mile of the journey.

This pleasant ride is too soon ended, and here, towards the highlands, as if we had been lifted on wings from the sea level, is Ballarat, the oldest gold field, save one, in Victoria-land. The precious ore was discovered on Anderson's Creek, near the site of this now splendid city as far back as 1841; but no successful mining operations were undertaken until August, 1851, ten years afterward, when extensive and profitable investments were made. Mount Alexander, on the other side of the mountains, was the central and most successful gold field, however, and still surpasses all other sections in the yield of the precious metal. If the railway should be extended from Ballarat to Mount Alexander, a distance of less than one hundred miles, the line would form a complete circle of about three hundred and fifty miles, with Melbourne, Geelong, Ballarat, and Mount Alexander, at almost equal distances apart, and the trains could go round and round this grand circumference, without the necessity for a turn-table for locomotives or cars with reversible seats. The surface gold of Ballarat was soon exhausted. Then came the era of machine mining, requiring capital, patience and skill. In 1872, no less than 215 steam engines, aggregating more than 6,000 horse power, were employed in the immediate vicinity of Ballarat, and mines as deep as the deepest coal mines of England were opened in the persistent search for gold.

It will be remembered that, in 1857, near this place, was found the great nugget of gold, valued at $50,000. A model of this rich creation is on exhibition at the British Museum. No wonder such an attraction brought thousands of people from the cities to the Bush.

The yield of gold is gradually decreasing, and the population of Ballarat is probably less at present than ten years ago, but it is still a busy, beautiful city of near 65,000 souls. The once comely hills round about bear the marks of the gold-diggers, being grooved, broken and yellow. The impetuous dash for money always mars the peaceful attitude of nature.

The railroads of Australia are conducted after the English plan, and built in an equally substantial manner. There are no doubtful embankments, no flimsy trestles, nor any perilous curves. Science has had a voice and genuine economy a hand, in every mile of the system.

At the station I was kindly met and escorted to the delightful home of George Smith, Esq., across the Park lake, a charming spot, indeed. On my way to the hospitable mansion of this new-found friend, I was pointed out the beauties of the city, such as the Town Hall, Opera house, Park lake, and Botanical Gardens. The Australian gardens excel all others I have seen in luxuriant foilage, brilliant flowers, and varied forms. I will not except our New York Central Park, or the parks of London or Paris. This great island of the southern seas has a climate peculiarly prolific of vegetable perfections. Nowhere else have I ever beheld such exquisite displays of the beautiful in form and hue and texture. I doubt whether the gardens of Solomon excelled these of the newest of the new worlds. The foliage of Tyre and Damascus in its prime could not have been more enchanting. Here were leaves in infinite variety: ovate, serrate, spiral, palmate, lobed and cleft. Here were finest interlacings of fibre and vein, living leaves, jeweled with diadems of dew, and armed with shining spears before the sun. Here were velvet and mossy leaves, gossamer and oval leaves, pendants and blades and spines, colored in emerald, in crimson, in purple, in white. Here were ferns in infinite variety, tendrils clinging to posts, curtain-leafed vines arching overhead, ground ivy, strange grasses, all seeming to live on air and dew and light. There was something almost spiritual in the magnificent array. The only thing lacking in the gardens was the odor, that sweet breathfulness, in some degree, even in the most beautiful flowers, being deficient.

My generous host, Mr. Smith, is a seedsman, having under the highest state of cultivation all sorts of flowers, shrubbery, and plants, with many small fruits, and he most thoroughly understands and enjoys his vocation. I was in good company to appreciate the luxury of the Australian gardens.

The principal street in the city is very wide, with a long, narrow park in the middle, and large, stately trees growing on each side, with a pebbled highway, made double by the intervening and ornamental park.

In the evening a large and intelligent-looking audience assembled to hear my singing; and although quite weary with sight-seeing through the day, and consequently disqualified from giving an ordinarily hearty service, yet the novelty of the occasion, or some strangely better infatuation of the gospel expressed, held the people in rapt attention for an hour and a half. The grace of God it was, and always is, and only that, which so wonderfully blesses the soul of the singer and the souls of the audience together. It is the pentecostal *one accord!* It is worship. In such service the angels above delight to engage. This form of adoration shall never cease.

The people of Australia are more demonstrative than the English or the Americans. They are scarcely willing to desist from outward manifestations of approbation, even when requested.

At Ballarat I met with a most enthusiastic photographer, an American by the name of Bardwell (he should have been a poet or a singer), who had prepared a splendid specimen ready for the World's Exhibition. Probably he received a premium, for he richly deserved recognition and reward.

VISIT TO CRESWICK.

From this place I proceeded to Creswick, about thirty miles away, a romantic little town of about three thousand inhabitants, nestled in the midst of rich gold-mining fields. Here I was entertained by the Wesleyan minister, the Rev. Mr. Crisp. In Creswick is an admirably managed hospital, besides a Mechanics' Institute, both well-supported by voluntary contributions. Indeed, as I learn, there is scarcely a town in all the colonies where there is not a merciful home for the unfortunate stranger. Here, as in England, is observed the "Hospital Sunday," which we in America ought to have introduced into our religious polity, but do not even pretend to a substitute. We can learn some essential lessons from the colonists of Victoria.

CHAPTER XVI.

SINGING IN AUSTRALIA.

THERE is one Sunday in each year in which a collection is taken in all the churches, of every denomination, throughout the country, for the benefit of the General Hospital Fund, large amounts thus being realized for these institutions, with but trifling expense for gathering the same. These comfortable, cleanly homes, many of which I visited, are to me the bright landmarks of future promise and usefulness in this interesting country, homes for the stranger who may be stricken down by accident or sickness, and which most have a strong influence in inviting emigration. These noble institutions and their conduct thoroughly impressed me with the thoroughness and excellence of Australian benevolence and charity.

The Mayor of this town kindly met me on my arrival and escorted me to his home where I was warmly and hospitably welcomed. In the evening I sang to a good audience, who seemed to enter into the enjoyment of the service with Christian spirit.

RELIGIOUS LIBERTY IN THE COLONIES.

Returning to Ballarat I gave my second service there in a large Wesleyan Chapel and to a fine audience, and was entertained by Rev. Mr. Watkins, at the Wesleyan Home. From his interesting converse I learned that one of the proudest boasts of Victoria, as a free country, was its privileges of perfect religious liberty. There is no state church, all enjoy their own religious opinions and follow the tenents and practices of their own creed, while no religious denomination enjoys privileges denied to any other.

THE WESLEYAN CONFERENCE AND ITS MANAGEMENT.

From this gentleman I also gleaned some facts relative to the working economy of the Wesleyans in this Colony which may be of interest to our good Methodists, as possibly worthy in example. The policy adopted by them is after the circuit or Wesleyan plan in England, over which it is a decided improvement, probably owing to the fact that the colony presents a more fruitful field for gospel labor than the old country. There are no Bishops, but instead a President of the Conference, who is elected each year, to which Conference each and every minister in the colony is a delegate, which body has lately been numerically increased by lay delegation. The appointments are made on the circuit plan, by a vote of all the ministers, with a chairman for each circuit, or as we should denominate it, district, and his duties resemble those of a presiding elder in the United States.

Their preaching appointments are published every quarter and are posted up throughout their several circuits. The local preachers are very much more active and popular than in America or England, and are earnest, faithful and indefatigable in their labors. Some of these districts keep horses, carriages and coachmen for the express purpose of conveying the preachers to fill their appointments. This vehicle is a sort of short omnibus, capable of comfortably seating six persons, and in Ballarat it is called by the people the "Gospel Chariot." I enjoyed the sights of the town while seated in it one charming afternoon, and learned from the coachman that he was accustomed to hitch up on Sunday and other mornings and drive from eight to twenty miles, dropping these men of God one by one at their respective places for holding divine service, and on the return, gathering them up again and conveying them home.

From these facts it will be readily and truthfully inferred that the Wesleyan churches in Australia have no settled pastors, and that the poorer and more scarcely populated localities outside the cities, towns and villages, have the same opportunity of hearing all the ministers and local preachers as the wealthier churches. The churches are new, comfortable and commodious and the parsonages very neat and pretty. I think the ministers are better paid, as a general thing, than in America, his average salary is about £200 or $1,000, with an addition or allowance of five guineas or thirty-two dollars per annum for the support and education of each of his children, which latter policy if adopted in America, would not only lighten the labor of many a devoted servant of the Master, but enable him to be more efficient in winning souls to Christ. Some of these ministers receive valuable presents at the close of their terms, and in a fine carriage thus presented Bro. Watkins, I took the first ride with him. I saw many such tokens of esteem from the people to their ministers in the many pleasant Wesleyan homes which I visited. From here I returned to my dear ones at Melbourne after a most interesting and successful week in what is called the "Bush."

On Sunday evening I gave my second song service at Emerald Hill Wesleyan Church before a large congregation. Here I met that multifarious Christian worker, Mr. John Bee, who not only superintended the Sabbath-school, and Orphan Asylum, but led the choir and filled many other positions connected with religious labor. In spite of myself there kept recurring to my mind that childhood couplet: "How doth the little busy bee improve each shining hour" for Christ.

At an after meeting at the close of the service, several persons came forward for prayers, among whom was a poor backslider, whose agonized pleadings to Jesus for pardon and restoration were so fervent, sad and pitiful, that he so wrought on my sympathies as to almost make me ill. Yet I was obliged to leave him while he was still crying:

"Where is my Saviour now,
Whose smiles I once possessed."

IN THE SUBURBS OF MELBOURNE.

For the next few days it was arranged for me to hold my evenings at Carlton, Prahan and Brighton, in the suburbs of Melbourne. In Brighton I was the guest of an ex-missionary from the Fiji Islands, an earnest, godly man, who instructed me very intelligently as to the manners and customs of the Cannibal Islands, and exhibited to me many curiosities which he had collected therein. I grew more and more encouraged as the people seem to grow more and more enthusiastic over my meetings, and are beginning to realize the object of my feeble efforts.

There must have been present some one thousand people at the interesting service at the Presbyterian Church in Carlton. I greatly enjoyed my short acquaintance with its pastor, Rev. Dr. McEchran, a model Scotch Presbyterian, thoroughly beloved for his eminent piety and earnest ministry. He was feeling very anxious to have Bros. Moody and Sankey visit Victoria and was then having correspondence with them in reference to this subject.

VISIT TO GEELONG.

My next week was spent in the country, and I gave my first service in Geelong, a town of some 30,000 inhabitants, which is beautifully situated on Corio Bay, forty-five miles distant from Melbourne by rail. It is noted for its fine public and private buildings, excellent harbor, public baths, woolen mills, and its surrounding country is taken up by farms, vineyards, and orchards. Here the first woolen mill in Victoria was built and received the government award of £1,500. It was for some time considered the second city in Victoria, but has been dispossessed of this pre-eminence by Ballarat. It is built on an inclined plane or smooth side hill and presents a most picturesque appearance either from the bay or from the hills above. The botanical gardens and parks of this town are beautiful beyond description. The former are cultivated by a most experienced man and noble Christian, Mr. J. Radensburg, who presented Mrs. Phillips on our departure from the place with a bouquet of rich exotic flowers and a package containing many varieties of choice seeds. The botanical gardens of this island are undoubtedly the most luxuriant in the world, the climate being peculiarly adapted to their culture, while in most of them are to be found fine collections of animals.

THE AUSTRALIAN EVANGELIST.

Geelong is also the home of the earnest and tireless Australian Evangelist, Matthew Burnett, who is so emphatically the Moody of the Southern hemisphere, and who seems to be always living in either a revival of temperance or salvation. Once shipwrecked on the isle of Malta, and obliged to remain there for several months to await the recovery of his wife, who received a severe shock when the vessel foundered, he at once commenced his Christian labors among the people, and under God's help was the direct means of bringing many souls to Christ. Known throughout England and this new continent as the Australian Evangelist, he is all aglow and desperate after the souls of men and travels the colony from end to end enticing men into the Kingdom of God.

I was entertained at Geelong by G. M. H. Hitchcock,

Esq., in a model Christian home not so costly in structure and ornament, as homelike and comfortable, and presided over by a most estimable Christian lady and wife, whose pleasure was pre-eminently that of her guests. A most intelligent company sat down to tea, and their goodly Christian fellowship and conversation made me feel to thank God for such dear friendships in a far off land.

From this town I returned to my dear family at Melbourne, and gave another service of song at old Brunswick Street Chapel to a large and appreciative audience. The words of encouragement given me on this occasion, by its pastor, Rev. Mr. Williams, and his wife, filled me with fresh zeal and renewed courage. How much good would be accomplished if Christians would occasionally speak words of comfort and good cheer to those who are engaged in earnest and tireless labor for Christ, both in the pulpit, the mission field and in other of the many posts of Christian work. On the following Sabbath I gave a song sermon at the Town Hall in Prahan, its subject being "Jesus." At the close of the service some nine persons professed to have come to the knowledge of his saving grace, one of whom was a Japanese of much prominence in that empire, who was on a visit of observation to these colonies. This evidence of the dear Savior's presence deeply impressed me that God means to use me in these services of Bible reading and sacred song. " Blessed be His name."

CASTLEMAINE, THE OLD GOLD FIELDS.

This town has about 18,000 inhabitants and was the locality where gold was first discovered in Australia, and for a long time its most important mining field. Its streets are well laid out, it is quite notable in public buildings, its water works are fine and very costly, and it has a spacious market building. The entire surface of the locality has been dug over and over again in search of the precious metal, and the ground in the vicinity is a mixture of red earth and gravel. Vine growing, and wine making is carried on to a considerable extent, the neighborhood where Rev. Mr. Daniels, my polite host, pointed out to me many fine vineyards, but informed me that the district relied principally on its mining and agricultural resources for its prosperity. My services were held in the theatre, which though uncongenial to me as a place to hold such, yet even here I could but feel it a privilege to raise the cross on the wings of sacred song, when Satan so often uses music to lull poor sinners into fancied security, or to excite them forward to fresh revels and forgetfulness. The audience was very attentive to the service, and at its close many of them desired me to come again and give them more information of America, and my travels about the world.

AN AUTHORSHIP DINNER.

From Castlemaine I was conveyed with my organ to Malden, an inland town of about three thousand inhabitants situated at the foot of Mt. Tarrangower, and on the banks of a creek by that name, and noted for its auriferous wealth. Alighting for dinner at a little village, I was delighted to hear some one singing "Home of the Soul."

The good lady of the house seemed to be glad of the privilege of welcoming the author of the favorite song she loved to sing; spread me an excellent dinner, and made me feel at home, as far as it was possible to do so, by her kindness and hospitality. I arrived at Malden in a drenching rain, and was entertained at the fine home of a local preacher and successful merchant, whose name I have forgotten, but whose modest hospitality and Christian fellowship I shall always remember.

NATURE AND SELF IN DUET.

Some two hundred and fifty persons assembled at the song service in the evening, but the torrents of rain falling upon the thin, corrugated iron roof, and which is much used in the colonies for building, made, much of the time, more noise than I could, that I was often compelled to yield the floor. Part of the time I would sing, then let the rain patter on these sounding boards, far excelling in sensitiveness those in the piano forte of any manufacturer, and thus I gave a duet concert, with nature and self in the role, the former really being master of ceremonies.

SANDHURST AND ITS GOLDEN ROCKS.

My next service was at Sandhurst, a leading town of Victoria, of forty thousand population, and at this time the most successful mining town in the colony. It is the headquarters of one hundred and forty square miles of country, containing seven hundred and fifty distinct gold bearing quartz rock reefs or ranges, in which about ten thousand miners and three hundred steam engines are employed in crushing out the ore. My first impression on entering the town was that every one was a digger for the precious metal, and I could only think of Bunyan's old "muck rake man," who could see nothing but the straws in his scramble for riches, while the beautiful sunshine and birds and flowers, and, more than all, a bright crown of his salvation, was within his reach just overhead.

Here I was entertained in a princely manner by Capt. Williams, a brother-in-law of the famous gold miner, John Watson. This genial host took me through and over the great quartz mills, where the massive machinery ground the rock into a dust as fine as flour, from which other machinery extracted every particle of the so prized metal. I confess I did not enjoy my first service at the church, and came to the conclusion that I was not adapted to sing of Christ to an eager gold-seeking community, for the thrift and enterprise and daring of the town would come creeping into my thoughts, and money-making and gold-getting evidently fully occupied most of theirs; and you know that music is often most needful to and appreciated by a heart filled with heaviness and disappointment, rather than in times of great worldly triumph and prosperity.

A FATHER IN THE ROLE OF DOMESTIC ECONOMIST.

On Saturday I rode about the city quite extensively with Rev. Mr. James, and took dinner at the parsonage. The dear brother was blessed with a large family, and the mother being absent, he was at the time presiding as the head of his domestic affairs. While he was absent for a short time from the dining room I asked these interesting children whom they liked best, father or mother, as I observed their efforts to get a good share of preserves during the absence of both parents. Two or three of them, with the strongest evidences of the goody on their lips, hurriedly replied: "I like father best, 'cause he gives me all the jam I want."

One could hardly fail to moralize over this life-like scene, in which mother was so evidently necessary to keep the larder from getting too quickly bare, and her children from the cramming which would necessitate the presence of a physician or an extra bill at the apothecary's. Then, too, in this conversation, father appeared to much better advantage in his true province as "bread winner," instead of "bread server" for this little flock.

A stroll through the city markets with Capt. Fletcher, who pointed out the many objects of interest, amused me for the time being, but the observations did not aid me in the work of singing with the spirit. Noisy crowds and dram and gambling shops were on every hand, the rich and dazzling specimens shone in many windows, while everything seemed to be wrapped in a blaze of glory and glitter. I was grateful when Sunday came,

"Sweet day, of all the week the best."

In the morning and afternoon I visited two large Sunday-schools, which were faithfully and earnestly taught. Although Satan is ever wide awake, so are the earnest Sunday-school teachers and Christians, who seemed to be so successfully battling him in this town, " brave soldiers of the cross, true followers of the lamb." I recognized that here was a desperate fight with Apolyon, and were it not for the holy influences and faithful teaching of the word on the Sabbath, locks and keys, or bolts and bars would not be able to hold this people in check. Sunday evening I gave a song sermon in the Golden Square Church, to an audience of nearly two thousand people. It was a precious hour, for God was in our midst, and Christ in song is ever sweet. What was better than gold or silver, at the conclusion a large number of Christians reconsecrated themselves to Christ and the work of saving souls. Contrary to my expectations, my experiences at Sandhurst were very satisfactory, and I shall always remember them as such.

THE RIVER MURRAY—AUSTRALIA'S AMAZON.

From this point I reached the banks of the River Murray, the largest and longest of the few navigable rivers of Australia, the absence of which is the greatest obstacle in the opening up of the country. This river is one thousand one hundred and twenty miles in length, but is only navigable for small boats and barges.

It is a low, muddy, sluggish stream, with the approaches infested with venomous serpents, and upon its banks in the interior live, in the rudest state, the aboriginal Australians.

They are a swarthy race, quite distinct from the Malay and African types, with coarse, bushy hair, small, lean stature, and in their natural state low, degraded, weak and miserable. They are certainly one of the meanest races on the face of the earth, a perfect description of whom would baffle even Darwin himself. Some of the tribes are cannibals. Even these, however, have been rescued by the power of the gospel, and here and there have begun the better life. But only by patient processes of education, by methods which shall attract and win and ultimately hold these heathen masses, is there any hope of success. Possibly the power of music, combined with the preaching of the word, a song-evangelism, indeed—the gospel, sweetened into ringing good news, as if heralded from the skies as at the beginning in Judea among the shepherds, when the messengers swept the midnight hills—may yet be blessed as the means of saving the multitudes in distant Australia.

CHAPTER XVII.

SINGING IN AUSTRALIA.

I NEXT sang at Echuea, the entrepot of the overland inter-colonial trade. It has a large business in red gum and wool, and a vineyard of sixty-six acres, is one of the sights of the place.
I shall never forget the great cordiality, sincere piety, and Christian hospitality of Rev. George Baker, then living in this place. My audience was large, although it was raining and muddy, the mud sticking even closer than that very clinging article found in the Western states of the United.

A VERY BIRD-LIKE HOME.

Eighty miles further on, and I am at Eaglehawk, which is called a "model borough," and has a population of 6,000 inhabitants. It is in a mining district and is four miles from Sandhurst with which it is connected by horse cars and omnibus. I was cordially received at the station by Rev. M. Ick, and driven to his delightful home, a model of comfort, graced by a most estimable wife, where, though everything was inexpensive and modest rather than luxurious, all was as neat as wax, to use that homely but expressive phrase. At my service in Eaglehawk, I was so interrupted by the falling of torrents of rain upon the iron roof of the church, that my voice and organ were nearly drowned at times, and I felt most uncomfortable at the situation, yet the kind audience endured to the end, although their politeness may have been due, in part, to the severity of the

tempest outside, which made the inside their only safe
shelter during its continuance. At five o'clock the next
morning, Mrs. Ick prepared me a warm breakfast. I was
then driven to the station, and took the cars to rejoin my
family at Melbourne.

SONG SERMON TO THE CHILDREN OF MELBOURNE.

When I arrived in the city, the first General Conference
of the Wesleyans was in session at the great Wesleyan
cathedral in Lonsdale Street, and they were holding exercises of exceeding interest to that denomination of Christians in this far off island of the south. Having been invited
to give a children's song sermon in the great town hall, in
the afternoon, although it proved to be rainy, yet there
were over three thousand youths present, and what was
far better, He who uttered those charming words: "Suffer
little children to come unto me, and forbid them not, for of
such is the kingdom of heaven," was in our midst also.

I felt very anxious to give those dear children a lesson
which would be profitable and which would be indelibly
impressed upon their minds, and to sow seed for the Master
in their tender hearts which should blossom into fruitfulness
in the after years. Therefore, I wrote a new tune to that
beautiful hymn,

"Jesus bids us shine,"

And taught it to those little ones. I tried to imprint upon
their minds the beauty of shining in their every-day lives,
and while I felt my own heart cheered and strengthened in
the work, I had reason to feel that these little souls were
profited thereby. Afterward I heard that a little six year-
old son of Rev. Mr. Watsford came down from his bed-
chamber the next morning, and said: "Papa, see me *shine*."
"Yes, sonny," said Mr. W., "but that is not what Mr.
Phillips meant by shining; what he meant was that when
little brother strikes you, that you must *shine* by not strik-

ing back." "Well, papa, tell brother not to strike me quite so hard and then I will shine that way!" This is simple lesson in practical Christianity, from which older and younger can draw a profitable example. The success of this song-sermon was very gratifying to me, and I feel it will never be forgotten by the bright-eyed children of Australia, who were present, and that it is still sounding sacred harmonies in their hearts and lives.

On Sunday evening I had a most precious season in a song-sermon at Hawthorne; a number came forward for prayers, and several found peace. The next day I attended the general conference; took dinner with some sixty members, at the Wesleyan Home, and led the singing at a missionary meeting in the evening under the auspices of the conference. At the latter service I became interested, for the speeches of the meeting were fervent, witty and full of fire and pathos. Probably there was no place in the world where such a field of missionary work was ever represented as at this gathering, and it thrilled me to hear these brave men of God relate how they had threaded the wilderness, walked over pathless plains and mountains, and forded and swam rivers, to break the bread of life to starving and perishing souls.

One of the missionary secretaries gave an account of his first preaching to the Fijians, when at the conclusion of his exhortation, the natives turned and ran to their homes, and returning immediately with many offerings and gifts, laid them on and within the altar.

The present year these very Fijian Islands had themselves contributed over four hundred pounds to the missionary cause. So encouraging appeared the work that the Wesleyan society, dating from the present year, 1876, has taken upon itself to give the gospel to all of the South Sea Islands. How appropriate that the largest island in the world should accept the mission of giving His word to the other islands of the remote sea. Truly, the Scripture is herein verified.

ACROSS THE RIVER MURRAY.

My next service was held just over the river Murray in Albury, and after a ride of one hundred and fifty miles, I was kindly met at the station by Dr. H. B. Hutchinson, a staunch and dignified Christian of Cornish birth, and one of Rev. William Taylor's converts. After quite a routine of examination in getting my organ through the customs, I was driven to my host's neat home, presided over by one of his prepossessing and intelligent daughters. I gave my songs that evening, as usual, to a good audience, and repeated the service the following night.

THE OVENS DISTRICT.

The next morning I returned to Victoria, to visit what is termed the Ovens district, and after a ride of ten miles reached Beechworth, a town of four thousand population. Here I was a guest of Rev. and Mrs. Flockheart, each lovely Christian characters. Mrs. Flockheart, as well as her husband, was fully alive in every good work, yet her household affairs were not in the least neglected. Cultivated, talented, yet simple and child-like, she gave you to feel that her home was your own, in the fullest sense of the word. Their little Bennie, eleven years old, seemed as much interested in Christian work as did his good mother, and I greatly enjoyed my ride with him to my next appointment, fifteen miles away. Sometime, in the near future, I expect to hear of Bennie as a faithful, earnest pastor in his island home.

THE AUSTRALIAN ELDORADO,

Or the village therein which bears this name, is inhabited by about one thousand people, and is located on the banks of Reed's creek, and is the centre of a large mining district, it being the only place in Victoria where tin ore is found.

In my ride thither, I stopped several times to converse with the miners, many of whom were Chinese, and to look at the precious stones which were exhibited by them. Here I stopped over Sabbath, and though feeling homesick to be with my family, yet kept occupied, though in a very quiet, lonely place, which seemed to me almost out of the world. After my service I slept soundly on my little couch, over which hung a picture of Rev. Wm. Taylor. Thoughts that after all I was in the footsteps of so good a man, acted as a soothing balm to my spirit. On Sunday evening I gave a song sermon which proved to be most profitab'e, one or two Catholics coming forward and asking the prayers of Christians, while the good minister seemed much encouraged in his work.

TEA-MEETING AT KILLMORE.

Ten more miles by train, and I reached Killmore, a small town of one thousand inhabitants, being a rich gold mining and agricultural locality. The church were holding a "tea-meeting" on my arrival, which gathering is quite common in the colonies, being somewhat after the style of our strawberry festivals; tickets of admission being sold, and the proceeds given to the church fund. The hall although small was thoroughly filled, and the audience seemed much pleased with my singing, at the close of which I was a guest at the parsonage. My thirty-fourth service was at Dinsmore, a little town of about fifteen hundred inhabitants, where I met two excellent ministers of the Presbyterian and Primitive Methodist churches, who were both earnest and tireless laborers for Christ in this far off land.

FROM THE COUNTRY TO THE CITY.

From Dinsmore I returned once more to Melbourne, and my dear family, deeply feeling the blessing of having them so near me. My next service was before a fine audience in a large church at the North Melbourne, several of the General Conference officers being present I felt somewhat nervous at the commencement, but soon recovered therefrom and became oblivious to all surroundings in the duties of this occasion. I next sang at St. Kilda, a fashionable watering place and suburb of Melbourne. As I took my place to conduct the service, I was greeted by some one hundred little children who charmingly rendered one of my songs which I had previously taught them in the town hall, "Jesus Bids us Shine." We had a pleasant service, and I thanked God and took courage. I was the next evening at Hawthorne, a neat little country town adjoining Melbourne, graced with many fine villas, and rich in the abundance of market gardens. Here is the home of Mr. Symons, who was the chief instrumentality in bringing me to Australia, and whom I had learned to love and respect, and whom on this occasion I especially desired to please; there was also, in my audience that evening a Mr. Nicholson, the chief clerk of the Wesleyan Publishing House, a gentleman most courteous and obliging to all who come within his personal or business presence.

All seemed pleased with the services which gave me great satisfaction.

On the Sabbath I gave a song sermon at the large Brunswick church, at which several professed to have found the Savior. I was rejoiced that the Lord seemed, in these services, to be using me as an instrument for His glory. On Monday evening a large and appreciative audience assembled at my service in the Gibbs street church, where I gave for the first time my new temperance song, "Self Deceived," which was well received. It is a peculiar delight to me when I can add a new and pleasing song to my programme, and my prayer is that God may bless this one to many a needy one. My next service was a song sermon in the Royal Alfred hall at Ballarat. No admission fee was charged, and as a consequence an hour before the commencement, 3,000 people had assembled while many were unable to obtain admittance. I did not enjoy the service much, for fear some accident might occur to the people, they were so crowded. A penny collection was taken up at the close and some thirty-one pounds or one hundred and fifty dollars was realized.

Returning to the suburban towns of the metropolis I sang at Northcoat and Footscray, where my efforts were well appreciated by my audiences, and where I felt in the best of spirits.

The following Sunday I gave a song sermon at North Melbourne, in connection with Rev. Mr. Fitchett, who is one of the most influential ministers in the Wesleyan denomination. At its close a collection was taken for the mission, and twenty pounds was the result.

ANOTHER VISIT TO THE INTERIOR.

My next service was at Daylesford, quite a distance into the mining districts, a thriving and desirable town of 4,000 inhabitants, and reached by twelve miles of stage, and eighty miles of railway travel. Here I was warmly greeted by the Wesleyan minister and a large and appreciative audience, many of whom were natives of Cornwall, England.

A FREE THOUGHT NEWSPAPER.

Thence I came on to Maryborough, having a population of about 3,000 people, and being the centre of eighty-two miles of gold bearing quartz reefs, giving in its many mines employment for over 10,000 workmen. Among other things the town is noted for having an editor and publisher of a newspaper devoted to free thought, in, as the world would generally term it, to the doctrine and sentiments of the "free and easy." Some eccentric ranger bequeathed five thousand pounds to disseminate these ideas throughout the colonies, and his newspaporial representative in the flesh, failing to find another locality, chose Maryborough for the fulcrum whereon to rest his lever to pry the great Island into his erratic line of thought and belief. This sheet gave no uncertain sound for the service of Satan in which it seemed to be so thoroughly engaged, for its abuse of the churches, and railing over the imaginary failings and shortcomings of Christians, always appeared in its leading editorials.

The town was very pleasant, and there were many noble and lovable people in it. My audience was a good one, and all seemed to be pleased, except this solitary editor who said in his newspaper "that he should have enjoyed the service better if when I had closed singing my song 'Scatter seeds of Kindness' I had scattered a few pounds over to him."

The great majority of our editors in city and in country are men who hold the name of God, and his earnest, faithful workers and followers in reverence and respect, and with their great facilities do much to build His kingdom upon this earth, and it is gratifying that one sordid and skeptical, as in the above instance, can rarely be found in civilized countries with hands upon the journalistic pen so mightier than the sword.

MY SERVICE IN THE SMALLER TOWNS.

My next destination was Talbot, a town of fifteen hundred people; from thence to Clunes, a thriving mining town of five thousand population, where I had a good audience and was kindly entertained by Rev. John Horsely, an estimable gentleman, who had worked so unceasingly in his field of Christian labor that he had evidently become somewhat broken in health. I am glad to know that he has since visited England, and has returned to his cherished work with restored vigor.

AN EARNEST CHRISTIAN IN HARNESS

My next appointment was in the mining and agricultural town of Bunningyong, near the great gold fields of Ballarat, with a population of three thousand. Here I was most cordially entertained by Mr. Robert Allan, a Scotchman by birth, and a noble Christian worker. A few facts in his history are as follows: Making his fortune in the earlier years of the island's settlement, he returned home to Scotland with the intention of spending the remainder of his days in his native land. After spending some time in his old home, the spirit of Christian zeal began to light up his soul so brightly and fervidly that he again took ship for Australia, where he has ever since devoted his whole talent, time and energy to Christian work. He has erected a model Sunday-school Institute, and under his novel and successful methods of instruction, with a heart desperately in earnest, his labors have been and are proving very fruitful, and nearly all of his flock have become Christians, and a few among the number called to preach the glad tidings. He is known throughout the length and breadth of the colonies as the most devoted and successful of Sunday-school teachers, and an earnest man of faith and good works. One of his school exercises is the writing of six questions upon a large slate in a plain, bold hand, and turning the same toward the school. Each scholar is also provided with a slate, upon which all write answers to these interrogations. Then the slates are gathered up, and each scholar's answers are drawn off into a book or report for future reference. It will be discerned at once that this exercise gives an interchange and expression of thought most interesting and instructive. Being certain that some may desire to receive his reports and methods of instruction, which he delights to forward to all those who apply for the same, I give his address in full: Robert Allan, Bunningyong, Victoria, Australia.

From this point I returned to my dear ones at Melbourne, where I gave a song sermon—the theme, " Sweetest note of Praise," in Rev. P. R. C. Usher's church. He is a devout man of God, and much interested in the doctrine of holiness, or the higher Christian life.

CHAPTER XVIII.

DEPARTURE FOR THE WESTERN DISTRICTS.

ON Tuesday, June 22, I took the steamer "Otway" for Warnambool. On board this steamer I was pained to witness the terrible effects of strong drink on the part of quite a number of passengers. One finely-dressed man became so thoroughly crazed under its influence as to compel his little son, only eleven years of age, to drink. It was one of the saddest sights I ever witnessed to see this inebriated father forcing this deadly poison upon the dear boy, to whom he was proving himself such an unnatural parent. Surely I could not help saying: "How much more provident and merciful to their young are the beasts of the field than those who wear the fateful chains of this body and soul-destroying vice."

This "western country," as they term it, seems to be the great farming district of Australia, and is really wonderful in its adaptability for the raising of potatoes, yielding immense crops of the largest and finest varieties of this popular esculent.

The town of Warnambool, well built and cleanly, is a seaport, located on Lady Bay; and has a population of four thousand. Here I had a fine audience, who seemed to enjoy the service, and I was entertained by Rev. Mr. Kings at the Wesleyan Home. From here I was driven twelve miles in the rain, and through the black mud, to the little village of Karoit, having a population of fifteen hundred souls, where I remained for the night, at the pleasant home of Mr. Miller, having previously sung to a small but a demonstrative audience.

A SURPRISE DINNER.

After a ride of five hours, rendered very unpleasant by the mud and rain, I came to the little town of McArthur, where I was invited to a splendid dinner, prepared for me by Mr. Joseph Law, who, knowing I was to pass that way, gave me this most pleasant surprise. He said that he felt like an old acquaintance of mine, having known me a long time by my songs, many of which I found upon his piano. Going forward to Belfast, I gave my next service to a large audience, but whom, I felt, had but little sympathy for my peculiar role of song.

CHASING KANGAROOS.

A ride of fifty-two miles, in a sort of mud-barge stage, brought me to Hamilton, the metropolis of the western interior, and eminently an agricultural and sheep-grazing land. I shall never forget that ride. Coming, as we did, upon a flock of kangaroos, the temptation fell upon me to try and catch one of these nimble jumpers, and I ordered the stage to a halt, to enable me to try the experiment. Not until after the excitement was over did I realize the ridiculousness of the adventure. The whole flock were facing me as I entered upon the chase, when suddenly the older members of the family began to put a hopeless distance between me and them by their immense leaps to the front, which were soon imitated by their younger relations to such an extent as to completely baffle my hunter instincts. Just then an adolescent kangaroo came upon my near vision, who seemed to be unmindful of my presence and intentions. Stealthily creeping upon him in the rear, I was about to clasp him in my arms as captive, when, taking in my person and evident purpose, with long, swift bounds, he passed into distance like a fleeting cloud. Arriving in the town after dark, I was met and delightfully entertained by Rev. Mr. Hunter, a most excellent minister, with whom I spent a most profitable day and evening in Christian conversation and interchange of thought. From what I observed in the streets, I had felt the people were greatly given over to drunkenness and debauchery, yet at my service on Sunday evening the good Lord was with us, and we felt blessed, and that much good had been accomplished. Fifty-three miles farther on, by wagon, over a fine highway called the "Metal Road," I reached Portland, an elegant little seaport, having a population of four thousand people. Here I was greeted by a large and intelligent audience, and being in good voice, I spent a pleasant hour and a half in song service. After the exercises I took passage in the steamer " Rob Roy," for Melbourne, one hundred and thirty miles distant, arriving next day at noon, and again found home with my waiting family, after my two weeks' delightful song trip to the new districts of West Victoria.

MY SONG CAMPAIGN IN NEW SOUTH WALES.

At two o'clock the same day I embarked on the steamer " City of Adelaide," for Sidney, the parent city of Australia and capital of the colony of New South Wales. I had only a few short moments with my dear ones who accompanied me to the wharf, and watched me and my steamer fade out sight on the bosom of the ocean. It was a great cross to me to thus be obliged to leave them one day sooner than I had expected, and I repaired sorrowfully to my cabin to peruse my pocket full of unread correspondence, almost overcome by feelings of loneliness.

I soon became acquainted with some of my fellow passengers, among them one of my countrymen, Hon. S. D. Hastings of Wisconsin, an earnest temperance advocate,

whose society I enjoyed during the trip. We reached the
beautiful harbor of Botany Bay at eleven o'clock, on the
evening of the third day and effected safe landing at Sidney. I was awaited at the wharf by the Rev. Richard
Sellers, secretary of the committee in charge of my services, was quartered at Petty's hotel, which proved a very
comfortable, pleasant home, and spent Saturday in attending to the preliminaries connected with my singing campaign.

SOME FACTS CONCERNING THE COLONY.

The name of New South Wales was given the colony by
Captain Cook in 1770, who discovered it, because of a fancied resemblance to South Wales, England, and in which
was established by the home government the first penal
settlement in Australia, at the famous Botany Bay. The
colony has a coast line of 800 miles, the greater part of
which offers a bold and dangerous front to the navigator.
A range of lofty hills runs parallel to the sea coast, at an
average distance of thirty miles therefrom, and divides the
colony into what is known as the eastern and western water
sheds, the surface of which is diversified with alternate
hills, valleys, and plains. It contains 323,437 square miles,
is 500 miles long with an average breadth of 850 miles.
It is divided into thirteen pastoral districts, and 118 counties and has a population of over 500,000 souls. Its principal river is the Murray, which rises in the Australian Alps,
which, receiving all its western waters, falls into the sea in
South Australia. It has several isolated mountains of great
height, and as it extends over eleven degrees of latitude,
every variety of climate can be found therein. Everything
which is grown in England is cultivated with care in this
colony, while its vast plains, or "runs" are very valuable
for the grazing of sheep. Gold, silver, tin, lead and iron
are mined, but its most extensive mineral is coal, of which
there are inexhaustible quantities.

JOKES AND JEALOUSY.

My first experience in New South Wales, was one of that peculiar humor which is so taking with an American, whether the subject be himself or another. On entering the market on the evening after my arrival in search of some fruit to regale and refresh myself with, my attention was attracted by a market man of such wonderful corporosity, as to draw from me an astonished smile. This the New Wales man greatly resented by reminding me that my nose was as much an object of prominence as his body. Taken all together the situation was so very droll and pat, not to deny his soft imputation, as to give me a genuine Yankee tickle. I was peculiarly struck with the seeming jealousy, which the people of the several different colonies cherish towards each other. One would tell you that his side of a colonial line was Paradise; and the other, Heaven, but coming down to a rigid examination of the informant, these terms would be invariably reversed, Paradise and Inferno.

THE CITY OF SIDNEY

Was founded by Captain Phillip in 1788, six days after his arrival at Botany Bay, with a fleet of convict and store ships, and is beautifully situated at the head of Sidney Cove, on the shores of Port Jackson, one of the finest harbors in the world. It lies about four miles from the ocean entrance, which is over a mile in width, and well lighted by beacons on its almost perpendicular cliffs. Its aspect bespeaks substantial wealth, advanced civilization and growing enterprise, so elegant are its public edifices, banking and mercantile buildings, while in many of its features it has a strong resemblance to an English town, some of its streets being narrow and the houses having an old fashioned look. Among its most costly structures are the university, new post office, town hall, government house and treasury building and the circular quay, which is thirteen hundred feet in length, and available for the largest vessels.

It has a population, including that of its immediate suburbs, of one hundred thousand. I gave my first service—a song sermon—on Sunday evening, for the children of Balmain, a suburb of Sydney, and the occasion was very precious. My first evening of song was given in the large Wesleyan church, York St., Rev. George Woolnough, pastor, as also chairman of the district, and my meeting. His remarks in introducing me, were very apropos, making me feel at home, and among my friends, and I was enabled to sing in excellent spirit and voice.

CELEBRATING MY NATIONAL BIRTH-DAY.

It being the Fourth of July, I took the liberty of presuming somewhat on English delicacy by mentioning the fact as follows: "You may not be aware that to-day is the glorious Fourth of July in my own land, and while, by my absence, I am prevented from participating in the bonfires, illuminations, and festivities of the day at home, I would ask the audience to join with me in singing a chorus —our national anthem set to the tune of England's. We change the words a trifle but it is nearly the same, and I have had the privilege of singing it to the words of 'God save the Queen,' in nearly every city of Great Britain, and in the city of Washington, when our people sang it as heartily as I ever heard it rendered in your native land, for we too, love and respect your noble Queen."

I then sang

"Who does not love his native land,
  The best of all on earth.
Its rulers who in justice stand,
  As guardians from our birth;
Let those who frown their country down,
  No right or prestige claim,
But all in love and peace abound
  With honor to its name."

All joined heartily in the annexed chorus, while the union of the English and American flags, literally covered my organ;

> "My country 'tis of thee
> Sweet land of liberty,
>   Of thee I sing.
> Long may our land be bright
> With freedom's holy light,
> Protect us by thy might
>   Great God, our king."

I then proceeded with the second verses:

> "And while our father-land we prize,
>   Its banner true we raise;
> Far up above the earth and skies
>   God and His Christ we'll praise.
> He rules the world in righteousness,
>   Before him angels fall,
> His name we'll praise, His cross we'll raise,
>   High up above them all."

Then the great congregation sang with thrilling power,

> "Jesus shall reign, where'er the sun
> Doth his successive journey run,
> His kingdom spread from shore to shore,
> 'Till sun shall rise, and set no more."

Three cheers were then proposed and given with hearty good will, and with Hon. S. D. Hastings at my side, we closed the exercises, with the audience by singing "God save the Queen." The *Sydney Morning Herald*, the oldest and leading paper in Australia spoke of my service in detail, and in most congratulatory terms. For several evenings following, I sang in different portions of the city, before large and enthusiastic audiences.

CHAPTER XIX.

THE COAL FIELDS OF AUSTRALIA.

MY NEXT point was New Castle, the principal shipping port on the northern coast, and most important town in the great coal regions of Australia. It has 10,000 population. The church in which I held my service was literally packed with people, and very many were unable to gain admittance. Draped over the pulpit were the Union Jack and Stars and Stripes with the words:

"May we ever be one."

My service here was a marked success and I was a guest of Rev. F. F. Firth, a staunch teetotaler, and a devoted minister of the gospel. The site of his church was one of the most conspicuous in the town, and I was told that sometimes the incoming ships took the edifice for a land-mark to guide them safe into port. Indeed, all our churches should be guiding stars to point the way to the safe haven of the celestial city, "Where the wicked cease from troubling, and the weary are at rest."

THE GRANARY OF THE COLONY.

I next arrived at Maitland, the productiveness of whose alluvial land, bordering on Hunter River, has caused the district to be called the "granary of New South Wales." It is a live inland town of 8,000 population, with several manufactures and a paper mill. It has been overflowed several times, the floods doing great damage; but, owing to these uprisings of the waters, it is said to owe much of its agricultural prosperity. My service was held in a large, high, gothic church, and, although I had a fine audience, and my efforts were kindly received, I found it a most difficult place in which to sing.

I was cordially met at the station by Mr. Robert Blair, a leading merchant and Christian, who escorted me to his home. Mrs. Blair was the joy of her household, beloved in the town, and the Aquilla of the church. These friends invited a choice Christian gathering to tea, my meeting with whom was most pleasurable.

BACK TO SYDNEY AND ITS SUBURBS.

From Maitland I took rail twenty miles, and boat seventy, and reached Sydney at six o'clock the same evening. Although the sea was not rough, I suffered much from nausea, and the tediousness of the voyage was only broken by the intelligent movements of the Captain's fine dog, who seemed to really understand the piloting of the ship. On Sunday evening there was a large attendance upon my service—"Gospel in Song"—several coming forward for prayers, and eight professing to have found peace in believing, which added new zest to my work.

On Monday evening I sang at Waverly, a nice little village in the Sydney suburbs, where I met with a hearty reception. Here I made the acquaintance of Rev. George Hurst, book steward, and Rev. William Curnow, editor of the *Christian Advocate*. The Christian men in position in all the Australian Colonies, are evidently the very bone and sinew of the gospel work, and as such I shall ever cherish them in my memory.

My next service was across the bay, on the western shores of Darling Harbor, called Balmain. Here I was entertained by Rev. R. Sellers, and was blessed and profited by his companionship. Together we visited the oldest minister in Australia, Rev. Bro. Watkins, who has three sons who have followed his example in entering the ministry. Here the service was well attended, and I had reason to believe, I was much appreciated.

OVER THE HILLS.

On the morning of July 14th I set out for Bathhurst, distant from Sidney one hundred and twenty miles, and twenty-five thousand feet above sea level, having a population of about sixteen thousand, and the third town of importance in the colony. I considered myself most fortunate in having for a companion, on this trip, the Rev. Dr. Kelynack, learned, eloquent and devout, and considered by all who know him to be the Punshon of Australia. The journey was made on the most famous zigzag railroad in the world, over rocky wasts, steep canons, deep gorges, perpendicular crags, wild hills, and is one of the greatest triumphs of the science of engineering which has ever been accomplished. With the great blue mountains in the distance, and the wonderful landscape of earth and sky, it was the most delightful journey by rail, which I experienced in the colonies. At length we reached the base of the hills, with which the lovely little town of Bathhurst is surrounded, and saw it standing out in charming perspective upon a gently sloping mountain plain. From the station I was driven to the delightful home of Hon. Mr. Webb, a member of the Provincial Parliament, and Mayor of the town, whose grounds were tastefully laid out with plots of shrubbery and flowering plants, fountains and minature lakes, in which latter, beautiful black and white swans and other aquatic birds disported. The kindness, thoughtfulness, and courtesy of this dear family, so thoroughly and effectively engaged in their several capacities in the forwarding of the Master's work will never grow dim in my memory. Here I sang two evenings to fine houses and with good success, and took the train back to Sydney over the same picturesque route. On the evening of the same day I gave a service at Newtown, and upon taking my seat at my organ found a note upon it saying "One of my sons was at one of your services, and is almost persuaded to be a Christian. If you would give an opportunity for him to be prayed for this evening, I believe he would give his heart to Christ." I earnestly endeavored to frame my service with a hope of winning his soul to Jesus, and at its close said to my audience that I should like to remain a short time after the benediction for prayers, and to hear the testimony of any who felt disposed to join me. To my astonishment and deep gratification nearly the entire audience tarried, while to the great joy of this widowed mother's heart, both her sons came forward and found peace in believing. They were the children of a minister of the gospel, and who shall say that the good news of that night, did not give joy in heaven as well as on the earth. Saturday evening was set apart to give me a collection for my mission hall fund, and at the close of my service of song, the large audience handsomely responded with the sum of twenty-six pounds or one hundred and ten dollars. On Sabbath I gave two song sermons, one to the children in the afternoon, and the other in the evening. My theme was Jesus, and the service was peculiarly refreshing, several gave their hearts to Christ, and it proved a season of grace and power. I held my next service at Goulburn, one hundred and sixty miles distant, the terminus of the great southern railway, being the principal depot of the southern inland trade, and having a population of six thousand. In this thoroughly active and energetic town, I was nicely entertained by Mr. Davis, one of its most prominent Christians and merchants.

The exercises were held in Wesleyan church, a fine, new structure, which was well filled by attentive listeners.

A MISSIONARY FAMILY.

The noted town of Paramatta was the locality of my next service—sixteen miles by steamer and railway from Sydney, and next to it, the oldest town in the colony. It has a population of over six thousand, is beautifully laid out, possesses many fine public and private buildings, and quite closely resembles an English town of the same size. It is noted for its beautiful scenery, and fertility of soil. It has a beautiful park reserved for the recreation of its inhabitants, whose walks are bordered with oaks, which are said to be the largest in the island. I was the guest of Rev. Jabez Waterhouse and his estimable wife, and most interesting cultivated and pious family. The father of this efficient gospel minister was an excellent clergyman in the mother country, and four of his sons became laborers in the missionary work in foreign fields. Of this remarkable family, I met one brother in the Hawaiian Islands, another in Tasmania, while I learned another was doing God's work Fiji.

ORANGERIES AND VINEYARDS.

This Paramatta district has a world wide reputation for fruit growing, over four thousand acres being devoted to the culture of the orange and grape, and here are believed to be the largest orange trees in the world. In the evening my host took me to visit the humble cottage of a parishioner, situated in these beautiful groves. Here we met a women all aglow with thanksgiving and praise that God had spared her a left arm, she having lost her right by amputation a few days previous. I sang her a few verses in this little house, and went away with deep gratitude in my heart to my Savior, for His wonderful mercies to me, feeling almost ashamed of my feeble praise, as compared with that of this poor woman, with but a single arm, and a large family of children dependent upon her for support. Returning to Sydney I greatly enjoyed my service at Rev. Dr. Robert Steele's church, the largest of the Presbyterian denomination in the city. The edifice was well filled, and the people seemed to be captivated by simple melodies, and the gospel sentiments embodied therein, although so firmly attached to their custom of singing the Psalms only in their worship, as to deem an innovation upon the same, as almost sacreligious.

I enjoyed my tea with Dr. Steele, and the the short time I was permitted to spend in his company, who although quite deaf, is probably the most noted clergyman in the colony; is the editor of the leading Presbyterian paper, and is beloved by all.

THE AUTHOR OF BOOMERANG.

My next service was in a large church at Wallarah, where I was entertained by Mr. George Hardee, of the firm of Hardee Bro., jewelers. Here I had the pleasure of meeting the well known author of "Boomerang,"—an interesting book, giving a graphic illustration of Australian life—and also a German gentleman, named Bassicott, both of whom were very congenial and entertaining.

There was a large attendance upon my temperance song service the following evening, which had for its subject, "Better than Wine." After each of the scriptural readings, short, pithy speeches were made by gentleman, and the exercises were very interesting and impressive. The service was arranged by Mr. McCoy, an active and aggressive teetotaler, and under his management proved a gratifying success.

On Sunday afternoon I gave a service at the Female Refuge or home for fallen women, and many of the inmates were moved to tears by my songs, following the same, with a service at Rev. Mr. Nolands, Bourke St. church, in the evening, which was densely crowded, and at which many rose for prayers at an after meeting.

Mr. John Hardee took me a delightful drive on Monday to the South Heads, where I had a fine view of Sydney and its beautiful harbor, and returning gave my twenty-third evening of song at the Bourke St. church, to a good audience, being occasionally interrupted by the whistles and steam from the locomotives in the adjacent depot.

I next gave a service in Newtown, a beautiful suburb, where much spiritual interest was manifest in the large audience, the exercises being followed with an interesting prayer meeting. From this point I paid a second visit to Paramatta, giving another service there, as well as at Windsor, being the guest of Mr. William Deans.

FAREWELL SERVICE IN NEW SOUTH WALES.

On the evening of my farewell service, the edifice was filled with my beloved new friends, who with hearty hand shaking, and cordial, parting words bade me good-bye. On this occasion the committee presented me with an elegant, illuminated farewell address, with their names attached, which read as follows:

"The committee under whose direction you have held your services of song in this country, desire at this last meeting to say that you have afforded them, and the people here, a great, and rare enjoyment; that in your public work, and private conduct you have been generously scattering seeds of kindness, for our reaping bye and bye. We gratefully record that by the blessing of God you have held twenty-four services in as many successive days, singing to an aggregate of more than twenty thousand people. We now commend you to God, praying that He may long spare you to serve Him and His church by your singing for Jesus."

GEO. WOOLNOUGH, M.A.,
RICHARD SELLERS,
BENJAMIN JAMES, JR.,
HENRY GORMAN,
JOHN CORKETT,
JOHN GARDINER,
THOS. COWLESHAW,
THOS. PIM,
JOHN HARDY,
C. W. CALDWELL,
W. E. BOURNE,
JOHN GRAHAM,
R. MCCOY,
JAS. A. WATKIN,
SAML. E. LEES,
W. B. HAIGH,
J. S. MCCOY,
W. G. KINGSLEY,

SYDNEY, New South Wales, July 25, 1875.

CHAPTER XX.

AN EXCURSION DOWN BOTANY BAY.

THE next day an excursion was planned and carried out to show me Sydney harbor, which is regarded as the most picturesque in the world, with its deep, clear waters studded with many charming little islands, covered with elegant villas, flower and fruit gardens. A trim little steamer had been chartered, and with the leading men of the Wesleyan church, and their wives on board, as also the mayor of the city, we moved off from the wharf, provided with a bountiful and delicious supply of refreshments. We touched at several of the most beautiful of the Islands, and at the Quarantine, at which latter a ship containing several hundred emigrants, were just coming in from sea. Passing so near we threw on board, oranges, cakes, and other dainties from our store, and had it not been for the influence of an official, excited on our behalf, we might have been quarantined with the new comers, having scraped so close an acquaintance, as to attract the attention of the governmental guardians of the health of the port.

A speech of welcome and farewell to our emigrant friends by Rev. George Woolnough, and we left for the shore. It was in fact the most memorable excursion of its kind, in which I even participated, and it was certainly the most pleasant in my experience, had my dear wife been with me to enjoy it. At length amid good-byes, and God bless you, from their lips and gifts of flowers and fruits from their hands, I depart for my steamer, for a five hundred and sixty miles sail of sixty three hours for Melbourne, while a cloud of waving handkerchiefs greet me as I leave the shore. Seven miles out what was my surprise and delight, to have some friend, come out upon the shore of a small island we were passing, and wave the stars and stripes in his good-bye, to remind me of my dear native land, as the shore of this new, faded from my sight.

With smiling skies and favorable winds, I was soon permitted to rejoin my family in Melbourne. I spent the next day after my arrival in letter reading and writing, giving a service of song the same evening in Williamstown, the port for all the steamers of the heaviest tonnage, touching at Melbourne harbor. The singing was held in the church of which Rev. John Harcourt, the president of the conference, and a man of great eloquence, ability and piety, was pastor, and although the night was stormy there was o fair attendance.

The following day we made several calls upon our friends, and among other places of interest, visited the large confectionery establishment of Mr. Burrows, who took great pains to show us over the same, and to instruct us in the details of "lolly" making, presenting us a fine box of candies, which literally sweetened us in our subsequent journeyings.

The following Sunday I gave a song sermon in the town hall at Prahran, having for its subject, "Thou shalt call his name Jesus, because he shall save his people from their sins." At the close many called for the prayers of God's people.

DEPARTURE FOR SOUTH AUSTRALIA.

On Monday, August 9, we took leave of our Melbourne home at Royal Terrace, and taking passage in the steamer "Alhambra" for Adelaide, in South Australia, moved off from the wharf at two o'clock, sailed up the river, through

St. Philip's Bay, and by nightfall we were rocking "in the cradle of the deep." The five hundred miles were accomplished after a rough passage of three days, and we were glad enough to reach harbor at Port Adelaide.

South Australia was first colonized in 1836, by bodies of emigrants from Great Britain, sent out under the auspices of the South Australia Colonization Society, but its growth was for some time retarded by the discovery of gold in Victoria. As originally formed, it was twice and a half as large as Great Britain and Ireland, and by subsequent additions was enlarged to 750,000 square miles. It contains a great variety of soils and scenery, and within its limits are to be found almost every description of landscape. Its northern portions are arid and barren, and perhaps will never be valuable for any purpose, but its extent of pastoral and agricultural land is of immense area. Its principal mineral is copper, of which it has rich mines, while some gold is to be found. The climate greatly resembles that of Sicily and Naples, being very agreeable during nine or ten months of the year, while in the other the sun attains great power, and with the hot winds from the interior, is very oppressive and uncomfortable. It has but few railroads, no high mountains, while its rivers are not navigable to any extent. The population at this writing is estimated at three hundred thousand souls.

We were met at our steamer by friends and kindly assisted through the customs and driven to the "Adair House," kept by Mrs. Couch. On the evening of my arrival, I gave a service in the large Wesleyan Church in Pierce street, to a full house. Having been so seasick on my trip, and not having fully recovered therefrom, for the first time I made an apology in the colonies, as follows: "A few hours ago I was so ill that I had about concluded to 'throw up'—my appointments in South Australia." My audience, seeing the application of "throw up " in its humorous connection, before I comprehended it, broke out into a hearty laugh, which seemed to aid me wonderfully in completing my programme. The "Morning Advertiser" gave a fine notice of my singing, and thus I made a successful debut in South Australia.

THE CITY OF ADELAIDE.

This charming city, the capital and seat of government of the colony, is built nearly in the form of a square, with its streets running at right angles, and is located on a large plain of the Mount Lofty range, which walls it on the eastern and southern sides. The entire city is bordered by four grand terraces, sloping to the north, south, east and west, which form a broad belt, or reservation of land, which enterely encompasses this beautiful metropolis. It is, as it were, a brilliant, wide ribbon of living greensward, surrounded with the finest of promenades, paths, and carriage ways. This entire area is the property and care of the government, as well as are the beautiful paddocks and gardens which line each bank of the River Torrens, which runs between North and South Adelaide, and which is crossed by two massive iron, and two wooden bridges.

No palatial edifices or great works of art could give the inviting effect of this intermarriage of civilization and nature, rendering the city's suburbs equally as charming and desirable as its centers, and giving its population health-laden breezes, quiet retreats from the noise and bustle of business, and recreation of soul and body on every hand. Adelaide has also extensive gardens and a fine park, and has a plentiful supply of water from two large reservoirs. It has a population of fifty thousand, and its public buildings, club and bath houses, markets and residences, are of striking magnificence. In fact, each colony seems to have an especial pride in having the best capital, public buildings, gardens, etc., and it is quite difficult to decide which excels in these particulars.

My second service was held in the large town hall, and the governor general, Sir Anthony Musgrove, with his body guard and staff, were advertised to be present, but for some reason the former was detained, although his staff and officers, Lady Musgrove, the mayor and city council occupied the front seats. I felt quite honored by their attendance and a trifle disturbed thereat, but I went through my exercises as usual. Lady Musgrove, to whom we were presented, is much esteemed, respected, and beloved in all the walks of her position, and is a sister of Cyrus W. Field, of our city. On Sunday evening I delivered my song sermon on " The Higher Christian Life," in the Wesleyan Church at Kent Town, a part of Adelaide, where I met that pious and earnest minister, Rev. W. P. Wells.

A PLEASANT RIDE.

The next day our good friends took us out for a drive, that we might enjoy the sights of their beautiful city, after which we were driven out to some of the luxuriant orange groves, where for the first time we saw the naval orange, a most delicious fruit, and without seeds. I had thought the oranges we found at Honolulu were perfection, but found them thoroughly rivaled here. We were kindly entertained at tea by Rev. T. B. Stephenson, one of the editors of the " Advocate," and pastor of the North Adelaide Church. This Stephenson family are quite noted, as another brother is a minister in Tasmania, and a cousin is the far-famed Rev. T. Bowman Stephenson, of London, and the founder of the " Children's Home."

Owing to my sight-seeing, I was much too tired to sing well before the large audience to whom I gave my service. I sang the next evening at Kent Town, in a spacious church, and before a good audience, and again had the pleasure of the society of Rev. Mr. Wells. Oh, for more such ministers of the Lord Jesus, to help us on our way and at our work.

A STAGE JOURNEY INLAND.

The next morning, with my son James, I took stage for Kadina, one hundred miles distant, a fine little city of 4,000 inhabitants; and noted for its rich mines of copper. My son, and myself both enjoyed the style of staging, as with two wheel horses, and three leaders, they almost ran the horses, but exchanged for fresh ones every ten miles. Considerable of the distance, the country was bushy and monotonous, although we often passed through large wheat fields, some of which were 1,000 acres in extent, it being claimed that the best wheat in the world is grown in this locality.

The gathering at my service was quite large, and seemed to be very satisfactory to the hardy, good people of this mining town.

By special invitation I then went to the far-famed "Moonta mines," and although there was but twelve hours' notice of my coming, yet I found over 800 people gathered in the Wesleyan church to listen to my songs. This place is in the very heart of the richest copper mines in the world, and its whole-souled, and demonstrative people were nearly all natives of old Cornwall, England. Here I was entertained by a noble man, of large heart, Captain R. V. Hancock, the superintendent of all this mining district, who seemed to enjoy the thorough respect of the men underground, as well as those upon the surface.

He presented me several rich specimens of copper ore, in its various grades; which added to the fine large specimens of malachite, presented my good wife by Captain Anthony of the Wallaroo mines, gives me a fine exhibition of Australian minerals for my cabinet, with which to hold in remembrance these far-off friends of toil and worth. God bless these noble men who do business in the bowels of the earth.

Here, where the spirit of Billy Bray, and Daniel Quorum seemed to be everywhere present to me, I gave a song sermon on Sunday evening, taking as my subject—" About Jesus." The exercises were both new and novel to this people, and they seemed to be greatly delighted and profited by it. The Moonta mines, are those bearing the name of the town, yield the richest of ores, and are worked by 1,300 men, directed by an able staff of officers. In a space of six months in 1873, 12,000 tons of ore, averaging twenty-five per cent. of pure copper, were raised from them, and constant discoveries of fresh lodes, indicate that the metal will last for many years to come.

Another trip of 112 miles brought us to Gawler, a pastoral, and agricultural town, and the oldest established port in connection with the trade of the river Murray, and its tributaries. Here we were entertained by Mr. Clements and sang to an audience of 1,000 people. Thence we passed to Kaponda, noted for its copper mines, and quarries of marble. Here I was entertained by Hon. James Price and his excellent family, a fine Christian gentleman, in high position, although in very poor health.

A NATIONAL WHISTLE FROM A MAGPIE.

A drive of forty miles and I reach the neat little town of Clare, located among the hills and blue gum trees, having a population of about 3,000, and famous for its cattle stations and stock raising. As I was alighting from my carriage at the place appointed for me to sing, an Australian magpie suddenly struck up a distinct whistle to the exact tune of "Yankee Doodle's come to town," as if in welcome of my arrival. I afterwards learned that an American resident had taught this singularly imitative little bird this popular air of our republic. I greatly enjoyed my next song service at the famous Burra copper mines, as also my entertainment at the residence of Mr. E. Lipsett. From this point we returned to Adelaide, my wife accompanying me the same evening to Port Adelaide, some four miles distant, where I held a service. We took tea at Mr. Rogans, who earnestly enquired of us after Rev. Dr. Kidder, of Drew Seminary, whom he met years ago, while in Brazil.

On Sabbath evening I gave a song sermon in Perre street church, which was thoroughly crowded; and at which the exercises were signally blessed; following it, on Monday evening, by a temperance service at the town hall, at which I caused no slight astonishment by stating the happy fact that I had never seen wine on our Christian tables in America.

FINAL TO THE INTERIOR.

The following day I traveled thirty miles by stage to Willunga, a small village of about 1,000 souls. From this place large quantities of slate are shipped, being the product of the southern quarries. I was kindly received by my audience, among whom was a lady who had ridden thirty-five miles on horse-back to hear me sing. Giving a song sermon on Sunday evening to a large audience at Archer Street church in Adelaide, on Monday I took stage for Strathalbyn, one of the most picturesque towns in the colony, having for one of its many pleasing features, the river Angus, whose banks, the corporation have lined with luxuriant shrubs and willows. Here I was the fortunate guest of Rev. Mr. Hobbs, a minister of thorough good taste, and of devout piety.

A song-sermon at Kent Town on Friday evening, I spent the following day in calling and driving about Adelaide with my family, giving my farewell service, in old

Pierre St. church, where a collection was taken for my mission hall fund. At the close of this service, which ended my never-to-be-forgotten visit to South Australia, the following address was presented to me, which read as follows:

To MR. PHILIP PHILLIPS,

Dear Sir:—On the eve of your departure from South Australia we desire to express the pleasure which your visit to our colony has given. Your fame as a singer and composer of sacred songs has made your name familiar long before we had any anticipation of seeing and hearing you for ourselves.

The great popularity of many of your Sunday-school and other songs, made the prospect of your visit a matter of public interest; and now that we have become familiar with your voice and face, as we were before with your compositions, we cannot do less than assure you that we believe your services have afforded both pleasure and profit to the large audiences that have assembled to hear you. In wishing you farewell we beg to assure you that you will have a place in our affectionate remembrance, and we sincerely hope you may long live to "sing for Jesus" in many places, and to contribute to our Sunday-school and congregational psalmody, songs as sweet and popular as any you have already composed.

On behalf of the committee we are, dear sir,
    Yours faithfully,
- JAMES BICKFORD,
  Prest. South Australia Conf.
  A. A. SCOTT,
  W. H. SHARLAND,
  THOS. MURDES,
  T. B. STEPHENSON.

We took the steamer, " Coorong," for Melbourne, September 7, and after a pleasant three days' passage, again reached that city. For the next few days we were busy preparing for our homeward trip, while in the evenings I gave song services in several of the churches.

ENGLISH LIFE IN INDIA.

CHAPTER XXI.

TASMANIA, OR VAN DIEMAN'S LAND.

ON Wednesday forenoon, September 15, we embarked for Tasmania in the steamer "Derwent," and after sailing twenty-four hours, reached the mouth of the River Tama at daybreak and sailed up its waters seventy miles to its head at Launceston. The only incident of the voyage was the meeting of a small boat, containing Capt. Marshall and the almost starved crew of the shipwrecked sailing vessel, "City of Cambridge," who had nothing to eat but a scanty mess of salt pork which they were cooking on a flat stone in the centre of their little craft, and whom we took on board.

A FEW FACTS CONCERNING THE COLONY.

Tasmania was discovered in 1642 by a Dutch navigator, Abel James Tasman, who was commissioned by Anthony Van Dieman, Governor-General of Batavia, to explore the continent now called Australia, but then termed "the great unknown South Land," who named it after his patron. Although touched at by several navigators, who had encounters with the hostile natives, it was not discovered to be separate from Australia until 1798, when Mr. George Bass, a surgeon in the royal navy, discovered the existence of a dividing channel. The first settlement was made at Hobart Town, and was followed by that at York Town and Launceston, and in 1813 its ports were opened to English commerce. The profits made on the first importations of English goods were enormous, and many men who have since counted their incomes by tens of thousands, and feasted royally at their tables, made their first money by shouldering a peddler's pack through the Tasmanian bush. The "Emerald," in 1820, brought the first emigrant families direct from England to this colony, together with sixteen pure Merino sheep, from which have descended the fine flocks of the east coast, which have supplanted the native sheep whose wool was coarse and of but little value. So limited were the supplies of the commoner articles, that upon the arrival of the Emerald, eleven poor wretches who had long been condemned to death by hanging, had rope supplied for the purpose by that vessel, to the authorities, there being nothing of the kind available on the island. The fourth Governor of the colony was Sir John Franklin, the unfortunate Arctic explorer, whose administration was eminently disinterested, and who, with Lady Franklin, did much to foster a taste for science, literature and art.

Tasmania is divided into eighteen counties, four of which are wholly unoccupied. The great Wellington range of mountains traverse the whole length of the island, and have been aptly termed the "backbone" of the colony. The loftiest eminence does not reach 6,000 feet elevation. All portions of the country not occupied by primary ranges, are generally hilly, the surface swelling into long and lofty ridges called "tiers," and from an eminence give to the landscape a very unequal and undulatory aspect. Where granite, quartz and micaceous rock is found, the soil is uniformly poor, while in the trapp rock districts which cover many thousands of square miles, nearly all the best lands are found, upon which most of the population of the country is settled, where agriculture alone flourishes and the live stock of the colony is supported. Passing from these, either east or west, settlements are few and far between, and the existence of man is hardly to be traced. The lands on which the forests stood with their massive gum, the musk, sassafras, silver wattle, laurel, the fern and the palm tree, and gorgeously beautiful flowering shrubs, are the richest from the accumulated soil of ages of decaying vegetation.

The Tasmanian lakes, which are principally upon the high plateau of central table lands of the Wellington range of mountains, are large natural reservoirs and flow over an area of seventy-five thousand acres. Of these the great lake, which is thirteen miles long by eight wide, and is a beautiful sheet of water, covers twenty-eight thousand acres. Its principal rivers are the Derwent and Tama, while the lesser streams and water courses are almost beyond numbering. The eastern coast scenery introduces the visitor to some of the grandest in the world, with its majestic crags, and cliffs, and mighty outposts of mountain ranges.

Added to this, the colony has one of the mildest and most agreeable climates known, though it is quite variable. Extreme heat is not present here, except in five or six hot winds in a year, lasting about as many hours, while extreme cold never reaches the lower lands, though the high lands have quite sharp winters, with considerable snow. The population of the Island is estimated at about one hundred and fifty thousand.

THE CITY OF LAUNCESTON.

At the mouth of the Tama we were joined by Mr. Birkshall, who accompanied us up the river, pointing out its beauties of lake and tributary, and that of the surrounding country, as we glided up that stately avenue of waters, draining, with its tributaries, a great territory of hill, mountain, valley and plain. Under his attentive escort, we landed at his beautiful island home. The city of Launceston has a population of about twelve thousand, and is at the head

of the Tama River and in the peninsula formed by the
junction of two rivers, the North and South Esk. Its appearance, as seen on entering it riverward, with its profusely wooded background, its hills studded with pretty villas, and majestic mountains in the distance, is exceedingly
picturesque. A pleasant feature is that almost every residence, even in the heart of the town, has its well-stocked
garden and fruits and flowers, and in the spring white blossoms are so profuse as to give the impression that everything
is snow-clad, and they mingle their perfume with the haw-
thorn and sweet briar, which crop out over the fences, in
the highways and by-ways, while the sweet songs of mi-
gratory birds give a charming home aspect to the place. It
is supplied with an abundance of water from St. Patrick
River, flowing through an artificial tunnel, to reservoirs on
an eminence two miles above the city, and conveyed thereto by pipes. It has elegant public buildings and churches,
a fine park, while its spacious botanical gardens are prettily
laid out, adorned with fountains and conservatories, and
filled with choice shrubbery and flowers.

A CHRISTIAN PHILANTHROPIST.

We were driven from the wharf to the residence of Mr.
Hart, where we made it our home during our stay in the
city. A short time after our arrival we received a visit from
Henry Reed, Esq., whose valued acquaintance I had made
at Harrogate, England, in 1872. He took us in his carriage to Mount Pleasant, his charming estate, situated some
two miles distant.

As this gentleman is so well known to the public of England and these colonies, for his remarkable deeds of Christian heroism and devotion, and shining example in evangelical work, the mention of some of his prominent traits of
character and methods of practical missionary labor may
not be amiss at this time. Years ago he was a most suc-

cessful hardware merchant in Launceston, where he succeeded in amassing a large fortune and retired from business. Returning to his native England, he resolved to employ his time, talent and means in trying to Christianize the people, first having built himself a palatial mansion at Tunbridge Wells, but some of the people whom he was endeavoring to bring to Christ said: "It is easy enough for a man to live a Christian life in such a palace, and surrounded with such luxury," and other remarks of like character. These expressions so smote him to the heart that he sold his place as soon as possible, resolving not to be a stumbling-block in the way of sinners. Proceeding thence to Harrogate, a famous English watering place he built a comfortable house, with a chapel attached, where he held daily meetings, which were attended by many frequenting this fashionable resort, and at which, almost daily, his labors were blest by conversions of these people to Christ.

During one summer season he was vitally aided and powerfully seconded in these meetings by a rich banker visiting the resort. So thoroughly grateful was he to this gentleman that he voluntarily told him that if, at any time, he could be of service to him, financially or otherwise, he would do so.

In the course of time, the wheels of fortune so turned with this friend that he stood on the brink of bankruptcy, when, remembering this promise, he appealed to Mr. Reed, who promptly kept his faith by giving to him all he possessed, to avert the disaster, and saved him from ruin by failure. But by his superior business capacity and courage Mr. Reed soon accumulated another large fortune, and with it devoted himself anew to home missionary work. An instance of his open kindness for the cause in which he was so ardently engaged occurred on the occasion of a tract distributor calling on him for a contribution of a few shillings to aid him in distributing the word in that form to the people. Satisfying himself of the worthiness of the applicant and his need of the same for the forwarding of his labor, he promptly drew and handed him a check for five hundred pounds, accompanied by a "God bless you."

At last, becoming convinced that his duty lay rather in Tasmania than in his native land, that he could accomplish more good in the far-off island of the south, with his estimable wife, who labors effectively with her husband, with her voice, in sacred song, he came back, across old ocean, to the home in which we now find him.

At this time Mr. Reed was making extensive improvements on his grounds, and had fifty men in his employ. He had just finished a neat little chapel, capable of seating two hundred persons, where it was his custom to hold two religious meetings each week, which were especially designed for the moral improvement of these workingmen and their families, and at the close of which he would often distribute some necessaries of life to the poorer of them.

I well remember his remarks at one of these meetings which were addressed to one of the audience: "Oh, you Yorkshire man! I never had a better mason than you are, and I feel in my heart that the day is soon coming when you will yield yourself to the Master." Thus he busied himself giving his men the "Bread of Life" as well as the bread that perisheth.

He was very reticent concerning his good deeds, and the above and other facts, I learned from his fellow Christians on the Island. From one of them I also learned that on a certain occasion he was detained at Cape Colony, in Africa, for quite a length of time on account of the breaking out of small-pox, and the consequent action of the government to confine its ravages to the part where it made its appearance; notwithstanding the urgent pleadings of his friends not to do so, he took his life in his hands, when no other could be found, to fill the post of Chaplain in one of the pest houses, where he comforted the sick and dying, and where God protected him and used him greatly in bringing many to the knowledge of the truth as it is in Jesus.

My service in the evening brought a goodly audience together, to whom I was introduced by Rev. Mr. Stevenson, and I had reason to feel that my efforts were well appreciated; for here, away in the farthest corners of the earth, were most noble Christian men and women.

STAGE JOURNEY TO HOBART TOWN.

From Launceston we took the royal stage-coach for Hobart Town, leaving at six o'clock in the morning and arriving just after sunset. Over a magnificent macadamized road bed of one hundred and twenty miles in length, constructed by convicts in the earlier penal history of the colony, a few of whom, who are now living, still bearing evidence in their walk and movements of the galling ball and chain, we were driven with great rapidity, with frequent and fresh relays of horses. This grand island avenue connecting these two most prominent cities, was literally bordered with the beautiful yellow blossoms of the wattle tree, whose branches seemed alive with the gay plumaged paroquettes, and other tropical toneless and tuneful birds, while now and then an innocent pair of fawns would look out at us from the shrubbery, with their almost human eyes.

At Newtown, a charming suburb of Hobart, we were entertained by Henry Marsh, Esq., and his genial Christian family, whose constant study seemed to be to give us pleasure and make us feel at home. The chattering of the clear-throated magpies at early morn, on a eucalyptus tree, which shaded this charming retreat, has a niche all to itself among our treasured memories of incidents of travel. My introduction in the city was a song sermon given at the spacious Melville church on Sabbath evening, to a great audience where the Lord vouchsafed His presence and blessing, leading several to ask for the prayers of his people.

THE TASMANIA CAPITOL.

The population of Hobart Town is about twenty thousand; approached by sea it presents some of the finest coast scenery extant; with its huge basaltic pillared cliffs in the foreground, the metropolis built upon hilly and undulating land, back of which looms up the often clouded and snow-capped pinnacle of Mount Wellington, in majestic grandeur. It is situated on the shores of a beautiful inlet called Sullivan's Cove, close to the mouth of the celebrated Derwent River which derives its source from the Tasmanian lakes.

The main streets of the city are of good width and finely macadamized, its public and business structures elegant and imposing, while its private residences seem to be built with an especial view to the good old English idea of comfort. The houses of Parliament occupy a commanding position facing the harbor. Its many fine churches, charitable institutions, and school buildings, together with the Tasmanian library, botanical gardens, and other mother-land features, give it quite the air of one of the older European cities. I think if my old friend, Linas W. Miller, of Chautauqua County, N. Y., who was sent here years ago by the authorities in Canada as an exile, could look upon this country now, he would not consider it a prison land, but a paradise of earthly beauty.

On Monday I gave my first evening of song at Wesley church, to a large, appreciative and demonstrative audience, who oftentimes became so enthusiastic as to stop me with their applause between the verses of my songs, and to whom I had been handsomely introduced by my chairman, Hon. Mr. Moore, a member of the provincial Parliament.

DELIGHTFUL NATURAL SCENERY.

The following day, in company with Mr. Marsh's family,

we were driven to that most romantic locality, the Fern
Tree Valleys, clothed in deep verdure of briar, shrub and
vegetation, and over-arched by the sun-excluding, feathery
fronds of great fern trees, bending in palm-like grandeur,
with every curve and leaflet instinct with lines of beauty,
and tints of color. Leaving our carriages at "Fern Tree
Inn," we traversed a path of about one mile in length
through Fern Tree Gully, where these mammoth ferns,
some of them one hundred feet high, and two feet through
at the base, with their umbrella-shaped tops, vied with the
eucalyptus or blue gum tree to hide the sun from piercing
the density of the shade; a bright, rapid streamlet came
gurgling under the fringing ferns, dropping from the rocky
margin, or leaping out into light, flinging its silvery waters
in glittering cascade over walls of perpendicular black
rocks, clad in livid green of moss, lichen, and cryptogamous
plant. Reaching the "Bower," a tent like little nook, with
a glorious canopy of fern branches, and provided with
comfortable sittings for the rest of pilgrims to this beautiful
shrine of nature, we were joined by my son James and
Master Marsh who had availed themselves of the early
morning hours, and visited the summit of Mt. Wellington and
were this far on their way back, bearing a snow-ball trophy
in hand, anxiously waiting our arrival.

Having entered the day spent in this ferny ravine among
the "white ones in our calendar," we wended our way
homeward. Among the grand views we caught in descending, was that of the Derwent river, flashing in the
sunlight, like a long sheet of burnished silver, stretching
far inland, while its broad bosom, and highland battlements,
reminded me of our own dear Hudson.

Giving a third service in the same church to as large
and appreciative an audience as before, we bade our dear
new friends an early "good-bye" the following morning,

and took the stage for Campbell Town, a distance of eighty-one miles, the central district of the colony, and its head quarters, agriculturally. Here we were most hospitably entertained by a Mr. Hart, but owing to the visit of a circus to the place, my audience was quite small. Here it was my pleasure to meet Rev. I. B. Richards, a gentleman universally loved and respected, who is president of Horton College, considered the finest school in Tasmania.

Returning to Launceston we were again kindly received by Mr. & Mrs. Hart, who accompanied us on board the steamer "Tamar" to Melbourne, on which we took passage the next day, I having given a song sermon, as my farewell service in that city the night before.

OUR LAST DAYS AT MELBOURNE.

Safely landed in the Victoria Metropolis again, we took up quarters at Scott's hotel. During our stay I gave several services in aid of temperance, orphan, and other charitable institutions, and of my mission hall fund, adding another one hundred dollar brick to that structure.

On Monday evening Oct. 4th I gave my farewell service of song in the great Lonsdale Church, where I held my first service in the colonies, March 30, having since my arrival, conducted one hundred and one song services, and given forty song sermons, by the grace of God having been able to fill every engagement. This great edifice was again filled with people, and at the close of the exercises, I was presented by Hon. Mr. Crouch, in behalf of the committee who invited me to Australia, a beautiful illuminated address, which read as follows:

Mr. Philip Phillips:

Dear Sir:—At the close of your services in Australia, we, the committee, in connection with whom they have been given, desire to express our entire satisfaction with the manner in which they have been conducted.

The evenings of sacred song in various parts of Victoria, New South Wales, South Australia and Tasmania, have contributed to the pleasure and profit of many thousands, and will, we believe, have the effect of exciting an increased attention to singing as a hand-maid to social, family and public worship.

The song sermons which you have given gratuitously on Sunday evenings, have, under God, been the means of leading many to the Savior, and of awakening deeper religious feeling in the hearts of great numbers.

Your name, as a composer and singer, had, of course, become familiar to us, and we were glad to have the opportunity of personal acquaintance and intercourse.

We anticipate permanent and beneficial results from the solo singing as a part of public worship, of which you have afforded us illustrations, and believe that it will open up a form of presenting divine truth to the hearts and consciences, of which the church has not hitherto fully availed itself.

Our personal intercourse with you, has been of a very happy and profitable kind, and we desire to bear testimony to the manner in which you have subordinated other considerations, to the chief object of doing good by singing the gospel.

We wish you, Mrs. Phillips and your sons, every blessing from our kind heavenly Father; we shall cherish many pleasant memories of your visit and labors among us; we shall follow with interest your continued efforts of Christian song; we shall pray that you and your family may be favored with a pleasant and safe voyage, by the will of God, to India and to your native land, and, trusting that you may be spared long to serve God and His church in the path which He has chosen for you, we are, dear sir, for the Committee:

   JOHN HARCOURT, President of Conference.
   JOHN COPE, Ex-President of Conference.
   JOHN C. LYMAN, Secretary of Conference.
     S. G. KING, J.P.,
     J. P. CROUCH, J.P.,
     JOHN G. MILLIARD,
     JOHN BEE,
     JAMES S. WAUGH,
     JAMES D. DODGSON,
     JOSEPH DARE,
     JOHN WATSFORD,
     ADAM NICOLS,
     WM. C. QUICK,
     J. T. HARCOURT, J.P.

CHAPTER XXII.

OFF FOR THE INDIAN OCEAN.

WE SPENT our last evening in Melbourne, taking leave of the committee and private friends, and on the morning of October 7, were accompanied by a number of them to Williamstown wharf, where, after a season of prayer on board the steamer "Nubia," in which God's blessing was besought for our prosperous voyage to India, and upon our services there—a precious hour full of tenderest emotions,—our farewells all spoken, the steamer moved oceanward, from whose deck we could see Dr Dare, Brothers Simmons, Crouch, Marsh, and others, waving their handkerchiefs until the shore faded from our view.

The "Nubia" was one of the largest and staunchest of the steamers of the Peninsular and Oriental Line, but was not a fast boat. For the first few days the waters were smooth and calm, when suddenly it set in so stormy and rough that the captain was unable to leave the mails and passengers for South Australia at the usual port, and after lying to all night outside the harbor, only succeeded in discharging them at a land-locked harbor at Kangaroo Island early the next afternoon.

STORM AT SEA.

As we neared the waters of King George's Sound the extremely "nasty" weather as the sailors termed it, culmina

ted one dark night in a fearful storm. As it approached in
its great strength, the whistling of the wind through the
rigging of the staunch old vessel, now rolling in an ocean
trough, blended with the hoarse, melancholy moaning of the
sea, struck upon the ear with terrible significance. Then
the great winds shook our good ship, which was nothing
but a feather in their giant grasp, upon this boundless waste
of waters, which it rolled up mountain high or plunged
down fathoms deep as if in wild wrath, and now and then
engulfed us in the embrace of a great crashing sea wave,
which filled our decks with Niagara rivers which it seemed
could never flow off therefrom, and which, penetrating the
hatchways to the cabin, drenched us to the skin, as if to
show us how feeble and helpless we were as opposed to its
mighty strength. I never passed a night on the ocean so
full of terrible anxiety, and fear for possible results, and was
never so thankful for the morning light when Jesus said to
these surging waters, as to those of Galilee—"peace, be
still!" How forcibly this perilous night brought to mind
the terror of the little sailor boy, on such a night as this,
whose feelings some forgotten poet has expressed in these
lines:

> "Oh pilot, 'tis a fearful night,
> There's danger on the deep,
> I'll come and pace the deck with thee,
> I do not dare to sleep.
>
> "Go down," the sailor cries, "go down,
> This is no place for thee;
> Fear not but trust in Providence
> Where ever thou may'st be."

THE COLONY OF WEST AUSTRALIA.

On the afternoon of Oct. 16, we glided in out of this
treacherous sea among the little Islands of King George's
Sound to Princess Royal Harbor, and came to a stand-still
along side the town of Albany. No sooner had our anchor
dropped, than that good Wesleyan Missionary, Rev. T. C.

Lawrence, boarded the vessel in search of myself and family, he having learned that I was about leaving Melbourne, thought I might be prevailed upon to give a service of song, to the people of his town, while the steamer was taking coal, which it could not accomplish before midnight. Accordingly with my little family and my peripatetic organ we were oared to shore in the little boat in which my brother came out. The church bells were at once sounded to give the people notice of the service at eight o'clock that evening, and we were conducted to the parsonage where we were so rested and refreshed after our rude jostling on the water, that this missionary home has ever been a bright spot in our memory. It seemed then, and has always seemed since, that such a cup of tea as Mrs. Lawrence had prepared for us, never was matched in tea-land itself, much less wherever in the wide world this wonderful leaf has been imported.

THE GENUINE ABORIGINAL AND HIS BOOMERANG.

After we had rested, our host took us out to see the sights in Albany, which is a pretty little hamlet, and a principal coaling station for the mail steamships. Here for the first time, as we were landing we saw about fifteen men, women, and children who had come down to sell kangaroo, opossum, and wombat skins to the sailors, who proved to be the genuine aborigines of Australia, whom we had feared our curiosity would never be gratified in beholding, but which in the end was abundantly satisfied.

Without doubt these people are of the lowest type of humanity on the face of the earth, subsisting as they principally do upon roots and herbs, and many of them without other covering or garment than the skins of animals which they wear loosely from their shoulders. Their skin is black, and to this feature is added the appearance of filth, evidently never adding to their toilet a wash or bath, which taken in connection with their almost fleshless limbs, and the peculiar odor attending their presence made their vicinage anything but agreeable to the Anglo-Saxon. Having often read of the famous "boomerang" and its dexterous management as a weapon of offence and defence, in the handling of which these native Australians are superior to all others, our good missionary friend induced some of them to go out into a large open field, and throw this instrument for our amusement, and we confess to never having been so thoroughly interested in a feat of dexterity. The boomerang resembles a hugh ox-rib in size and shape, being carved on an angle of one hundred to one hundred and forty degrees and beveled sharp at each edge and end. It is made of iron wood, which is hard enough to cut, but not to batter or break. It is usually from twenty to thirty inches in length, an inch and a half wide, and about one half inch through the thickest part, and is thrown from the hand with a quick rotary motion, describing very remarkable curve, and returning drops at the actor's feet. In our presence they hurled it a distance of ten rods into the air, where after spinning round and round it returned to the thrower and was picked up by the children and handed to him. Several times they threw it so that it described a circle around a tree, coming back with force enough to kill a man if it had hit him. So correct is the aim of the natives with this curious instrument that it is in constant use for killing game, and as a weapon of warfare.

These natives also throw the spear with great accuracy of aim, which they fully proved to us by hitting three times in succession four shilling pieces, which we set up on the top of a split stick at a distance of five rods, relieving our pockets of an even dollar.

LAUGHABLE OPINIONS.

Notwithstanding railroads, steamboats, and telegraphs

have brought the lands and the nations so near to each
other, still some very queer ideas linger in the minds of
some of the people of each and every more remote land concerning their far off brethren.

In my own country I have found many people who imagined that Australia was mostly populated by the blacks,
when the fact is we met with them as scarcely as we see
the Indian east of the Mississippi river; while others have
talked of this great island as though nearly all its whole
population were convicts, which had been annually sent
there from Great Britain, but who are now in fact about as
scarce as the aboriginals themselves; on the other hand I
found quite a number of intelligent people in Australia, who
are laboring under the idea that the mass of the population
of America were Indians, and were surprised that I was
not versed in the vernacular of the wild Indians of the
west. Imagine the feelings of injured, western, metropolitan pride of a gentleman friend from Chicago, who was
about to land at Bombay, at being asked by an Australian
lady " if Chicago had any stores or shops, or if the goods
were all sold in bazaars kept by native Indians?"

CROSSING THE EQUATOR.

After the service of song, Mr. Lawrence took us off to
the steamer in his little boat. Here he walked the deck
with us in pleasant and profitable conversation, until the signal gun was fired to announce the vessel's departure, when
in the solemn midnight he bade us good-bye, giving me a
beautiful cane in token of remembrance.

After a passage of fourteen days with a goodly company
of passengers, and with but little to disturb the monotony,
we came in sight of the palm-tree girdled shores of the
Island of Ceylon, just before nightfall, so were obliged to
stop outside the harbor, but being unable to anchor, drifted
back with the current, and when the morning dawned we

found ourselves quite out of sight of the coveted haven. How wonderfully similar to our progress, many times, in the Christian life, in which so often the anchors of our faith loosen while gazing upon the very turrets of the heavenly city, leaving us in darkness and doubt, to struggle back to the haven of our hopes, from which we have so unconsciously drifted in our fancied security.

CHAPTER XXIII.

THE ISLAND OF CEYLON.

AT noon we were safely anchored in the exquisite bay, off Point de Galle, which is encircled by wooded hills of lovely tropical growth, chief among them the beautiful palm tree, that, inclining toward the sea, bend their crowns above the water. I shall never forget my first impressions as I gazed upon the scenes which were here spread before me; everything was so intensely fascinating and interesting, and so thoroughly unlike what I had pictured in my imagination, that I was fain to believe my own eyes. Almost the moment the Nubia came to anchor it was surrounded by native boats and boarded by scores of dark and yellow-visaged natives, looking like so many pieces of bronzed statuary, who came swarming over the bulwarks, eager to sell their carved curiosities of ebony, ivory and tortoise shell, and many of them so persistent in entreating passengers to go ashore in their little crafts as to oblige the ship's officers to drive them away with a whip.

We were kindly met on board by a native minister, Rev. William Willemburg, who, after seeing our luggage safe, guided us, in his queer little boat, through crowds of the Tamil and Cingalese, safely to shore, where he had a carriage, or "bandy," in waiting to take us along the banks of a rill bordered with palm trees, and through streets and groves fairly alive with bustling, clattering, wriggling natives—a locality crowded with confusion and the wrestling noises of a strange humanity—to the "Wesleyan Home," on "Richmond Hill," the quiet and charming residence of Rev. George Baugh, the superintendent of missions, situated in the center of an elevated compound of several acres. From this point we could look down upon sloping, green-canopied grove tops of the magnificent cocoanut palm, catching, now and then, bright glimpses of the waters of the bay, while through the tropic air we could almost catch the poetical strains of Heber, which ever breathe so softly o'er Ceylon's isle.

The beautiful twilight soon came, but sooner passed away, for darkness cometh here upon the land immediately after the sun sets, even as though a thick mantle were suddenly cast over the face of the earth. Through the darkness strange murmurings and noises come to our ears from all sides, while lights are seen flashing and disappearing in all directions below and around us. The wild chattering of the mischievous monkeys in the jungles and groves were amusing to the unpracticed ear, while thoughts of the venomous reptiles crawling upon the roof, and liable to enter our room from the open crevices beneath the eaves, and the rustling footsteps of the brown lizards promenading our matted floor, were anything but soothing to our nerves, somewhat startled as they had been by the good missionary's story of a deadly cobra snake which had crawled into an adjoining room but a few months before, and which relation he ended with the timely suggestion, "It is always well to look under your pillows, to dislodge poisonous reptiles, before lying down." Added to these mental anti-æsthetics came the weird noise of the poor heathen's "tom-tom," vainly trying to wake up his inanimate idols, so sad and pitiful to hear by those who worship the true and living God, "whose eye never slumbers nor sleeps."

THE MISSIONARY'S LIFE INSURANCE POLICY.

The hour for retiring came at last, and our host, remark-

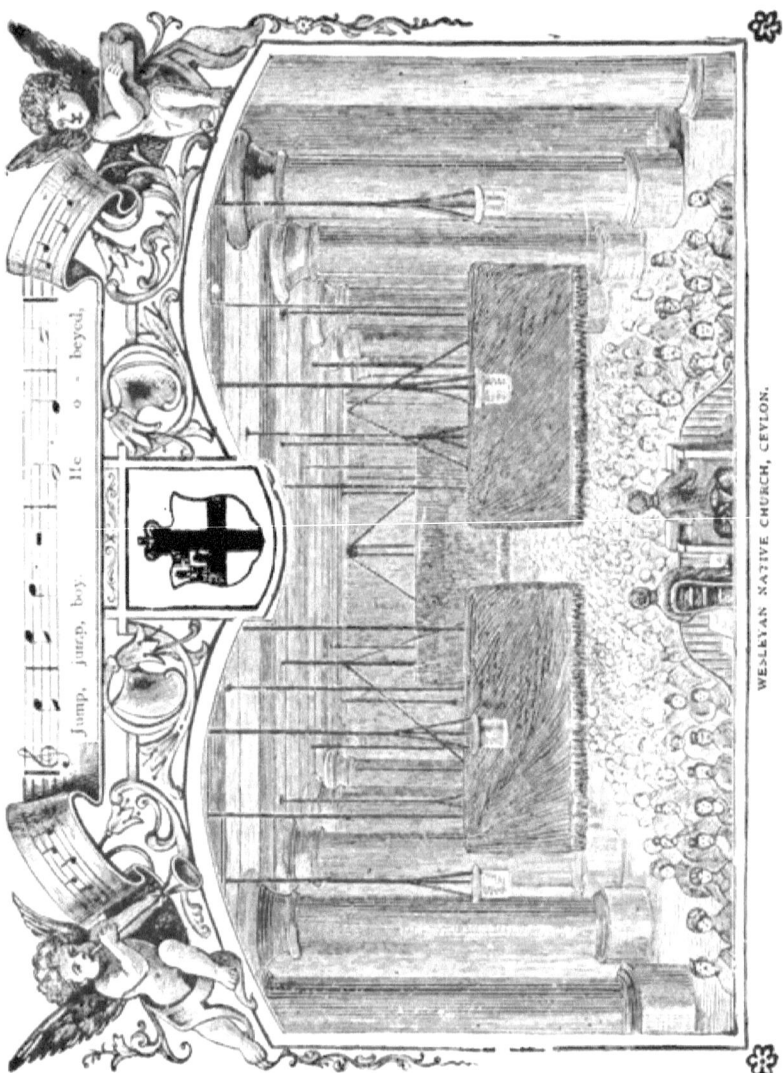

WESLEYAN NATIVE CHURCH, CEYLON.

ing, "You will please pray after I read," turned to the 121st Psalm, which seemed to me to be a veritable life insurance policy, formed by Deity itself, for the missionaries who should proclaim his word and his glory in the tropical climes of the earth:

"I will lift up mine eyes unto the hills, from whence cometh my help.

"My help cometh from the Lord, which made heaven and earth.

"He will not suffer thy foot to be moved; He that keepeth thee will not slumber.

"Behold, He that keepeth Israel shall neither slumber nor sleep.

"The Lord is thy keeper; the Lord is thy shade upon thy right hand.

"The sun shall not smite thee by day, nor the moon by night.

"The Lord shall preserve thee from all evil; He shall preserve thy soul.

"The Lord shall preserve thy going out and thy coming in from this time forth, and even for ever more."

How could we be otherwise than comforted, calmed and blessed by these beautiful lines of the psalmist and the refreshment which followed their reading in that "sweet hour of prayer?"

We retired to our beds and slept soundly and sweetly until the morning dawned, when, as I lifted my coat from the wall and was about putting it on, my wife discovered what she thought an enormous spider on the sleeve, but, calling our hostess' attention to it, was told that it was a venomous scorpion. I was not long in dispatching it. "Behold, I give unto you power to tread on serpents and scorpions."

SONG SERVICE IN CEYLON.

The second day after my arrival I gave my first service

in the Wesleyan Church at Point de Galle, before an audience of three hundred people, the most of whom spoke the English language, and gave every evidence of appreciation of the exercises. The day following I took stage for Matura, some twenty-eight miles distant, situated on the extreme southern coast of the island; the most of its population is native. The drive along the coast through groves of palm trees, meeting at every turn the nicely shaved, and beautiful combed Cingalese, with his Japanese umbrella always spread above him; the priests with long yellow gowns, smoothly shaved heads, and always carrying a palm leaf fan, together with the hundreds of native population in all styles of native dress and undress, was novel and strange.

At Matura I was made most welcome by Rev. Mr. Nicholson and his estimable lady, whose kind hospitality and society I had greatly enjoyed four years before while in Paris.

Preparations which had been made by these good missionaries for my comfort and pleasure seemed to greet me on every hand, while every preliminary had been arranged by them for my evening of song. After a refreshing nap at mid-day, I was awakened for a delightful dinner with several of Mr. Nicholson's native workers, who had come in from their respective fields of missionary labor to hear me sing hymns of "Jesus and his love." The little church was decorated with beautiful flowers, the perfume of the little blossom called the "temple flower" filling the structure with a fragrance which outvied the "spicy breezes" themselves. Here were gathered a goodly number of attentive listeners, upon whose ears my songs seemed to fall like old acquaintances, as many of them had been translated into the Tamil and Cingalese language; and they listened with the deepest attention and interest. The next morning we visited

THE HEATHEN CITY OF THE GODS,

And "Doudra," said to be the oldest Buddhist temple in Ceylon, some of the inscriptions upon the tablets and pillars of which are readily deciphered. The temple is on the summit of a steep eminence, and incloses a collossal statue of Buddha in a reclining posture, which is built of brick and mortar, and is gorgeously painted. In front of this statue is a table containing floral offerings, prominent among which was the temple flower, a beautiful, white, and wonderfully fragrant blossom, somewhat resembling our cape jasmine. We paid a visit to a wealthy native whose residence is on a point of land extending quite into the sea, and who has given Bro. Nicholson ground whereon to build his new school. Here we had a fine view of the sea, with its huge breakers rolling up against the rocks, and splashing their briny foam at our feet; while the cocoanut, banana, bread fruit, and palm trees were on every hand, the latter ever inclining their tufted heads toward the water, as if in grateful recognition to that prolific element of their life and growth. After a very pleasant forenoon, we were invited to lunch with the Presbyterian minister, and went home with our friends to dinner at six o'clock, returning next morning to our pleasant quarters at "Richmond Hill." After a noon-day nap and "tiffin" we seated ourselves on the wide pleasant verandah, which encircled the whole house, and whose overhanging roof formed a comforting shade. While we were looking at some coffee bushes, one of the native servants climbed a cocoanut tree for our amusement. He fastened small wisps of the cocoanut bark to his ankles, tying them together, and clasping the tree with his hands, and the soles of his feet, with a series of hops and jumps he ascended it as easily as a squirrel and as nimbly as a frog, throwing the greatly prized fruit at our feet. The floors of the English houses are covered with a carpet or matting woven from the cocoa bark; the native vehicles are covered with its leaves; and the houses of the natives thatched with them; cocoa oil is burned in their lamps, curry is combined with the flesh of the nut, making a most palatable dish, and its milk is considered a great luxury.

We saw the Areca palm growing in every native garden, being planted near the walls or water courses, with its thin, polished stem, and crown of green leaves, after running to the heigth of forty feet. Just beneath its leaves are its nuts which the natives prepare with a lime made from calcined shells, and the leaf of the betal pepper, for the purpose of chewing. If possible it is more offensive than American tobacco, as the combined articles color the saliva so deep a red, that the lips and teeth look as though they were bathed in blood.

After a pleasant day in this angel land, but not land of angels, we gave our second song service in Point de Galle to a large audience, and I greatly enjoyed the sweet Christian spirit which pervaded all present. Here I was deeply impressed with the truth that the language of Christ and his religion is the same the wide world over; while the name of Jesus has the same sweet sound, and significance.

OUR VISIT TO COLUMBO.

The next morning as the regular stage had overlooked our order, we were assisted by Bros. Baugh and Willemburg in hiring a special one to take us to Columbo. We started about eleven o'clock, with a driver—and a boy to blow the stage horn as we advanced to give the natives warning to get out of the way and avoid being run over.

About seven miles out I was pleasantly surprised to have a good native brother, who had attended my service the evening before, bring out to the coach presents of choice tropical fruits of several kinds, cakes and sweet-meats, and with many expressions of pleasure and good will wished us.

"God speed." I am sorry I have forgotten his name, but I shall never forget his kindly countenance as he handed me up these tokens of his friendship and love in this far-off land. Our entire drive—a distance of seventy-four miles—lay along by the sea, through avenues of palm trees; native houses and villages being scattered thickly all the way. We were meeting and passing such crowds of humanity all the time that it seemed to us like a great fair or parade day. We changed horses several times and stopped once at a government house called "house of rest," for lunch or "tiffin." It was very odd to see these black people standing in the waters of the brooks and little inlets, pouring water upon their heads from little earthen cups called "chatties," their bodies being previously anointed with cocoanut oil.

We arrived at Columbo at eight o'clock in the evening, thoroughly fatigued, and with thoroughly aroused appetites. We were at once made at home at the residence of Rev. John Scott, the superintendent of the Wesleyan Mission, where, with delicious soup, curry and rice, tender roast of beef, etc., our cravings were speedily satisfied.

This home is pleasantly situated near the water, its compound extending to the sea beach; the grateful breezes from these waters, and the lullaby of the surf, as it beat upon the pebbly shore, soon brought us the sweetest and most refreshing slumber. We arose greatly invigorated on the following morning and the day proved to us a memorable Sabbath. Early in the day we attended a Sabbath-school session or Bible class, conducted by Miss Scott, a lady of rare mental gifts, and cheerful, and loving in her work. The chapel was in the same compound as the home, and here we heard our American Sunday-school songs sung by the children of Ceylon. The season was most precious and refreshing, and we all worshiped with the same books, and the same songs, the same Savior.

In the evening we listened to a most excellent sermon by Rev. I. Landon, and, just previous, as the twilight was falling, I gave my song sermon, "About Jesus, our Savior." My little slips were well distributed, and many who came were unable to gain admission on account of the chapel having been filled a few minutes after the door was opened. So new was the character of the exercises, and so eager and attentive were the people present, the children being especially attentive and participative, that all seemed loth to leave the edifice, while I gained new confidence that through the voice of song the gospel truths would eventually reach the hearts of the heathen of every land and clime.

We spent some time on Monday in looking at the sights in and about Columbo, which has a population of 100,000, is the capital of Ceylon, and is its principal seaport. One portion of the town is open, while the other is fortified. The interior has some appearance of an English town. Its harbor, which is small, is defended by several forts.

In the afternoon, taking my eldest son, we loaded my organ on a wagon to visit Mortura to give my first evening of song in that city. On the road we encountered a religious procession, composed of several hundred natives, making the loudest and most discordant sounds, on all sorts of rude instruments, which evidently seemed to emit the grandest noise to them. I could not help thinking that this was a strange prelude to my singing; but it it fired my heart to sing with new ardor the sweet, old story of His love. Passing by a number of cinnamon groves, our curiosity led us to stop at one of them, where we peeled off the green bark from one of the shrubs, and took it away as a curiosity. The soil where this shrub grows most luxuriously, has a white appearance, which reminds one of the famous alkaline beds which we see in crossing our own continent.

MEN WEARING COMBS.

On arriving at the Wesleyan church, we found it filled with an audience of three hundred, composed entirely of Cingalese and Tamil, and that the missionary, my son and myself, were the only ones present who could speak English. They sat before me for two hours, as straight and attentive as so many sphinx, the men presenting a queer appearance, with their long hair gathered on the back of their heads in a knot or chignon, as the ladies would term it, with beautiful, tortoise-shell, round combs, the finely carved rims of which rose like a frontlet over their foreheads. The Rev. Bro. Carter interpreted my service as nearly as possible, and we sang two or three songs in English, Tamil, and Cingalese in concert, among which was "Happy Land," "I will Sing for Jesus," and "Rock of Ages." In the course of this exercise the old familiar verse kept recurring to my mind:

"Ten thousand, thousand are their tongues,
But all their joys are one."

The church was built of brick and mortar, after the style of adobe, as they call such buildings in California. The roof was very heavy, and supported by great strong beams running horizontally, and the whole of a thickness to completely baffle the penetrating heat of the sun.

Immediately below these beams is seen the punka or long fan extending the length of the church, being a wooden frame to which canvas or muslin is attached, and which is kept swinging from the vestibule or outside with a cord and pully by the native boys, thus giving comfort to the audience during hours of service.

This punka is one of the luxuries quite peculiar to tropical climes, and to a European has a more grateful remembrance than even "spicy breezes." We drove back at the close of the services to our pleasant home with brother Scott, the soft air and moonlight being especially delightful, and the next day received a call from Rev. J. I. Jones, the bishop's commissary for Columbo, who was one of the most devout and agreeable men I ever had the pleasure of meeting. In his charming company outer robes and ecclesiastical differences were lost sight of, and the robes of righteousness which so palpably clothed his life and character were only visible. According to previous arrangement we completed the preliminaries in regard to holding an evening of song under his auspices in the large club room. Had it not been for a severe storm of thunder and rain we should have had a crowded house, but as it was, a very elite audience of nearly all the English speaking people were in attendance. Before entering the room the reverend gentleman drew me aside to a private ante-room saying, "we are now alone, let us ask God's blessing upon the service." We knelt together and fervently addressed the throne of grace and felt as though our petitions had been answered during the entire meeting.

"O'ER HILLS WITH VERDURE CLAD."

On Thursday, Nov. 11th, we took train for Kandy, the ancient capital of Ceylon, accomplishing the ride of seventy miles in four hours and a half. The scenery on this trip was most enchanting, combining as it did the grandeur of the Alpine view, with the splendor of tropical vegetation. It was a perfect panorama of mountain, hill, valley, plain, gorge, ravine and cascade, of foliage, fruit and flower, with great "paddi" or rice fields, and coffee bush plantations on every hand, in which were to be seen the natives at their accustomed toil. The resident missionary, Rev. Mr. Tebb, was awaiting at the station, and escorted us to his home.

THE PEREDENIA GARDENS.

On Friday morning our kind host took us to the public gardens, which overlook the river on three sides, and though not remarkable for their display of flowers or artificial beauty, were grand in their wealth of stately, tropical trees, planted on an area of one hundred and fifty acres. We entered the grounds through an avenue of Indian rubber or Cantuche trees, whose formidable array of red roots above ground, looked like brick piled up in many fanciful and grotesque shapes. On every hand were the Taliput, the Palmyra, the Katool and the slender Arica palm trees, and the famous Travelers tree of Madagascar, which in many instances grew fifty feet in height. We were also much interested with the display of flowering, creeping vines, and the "jungle rope" whose strong vegetable sinews spread from trunk to trunk, and clasped them together in serpent like coils.

In the evening I gave my service to a most attentive and intelligent English speaking audience, who made evident their enjoyment during the hour and a half of song, which was followed by another service the succeeding evening, at which also my novel service seemed to give great satisfaction and pleasure to a still larger audience. In this connection I must not omit that Kandy is the home of Hon. J. H. Eaton, a most able man of letters, of extensive European travel, and who was educated in one of the finest universities of Great Britain. Not only is he a lawyer or barrister of legal reputation, but also an able and eloquent local preacher and *advocate* of the cause of Christ.

THE COFFEE ESTATE OF "ROSENATH."

Our hostess kindly took us in a "bandy" some three miles distant, to the large coffee estates of her brother. After winding round and round the hills, and stopping to gaze from terrace to terrace in our ascent, from which we caught charming glimpses of the little lake, park, and town at our feet, and the peak of old Mount Adams in the distance, we approached the pleasantest little spot imaginable, most pleasingly located upon a tree-embowered terrace, with delightful rising grounds in the rear, which were gemmed with flowering shrubs and plants, where stood the residence of our host, its roof and sides completely covered with three varieties of creeping roses, which were then in full bloom, and from which the estate had evidently received its pretty name.

Here we took tiffin with I. L. Dewer, Esq., a courteous and wealthy gentleman, who both owned and managed his extensive estates, at which the richest and rarest food and fruit of the tropics was set before us. We were then shown the coffee in its different stages of growth and preparation for the market, and looked upon the dark green foliage of this evergreen tree or shrub, whose gray-barked trunk is generally from two to four feet high, and whose long branches are covered with beautiful leaves and white blossoms, in thick clusters, nature's process of budding, flowering and ripening going on upon the same branches and twigs at all seasons of the year. Returning to the verandah of the house, we passed a pleasant hour, which was only disturbed by an occasional thumping upon the roof, which excited my curiosity to the extent of venturing an inquiry as to its cause, when I was very quietly and unconcernedly informed that it was a snake. Verily, "there is no rose without a thorn," even in such a delightful spot as this.

Well, the glorious Sabbath is with us once again in this famous island, and here, as elsewhere, we have the privilege of attending divine worship. Some three hundred worshipers assembled, and we are listening to the dear old gospel. Our preacher is Advocate Eaton, the first native minister in Ceylon, and a fine spiritual sermon he gives us from the text: " Awake, thou that sleepest."

A large congregation was in attendance upon my song sermon in the evening, nearly all of whom audibly responded to the Bible readings and the singing of the old hymns, and at the prayer and inquiry meeting which followed, two or three professed to find peace in believing.

On Monday we returned to Columbo, where, the same evening, I gave a service to the children at the Petty schools and church. The little Cingalese seemed just as susceptible to the songs and the word as children in any part of the world, and joined as heartily in the service, Mr. L. Isaacs d' Silva, editor of the "Ceylon Friend," having translated several of my songs for their especial benefit. This school is one of the best in Ceylon, and the little ones were under the best of discipline, having for their superintendent Rev. S. R. Wilkins. While most of the older people of Ceylon still blindly adhere to the idolatrous rites of their fathers, the children seem wonderfully attracted to the gospel through the medium of sacred song.

SERVICE IN A "REST HOUSE."

On the route back to Point de Galle, we stopped some eighteen miles from Columbo, to give a service at Kaltura, a mission station under the care of Rev. I. A. Spaar. Here we were entertained at a "rest house," which are so frequently to be found in Ceylon, wherein travelers, when wearied, can enter and escape the torrid rays of the sun. Some of these places are really country hotels, as was the case with this.

After my dear, tired wife and boys had retired to rest, overcome by fatigue, I gave my service in one of the rooms of the house, which had been improvised for the occasion, and furnished with a motley collection of chairs, stools, and blocks of wood for seats. How wonderfully weird it was to look down upon this closely seated assemblage, whose bare shoulders shone like bronze, and whose sharp, black eyes from stolid, upturned faces, pierced me from every side, as I sang amid an almost breathless silence, the "Old, old Story."

The following morning, by special invitation, we breakfasted with Mr. and Mrs. Spaar, and a novel meal it was to us, on account of the addition of "Hoppers" to a usual breakfast, a most delicious cake made of cocoanut and rice, and usually served with sugar or syrup. On this occasion one variety was made of pounded rice and grated cocoanut and a little arrak; another of the cocoanut shredded; another with an egg broken and dropped in the centre of the cake, and each baked in chattys, a small earthen cup.

We reached our old quarters at "Richmond Hill," in the evening, glad to avail ourselves of an early hour for rest and sleep.

The next day we dined with a number of Wesleyan native ministers, and in the evening I gave my farewell song sermon to a large gathering of people, who manifested intense interest from the opening to its close. Then taking our luggage, we repaired to a hotel near the steamboat landing, for an early start for India the following morning.

THE GRAND OLD SHIP, MIRZAPORE.

Along came this great steamer of the Peninsula and Oriental Line, under the command of Commodore Parish, a thorough and skillful seaman, and an earnest Christian, who held prayers in the saloons as regular as the striking of the morning bells.

Never did we enjoy a ride on an ocean steamship as this, with its noble captain, pleasant passengers, refreshing punkas, spacious saloons, airy and pleasant cabins and inviting tables. Greatly adding to the pleasures of the voyage, was our meeting with Hon. I. M. Francis, U. S. Minister to Greece, as well as the veteran editor of the Troy *Daily Times*, in my own native state of New York, and his wife, together with two other American ladies traveling with them en route from China.

OLD COURT HOUSE STREET, DALHOUSIE SQUARE, CALCUTTA.

GOVERNOR GENERAL'S PALACE, CALCUTTA.

CHAPTER XXIV.

TO AND AT CALCUTTA.

A THREE days' sail brought us along side Madras, where our ship dropped anchor and remained eight hours. On approaching the city we were quite alarmed at seeing our dear country's flag at half mast over the office of our resident Consul there, and soon learned from the papers brought on board, of the death of our Vice President, Henry Wilson. Hardly had our steamer's engines ceased their motion, when swarms of the Tamil men came shouting over the high surfs, in their frail bark canoes, and clambered on board our vessel, eager and anxious to dispose of their wares, consisting of embroideries, sandal wood fans, carved images of animals, and various articles, for all of which we soon learned the purchaser sets the correct price of them, and not the vender. A number of native jugglers came on board and performed most wonderful feats of jugglery, which almost led us to repudiate the laws of nature and those which govern the human body, and which would, I am sure, put to shame all the feeble attempts at the supernatural practiced by the so-called spiritual mediums of my own country. Not only would they eat knives, take out their eyes, grow plants, swallow snakes, but would drink water mingled with three different colors of paint, to spit the decoction from their mouths into three separate piles of colored dry sand.

Madras was a very cheerless looking city from the deck of our steamer, and it seems strange that it should have been built down so closely to the shores of the sea, without any kind of a harbor whatever. Taking on a supply of ice and fruits, we sailed away up the Bay of Bengal with slight head winds, at the rate of nine knots an hour, and on the following day we find recorded in our journal, "the most pleasant day we ever spent on ocean wave." Awnings were spread over the entire deck, and hanging half way down the ship's sides, protected us from the fearful rays and glare of the burning sun, and the cool, grateful ripples of air produced by noiseless waving of the punkas, with an atmosphere of velvet softness, and a calm still sea, in whose waters were prismed all the colors of the light, there is no adjective in our store of language to adequately describe the beauty, comfort and tranquillity of these hours."

Another lovely day, and blessed one, for it is the holy Sabbath. In the morning the entire ship's crew, except those required on duty at the time, came up on deck, in full nautical dress suit, for review, each one raising his right hand and bowing to the captain as he marched down in their front as they stood in file, the native sailors being dressed in loose white gowns each carrying a bright pocket handkerchief in his hand. Divine service was held both morning and evening. We found it a real pleasure to use the piano on board this ship, for, unlike most instruments at sea, it was a good one and in tune.

THE HOOGLY OR GANGES,

Early on the morning of Nov. 29, we were in sight of the lighthouses and island at the mouth of this mighty river of which so much has been written by both missionary and tourist. But owing to the absence of flood-tide we were obliged to anchor between the capes which guard the river's entrance into the bay of Bengal, until eight o'clock the next morning, when we had a charming sail up the stream, the scenery upon whose banks, though not particularly tropical, was very pretty, although not enhanced by the many brick kilns scattered here and there.

CALCUTTA, THE CITY OF PALACES.

As we near Calcutta on these waters held in pagan veneration for so many centuries, and in which so many lives have been sacrificed to superstition and in idolatrous worship, we find them to resemble in depth and width our Hudson, as it appears above West Point. Landing in boats at the wharf, amid a babel of chattering unknown tongues, and a din of noise which is entirely new and novel to our ears, we were met by Rev. J. M. Thoburn, bearing to us, from the ladies of the "Union Missionary American Home," the very kind invitation to make *their* home *ours* while in Calcutta.

Dr. Thoburn kindly escorted us thither, where the first to greet us was Miss Josie Kimball whom we had often seen at her home in New York, and who is now engaged as a missionary teacher, doing efficient and successful work for the Master. Here we were soon domiciled in spacious comfortable apartments, furnished both after the American and Oriental style. This home under the supervision of "The Woman's Union Mission Society of America for heathen lands," was established thirteen years previous to our visit, by Miss Brittan its present president or manager, who has associated with her twelve American ladies as teachers. They have already instructed seventy native women, who have become assistant teachers, thus bringing into execution a practical plan for the restoration of women, here in India, to her lawful sphere. My good wife was often invited by Miss Brittan or her associates to accompany them to the "Zenanas" or homes of the wealthy Baboos, as well as to the dwellings of those of inferior caste and had thereby a rare opportunity of gaining some knowledge of the details of this Zenana mission work.

First, these teachers gain access to the families of a household by teaching embroidery, fancy needle work, and elementary lessons. These families are often quite large, from the fact that the betrothed of the sons, live with the intended step-mother from childhood up to, and after marriage, and in many cases fifty persons, consisting of the Baboo and wife, their married sons and their wives and children, their unmarried sons and their betrothed wives, the widows and children of deceased sons, are to be found living under one roof, the female portion of which household, is secluded from the outside world by bars and veils. In the course of this needle instruction, the teacher having previously mastered the language, seeks to impress upon these women that industry is preferable to idleness, and that knowledge is one of the gifts as necessary to them, as to their husbands, sons, and brothers, which acquirements will make them happier, and better as well as thoroughly useful in whatever sphere of life they may be placed. Mrs. Phillips was kindly received in these homes in company with the teachers, and freely conversed with the occupants, and heard their simple instruction by interpretation. These women seemed pleased to show her their toilets and jewels, but in no case was she allowed to handle them, as the touch of a Christian is considered to so pollute these articles as to necessitate a thorough cleansing, if not their destruction.

The sad fate of the widows of these people called out her deep sympathy; they are consigned to an almost solitary life in the most wretched apartments of the father-in-law's home, and they are not allowed to wear jewels, so evidently one of the greatest privileges of the women of Hindostan. The mothers consider themselves very unfortunate by the birth of a daughter, who, whatever their affection for, is taken from them and affianced when but a few years old, and are correspondingly greatly rejoiced in giving birth to a son, for he can remain with her as long as she lives.

While the missionaries of India are well housed, and have no trouble in obtaining food, and have it prepared for them without any trouble of their own, their efforts to overcome caste, and to find means of approach to the hearts of the people, wherein to sow the precious seed of the gospel, are full of anxious care, great trial and perplexity, whose depths cannot be described by pen.

OUR FIRST DAYS IN HINDOSTAN.

At an early hour each morning we were awakened by our soft-footed waiter who tapped gently on the lattice door of our room, bringing to us our "chotohazra" or early breakfast, consisting of tea, toast, oranges and bananas, which we were supposed to eat sitting in our beds, after which we arose and took our baths, and after completing our toilets were ready to receive the early morning call which is so common in India. We breakfast at eleven o'clock, dine at five and have tea at seven, served in the drawing-room or verandas, and have supper at ten.

On Wednesday evening, Dec. 1, I gave my first song service to a gathering of about four hundred people, most of whom spoke the English language, and among whom were quite a number of missionaries who seemed to greatly enjoy the hour of song, while I thanked God for the privilege of singing songs of peace and glory in the great Hindostan capital. The next morning Mr. William Meyers called to take us to visit the markets, a long and commodious structure one-half of which was occupied by native venders, and the other half by European. My wife and little son riding home therefrom in a palanquin carried on the shoulders of four natives.

The same day we visited some English stores for articles

of which we stood in need, also purchasing "sun topeys," a sort of cork hat for protecting the head from the fierce rays of that orb, to whom it was never safe to expose that portion of the body. In the evening we spent a most pleasant hour with Miss Leslie, author of "One By One," "Guard Thy Tongue," and other poems of equal merit.

BANYAN TREE.

In company with Dr. Thoburn, Miss Brittan, and a party of twelve, we sailed down the Hoogly six miles in a boat chartered for the purpose to the garden which is called Eden, named after an accomplished sister of a former governor-general and not after paradise. It is the great resort for promenade of Calcutta for European and native citizens alike. On entering the garden we saw a live cobra de capello whose bite is deadly poison. Dr. Thoburn pinned it to the ground with the point of his umbrella until we all had an opportunity of seeing its distended hood and then himself dispatched it, not being able to call on certain Hindoo servants to kill this reptile, as they think the spirits of their deceased relatives dwell in animals, reptiles and insects, and they might in this act be slaying their fathers or grandfathers.

The five servants who accompanied us spread our luncheon beneath a banyan tree covering over an acre of ground, presenting with its huge parent trunk and myriad tree-column supported branches, one of the most curious sights we ever gazed upon. That evening, in company with Dr. Thoburn, I took dinner with Sir Richard Muir, a government officer in British India.

Our first Sabbath in this city we attended morning service at the M. E. Church in Dhuremtollah Street and listened to a deeply interesting and spiritual sermon by Rev. Dr. J. M. Thoburn, who is the superintendent of American missions in Calcutta, and who is eminently successful in carrying out the work which was inaugurated by the world's evangelist, Rev. William Taylor.

In the evening I gave my first song sermon in this church, which was attended by an immense audience and at which four persons rose for prayers. I felt quite anxious to know how many of my hearers were professed Christians; and having requested such to rise great was my astonishment to have the entire assembly stand up. Not till then did I learn that their idea of a Christian was any one who wears European clothing or garments.

REVIVAL SERVICES.

My friends thinking my singing the songs of Jesus in this old city of heathen temples and idolatry, seemed to warrant a special effort, it was concluded to commence holding two meetings a day; one in the morning at seven o'clock, and the other in the evening. These were all held in the Methodist Episcopal Chapel, which seats six hundred, has no ceilings, but an overhanging roof, beneath the eaves of which ventilation is given the structure on all sides, and being without glass windows, but with latticed blinds, was as free to the birds of the air, as to the people. For a while but few of the natives attended these services at which Dr. Thoburn preached and I sang, while the English people seemed to manifest that indifference so peculiar to large centres, in which it is so difficult to reach the masses with the preached word. Yet greatly aided by Christian workers we persevered until the interest began to increase, and many expressed a desire for the prayers of God's people. These meetings in Calcutta did not compare with those held in the cities of our own land, but taking the surroundings and influences into consideration, they seemed to result even more successfully, than many held in our more civilized and highly favored land. After one of the morning services a native came to me and asked for a Bible, which I gave him with an earnest prayer that it might open up to him the way of salvation. On taking it into his hands he manifested the greatest delight, and moved off looking at it as gratified as a lad with his first top.

IDOLATROUS SCENES AND LOCALITIES.

One morning after service, with a party of " workers " from the " home," we visited the Kali Ghaut, where poor deluded souls were bowing down to inanimate images of wood and stone.

We were under the guidance of Rev. Mr. Muckagee, a converted Brahim. Once this excellent preacher of the gospel, a man of great faith and piety, muttered the same prayers and bowed down at the same shrines, which we now saw his countryman doing, and it was most pitiful to witness his sadness, as we together looked upon them in these acts of idolatrous worship, for the abandonment of which and acceptance of the Savior, he had been forsaken by his parents, and kindred. Here we saw the natives bathing in the waters of the supposed sacred Ganges, and dipping in or sprinkling with its waters the young kids and other offerings they were about to lay at the feet of their different idols. Here animals were being slain, flowers borne, beads counted, and self infliction made upon the body.

Here too we came upon a wretched Fakir, sitting motionless over a slow fire, all covered with ashes from the burning embers beneath him, receiving their smoke in his eyes until the tears therefrom had worn channels down his wan and sunken cheeks. We talked with this poor misguided creature, and learned that for some sixteen years, he had repaired to this place for this daily torture. In this miserable locality where crowds were kneeling before their shrines, and offering up sacrifices and gifts to their idols, we were importuned by most wretched beggars, many of them fearfully deformed, and uttering the most pitiful cries for help.

NATIVE LIFE IN INDIA

DESCRIPTION OF THE IDOLS.

The following description of some of the principal idols worshiped in India was given me by brother Muckagee:

"The idol Juggernauth, by whose huge car worshipers consider it a great merit to be run over and crushed to death, and which has been suppressed by British laws, is represented by the dark-faced figure of Juggernauth on the right, with his green-faced brother on the left, and yellow-faced sister between them, with ornamental bands or collars of crimson, yellow and green hanging from their necks.

The heathen god Kishna is represented standing upon the red-hooded head of the blue serpent Kaligua in upright coil. Two forms on either side of this god, with female heads, breasts and arms attached to serpent tails, are the wives of Kaligua, whom Kishna is said to have destroyed. There is much that is mysterious connected with Hindoo mythology, and the representation of the incarnate Kishna, standing upon the head of a huge serpent, and totally destroying it, reminds one of the "old serpent" having his head bruised by the seed of the women. Yet the Hindoos themselves know nothing of the typical meaning which seems to be attached to some of their idols, but worship them blindly without being able to give any explanation or reason therefor.

Doorga, the ten-handed goddess, was much worshiped in Bengal in September and October, is represented with her hands full of warlike weapons, among which the bow and spear are prominent, and as standing with one foot upon the back of a lion, with the other resting upon the shoulder of the giant Azoor, whose breast the raging lion is rending with his teeth and claws. Doorga is also worshiped with her elephant-headed son, Ganesh, seated in her lap, with his arms clasped about her body, which son the devotee is commanded to invoke before the mother, lest he be despised on account of his deformity and uncouth appearance.

The goddess Kali is the wife of Mohedena, the third person in the Hindoo idol triad, and is so generally worshiped throughout India that her image is to be seen in almost every Hindoo home, except among the devotees of Kishna. She assumes different forms on different occasions, is exceedingly bloodthirsty, and is represented in one form with a great knife in the left hand, with a crimson clot of blood upon her right hand and foot, while with the toes of the left foot she holds a severed human head suspended by the hair. The most revolting human sacrifices were formerly offered to her, but the cruel practice has been discontinued by an edict of the British government. Thieves and robbers always invoke this goddess before going out on their predatory excursions.

Sharasnati, the goddess of learning, is represented as sitting among the leaves of a lotus tree and playing upon a guitar, while one of her feet rests upon an expanded flower. Young Hindoo students worship her at certain seasons of the year, she being pictured out on their desks, inkstands and pens. But those who commence the study of the English language soon discontinue doing her reverence, finding in industry and perseverance a surer and a better way of acquiring knowledge.

Mohedena, or the great god, is represented in a sitting posture, clothed in tiger skins, and intoxicated with the fumes of burning hemp, the smoke of which is curling about his head. He is worshiped in several other forms, however, and much that is revolting and indecent is connected with these rites.

The monkey god is worshiped because, when his devotion and loyalty to his master was questioned he tore open his breast and showed his heart, in which the idols Rama and his wife were to be seen enthroned. In honor of this proof of devoted service to Rama, all monkeys are held sacred by the Hindoos, who suffer them to commit all kinds of depredations upon their property without molestation or retaliation.

Garoier, a horrid-looking, yellow-bodied, green-winged old bird, with web feet, an old friend of Rama and his father, who imprisoned Raban, the king of Lanka, or Ceylon, together with his chariot and horses, in his monstrous beak, as he was kidnapping Sista, the wife of Rama, and who had to be slain before that king was rescued, is also an object of devout worship.

Jagatdhata, who is believed to support or hold up the earth, is a four-armed goddess, and is represented as seated upon the back of a human-faced tiger, who, in turn, is standing upon the head of an elephant. She is another form of Shera's wife, and is accredited as having slain a giant who was a terror to men and gods alike.

Other Hindoo idols are a representation of Mohedena begging rice from his wife, who has assumed a form known and worshiped as Annapurna, signifying full of rice and alms; Lakshmi, the goddess of wealth, and Saraswati, the goddess of learning, both the reputed daughters of Mohedena and Doorga, standing together on blossoms of the lotus tree, as also Krishna and his wife, Radhika, who are pictured out in the act of dancing beneath the branches of a palm."

After leaving these pagan sights behind we visited the China and Borrough bazaars, where, in little, narrow streets, the natives display their merchandise, sitting about like so many tailors on their benches, and where, among other trifles, we purchased several pictures representing their heathen deities. We took tea with Mr. Myers, a gentleman of wealth, who, with his wife, had been converted from the Jewish faith, and who were most generous and faithful Christians. His partner in business, though a Catholic, was a constant attendant upon our services, and has since joined the Methodist Church.

In the evening we came together again in our services, in which the interest increased, and where three persons acknowledged finding peace as it is in Jesus, and this made our hearts thankful. The members of Dr. Thoburn's church seemed full of activity and willingness in the work, in which we were strongly supported by Mrs. May and several other efficient and influential workers, prominent among whom was a young Mr. Oakes, by whose untiring efforts a large seaman's church has since been organized in that city, and whose preliminary work in this direction was the boarding of vessels as they came into harbor and obtaining permission to hold services on board while in port, by this means bringing many sailors to Christ. He afterward came to Drew Theological Seminary, in New Jersey, and there fitted for still greater efficiency in the gospel ministry.

THE BURNING GHATS.

The next afternoon we went to the enclosure where the natives burn their dead on the funeral pile, and saw several bodies thus publicly cremated. One husband was in the act of burning the body of his wife which had been laid upon the pile, covered with sandal-wood, her beautiful long hair depending from the ghastly pile. He muttered over some rite, when placing rice upon her mouth, he ignited a sort of bamboo broom, touched the flaming torch to her hair and ran swiftly around the fiercely burning mound three times. He then turned to me and said "My duty is done. Can you tell me any better way? She was a good woman, etc." I was so filled with horror that I could make no reply, and stood there in silence; my wife not desiring to look any longer upon such scenes we turned away.

The following forenoon we attended Miss Leslie's school examination and heard some most excellent papers read by native young ladies who had been placed under her careful tuition for months, and some of them for years, previous. My good wife had the honor of being selected to distribute the prizes upon this occasion. The same day we attended the closing exercises of a free school for native children, under the direction of the Wesleyans, and the principal was assisted by native teachers, who sent their servants for the little girls each morning, and returned them to their homes when their tasks were ended. Prizes were awarded at this school for the best specimen of fancy work in worsted, as well as for achievements in a mental direction.

On this day we were invited to dine with a number of pleasant people, at the residence of Dr. N. Naylor, a most estimable man and earnest Christian, and whose generosity I have tangible reasons for remembering, because of his unsolicited gift of ten pounds to my mission hall fund.

NONE TO BELIEVE HIM BUT JESUS.

On Friday evening, Dec. 17, I gave my final song sermon in Calcutta, in Dr. Thoburn's church, taking for its subject "The Way of Salvation." At its close a very notoriously wicked man arose and said, "since I joined this meeting I no more do my business, which is a wretched one of swearing people into prison, and then swearing them out again for money; you know me. I begin to-day to do better."

Dr. Thoburn took pains to enquire after this man, and found that his assertions regarding his nefarious business were true. I felt thankful to hear such a resolve from even such a man, and although I do not know whether this poor sinner ever came out into the great liberty of Christ's followers, I know that the forgiving Lord hath taken his word if it was uttered in sincerity and faith.

Before leaving the city several of my friends desired me to give a few evenings of song in aid of their work, dividing the proceeds. This I did in Dr. Miln's Presbyterian church, Rev. Mr. Ross' Baptist church, and in Rev. Mr. Hollam's, as also in the English Wesleyan church, which were all well attended.

On account of the general occupation of the people in preparing for the reception of the Prince of Wales, we were obliged to discontinue our day meetings, and having hired the large theatre for Sabbath evening Dr. Thoburn preached and I led the singing. At least one thousand people were assembled, and several requested the prayers of God's people.

My final evening of song was to a goodly attendance in Rev. C. Hollam's Baptist church, and I was never in better voice and spirits.

ARRIVAL OF THE PRINCE OF WALES.

By this time the city was thoroughly aglow with expectancy of the arrival of the Prince of Wales, the future Emperor of India, and all other matters were set aside in order to do becoming " honor to the King." The preparations which had been and were being made were on the most gigantic scale. Triumphal arches of great width and many feet in height had been reared at the entrances of the most prominent streets, grand displays were upon every street corner, while miles on miles of public and private buildings were festooned, garlanded and decorated with the richest magnificence. The Hoogly river was crowded for a long distance above and below the city with greater and lesser ships, whose sides and rigging were literally clothed with bunting, with the flags of all nations flying from their masts.

The great British man-of-war Serapsis, has come to anchor with the Prince on board, and, preparations for his landing have commenced. The wharves and streets are closely packed with at least one hundred thousand people, of all nations, lands and climes, who mingled with the gaily dressed natives from all parts of India, turbaned with the brightest colors, present a strange and novel spectacle. The Maharajas and Rajahs, native kings and princes, sparkling from head to foot with glittering gems, clad in rich velvet and satin vestments, broidered with silver and gold, proudly wait upon their finely caparisoned steeds at the front of their bronze-faced retinues, with the finest feathers pinned to their turbans with diamonds which gleam out of the throng like so many resplendent stars.

The reception committee have strewn the walk on which the Prince is to pass from the landing to his carriage with the rarest tropical flowers, while a bower of evergreen garlanded with beautiful scarlet blossoms is to shield his royal person from the rays of the sun now driving his fiery chariot in mid-heaven. The moment has come when his feet first press the soil of India when the cannon from a hundred ships and the many fortifications welcome him with hoarse-throated thunders which cause the earth to quake and fill the air with trembling, while great hot columns of smoke roll into the fervent sky from land and sea. The occasion and its attendant pomp and circumstance was replete with human power and grandeur, which was greatly enhanced by the presence of the native royalty in force, with their numerous bands of bronze-faced soldiery, clad in gorgeous robes and uniform of every color of the prism, while their piercing black eyes gleamed with brilliant intensity as they stood in serried rank headed by tawny-hued prince and potentate of this famed Eastern Empire.

The Bishop of Calcutta accompanied by Lord Northcote, the Viceroy of India and a large retinue of prominent officials and native kings and princes, were the first to greet the Prince, and the former read to him the address of welcome which was carried in the procession by a sentinel, bearing it upon a pillow of velvet, the document being inclosed in a box of gold. After the address came the introductions and hand-shaking, while the bands made the air resonant with the national "God save the Queen." The great assemblage then formed in procession and moved through the principal streets, passing under the triumphal arches and their loyal inscriptions, with the Prince at the front, who was received with the waving of flags, banners and handkerchiefs while the air was filled with the music and cheers. The Prince appeared in the uniform of an English soldier having on his head a helmet surmounted with his three feathered plume. His carriage was immediately followed by the English and native regiments of the line and by the respective commands of the Maharajas and Rajahs, it being drawn by four beautiful white horses.

The exercises and festivities of the evening were even more grand and imposing that those of the day, the whole city being lighted with a blaze of illumination, to accomplish which every device for turning darkness into light was brought into use. Mile after mile of streets glowed with streams of fire, and the buildings thereon were fairly wreathed with millions of Chinese lanterns of variegated colors, while great banners lettered in flame bore the inscriptions "God bless the noble Prince," "God keep the absent Princess," "God bless our future King." It was in all a day and a night never to be forgotten by the people of the palace city of the Indian Empire, and as I looked upon its pageantry and heard the multitude hail their future monarch, I could not help thinking what a day that will be when the Great Ruler of the Universe, the Prince of Peace, shall come to claim his own.

Finally, tired in limb and weary in brain, we repaired to our beds, but far too much excited by the day's proceedings to enjoy quiet sleep, although the next day was to witness our departure for the up-country.

THE NAUTCH DANCE, JEYPORE, INDIA.

CHAPTER XXV.

NORTH INDIA, INCLUDING BENARES, LUCKNOW, AGRA, CAWNPORE, ETC.

AT e'even o'clock on the evening of Dec. 29, after bidding the good ladies at the "Home" good-bye, and taking leave of quite a number of friends who had assembled at the depot, we took the train for Benares, 760 miles distant, this being our first railroad ride in India. Most of the people avail themselves of night travel in this country, it being so hot and dusty in the day; so, with pillows, blankets, lunch baskets, and my dear ones at my side, we took our compartments in the English built, first-class car, and soon were speeding on our way tired enough to go to sleep without being rocked or lullabyed. The scenery along the route was for the most part quite monotonous. Indeed, had it not been for the mud houses, and ox-carts with their many yokes of toiling cattle, their bronze-faced drivers, and the immense fields of the castor bean, barring the appearance of the carriages in which we were locked, we could have imagined ourselves in some portions of Illinois.

From our compartments we also had a view of the awkward implements still used by the Hindoos for cultivating and irrigating the soil, for gathering and grinding grain, for cutting and sawing timber, for spinning and weaving cotton, silk and wool, so thoroughly simple as never to have taxed inventive genius, and never improved since first brought into use a thousand years ago, and which completely scattered our morning fancies as to our being in the great rail arteries of industry in our own great west.

At eight o'clock the evening following our departure from Calcutta, we came in sight of the tall spires, stately domes, and myriad pagodas, and minarets of this famed city of pagan temples.

Alighting at the depot we were welcomed by Rev. M. O. Sherring, who insisted on our being his guests during our stay, and whose kindness and hospitality made us feel perfectly at home.

SONG SERVICE AT NOON.

It seemed very strange to me to hold my service of song at mid-day, yet when I saw the large church compound filled with gharrys and palanquins I was somewhat relieved, and on entering the edifice found a very appreciative audience assembled, who as time passed, seemed to thoroughly enjoy the new and novel exercises.

Benares is considered the most holy city by the Hindoos, who call it the Lotus of the world, and insist that it is perched upon one of the prongs of the idol Shiva's trident. To bathe here in the sacred Ganges, will, they believe, bring blessing and purification, almost inconceivable and the town teems with Brahmin priests, and mendicant fakirs, who subsist upon the gifts of the faithful.

This idolatrous stream which is sixteen hundred miles from its source to its mouth at the bay of Bengal, is worshiped by millions of Hindoos, and thousands die in, or have their ashes strewn upon it annually, expecting to obtain eternal life through the efficacy of its waters.

A bath or dip in it is supposed to heal the sick, comfort the dying, and cleanse from sin however black and heinous, while thoughts of it from afar will remove the foul effects of sin.

In company with our good missionary friend, Rev. Dr. Richardson, we visited several of the Hindoo temples, and saw the sacred oxen and pea fowls. The monkey temple also claimed considerable attention, in which a colony of hundreds of monkeys, held most sacred by the Hindoos, are housed, which are looked after by attendant priests, and are so tame that they come up to receive food from visitors.

From this spot we sailed down the Ganges in a "dinga" or small boat, and when just below one of the most prominent localities of pagan worship, our little craft was literally surrounded with a huge bed of floating flowers, the greater number of which was the fragrant temple blossoms, all having been swept from the shrines on which they had been offered to their respective idols, and cast into the sacred waters by the priests. Near by on the banks of the river was situated the burning Ghat, where after dipping the dead in the sacred waters they are laid upon their funeral pile and consumed, their ashes being gathered and consigned to that stream on miniature boats or crafts or sprinkled upon its bosom.

We witnessed several of these scenes, thankful that even the country had been subjugated so as to accomplish the discontinuance of the cruel custom of burning the living with the dead.

Here we found a most miserable and distressed company of Fakirs engaged in mortifying the flesh by self inflicted torture. Through Dr. Richardson I asked one of them, if he had ever heard of Jesus. "Jesus, who is he?" he replied. I said "the only Savior from sins." How pitiful and sad to hear him answer "I am holy, sins I have none." Nearly all these temples of idolatry are built upon the banks of the Ganges.

Now that the English control the government, no money can be had to build either new heathen temples or even to repair the old ones, the consequence of which is that many of these structures are rapidly going to decay. The ground floors of some of them are sunken several feet under water. The Ganges is the river of the Almighty God, and its ebb, and flow, and flood, so silently, and rapidly undermining and causing the destruction of those ancient monuments and shrines of heathenism, brings forcibly to mind the scriptural passage, "and the idols he shall utterly abolish."

Close by these structures to false gods, but further removed from old Ganges' treacherous waves, stands a Christian church, where the gospel is preached every Sabbath, and where the white and black alike, whose faith is founded on the rock Christ Jesus, instead of upon imaginary spirits dwelling in idols and temples builded on the sand, meet to praise and glorify his name.

Thus God's plan and purposes of salvation are marching on in Benares, the very throne of oriental idolatry.

How strange it does seem that this beautiful land, suggesting in its richness of climate and food, forest and flower, the very portal of paradise, should be to humanity the very gates of perdition.

To my service of song that evening there was a goodly gathering, and the two hours seemed to give those attendant thorough pleasure.

The next day we walked through many of the narrow streets, darkened by the tall buildings, and witnessed many curious sights, among which was a native funeral procession, the wails of the women therein falling sadly upon our ears.

By this time the great preparations were in progress for the reception, and entertainment of the Prince of Wales, large numbers of elephants were being brought in from all parts, for the grand procession, the streets were being decorated with flags and evergreens.

It was thus we left Benares, our visit having been one of intense interest, while the scenes and interests thereof will ever remain indelibly fixed in our memory.

THE CITY OF ALLAHABAD.

On the afternoon of January first we took a gharry, drawn by a pair of the most emaciated little horses which excited our deepest commiseration, and which were a correct type of the horses usually seen here, and started for the depot, to reach which we crossed the Ganges on a bridge of boats. We were met at Allahabad at ten o'clock that evening by Rev. J. H. Anderson, a Baptist missionary and escorted to the American Zenana home, to which place we had been previously invited, and where we were most kindly received and found delightful quiet. The house was quite large, and the compound spacious, the latter being irrigated with water drawn by oxen from wells, while natives with the skins of goats, filled with water, under their left arms were seen throwing it therefrom, sprinkling the flowers and gardens which are ten inches below the raised avenues or paths leading through the grounds.

On the Sabbath I gave two services of praise; at the Baptist church in the morning and the Methodist in the evening, both of which was crowded, and which the Lord made of great interest and enjoyment.

On Monday forenoon I gave a children's service which was largely attended by both young and old, and after tea at Dr. Anderson's, where I met several missionaries located in this great field of Christian labor, gave an evening of song to a large and thoroughly appreciative audience.

RIDING ON AN ELEPHANT.

At the close of my evening service, an English officer invited myself and family to ride about the city next day. Judge of our surprise at being called out at an early hour next morning to take a seat on a large and gorgeously caparisoned elephant, from which elevation we took in the sights of Allahabad. This was formerly a Mohammedan town, and called by them the city of God, but it has now relapsed from that faith into that of Brahma. It is located on the banks of the River Jumma, just before its entrance into the Ganges; is the junction of the Bombay and Calcutta lines of railway with those of northern India, and the capital of the northwestern provinces. Through its streets we now pass, on a level with its second-story windows, our native driver guiding this mammoth and intelligent king of the larger beasts by touching his ears with an iron hook.

We ride through the native portion of the city, with its clay walls, which seem strong enough in dry weather, but crumble and fall in wet seasons; to the old fort, and to the blood tree, which many of the Hindoos worship.

Then we are jostled, on the back of this great servant of mankind, through the English portion of the place, which appears to much advantage, and in which the trees gave refreshing shade.

THE TRIP TO AGRA.

After giving an evening of song, we took train for Agra at midnight, the richness and architecture of whose tombs excel those of any other land or clime. On the wide seats of the cars we spread our comforts and pillows, awakening in the early morning to enjoy a view of a most interesting country, as far as natural beauty was concerned, and most intensely so on account of the appearance of the people and the agricultural employments in which they were indolently engaged, aided by the use of the rudest implements for tilling and irrigating the soil. Here we saw vast wheat fields which were watered from hundreds of wells, from which the water was drawn by ox power and caught in leather bags or buckets, and thus conducted over them; as also large, purple-hued plantations of the castor bean, from which the oil is expressed, and which is also planted and harvested with the most ancient of tools and appliances. We were also much amused at the methods used by the natives in making excavations in the soil or clay, carrying away from or out of them all the debris in baskets on their heads, while small columns of earth were left standing beside these wells or holes, which indicated their depth, the excavators being so dishonest that their employers had to compel them to keep this kind of "double entry" of depth so as to ascertain the exact amount due them for their labor, and not be cheated by them in the work.

Arriving at the city at noon, we were met at the station by Mr. T. Bailey and conveyed to his pleasant home, where we found everything most charmingly arranged for health and comfort in this tropical climate, and where we were most hospitably entertained by this Christian banker and his wife and two lovely daughters. After a refreshing night's rest, our host gave us a splendid morning drive about the city, in which we visited the fort, a circular wall of massive red sandstone, one mile and a half in circumference, seventy feet in height, and once the residence of an ancient Indian king. Within the fort we came upon the crumbling ruins of some of the finest architecture extant, but of which only the imperial palace and Pearl Mosque remain in a state to give one an idea of their past regal grandeur and magnificence. In the evening I gave a song service to a good audience, and a pleasant occasion was the result. The following morning we made our visit to the

TAJ MAHAL,

The grandest monument builded from the materials of earth and adorned with the highest intelligence of human skill and craft, of the spiritual love of man for woman. It was Shah Jehan, a grandson of the mighty King Akbar, the Cæsar of India, who extended the Mogul Empire from Indus to the Bay of Bengal, and who not only built the fort of Agra, the great and massive tomb Futtehpore Sikra, to Sheik Selim Christi, his religious monitor, but also his own imposing and wonderful tomb at Secundra; who outrivaled his great ancestor and both the ancient and modern world in the erection of this beautiful tomb palace over the ashes of his sultana, Bunoo Begam, whom, in life and death, he loved with a surpassing love.

Tradition has it that this beloved and loving woman exacted a promise from Shah Jehan at her death that he would build her the most beautiful tomb on earth, and also that he would not marry again. But those most familiar with the emotions of the human heart reject this latter request as improbable from a woman who could inspire in her lifetime such lasting affection and fidelity as exhibited by her bereaved lord after she had passed away in her loveliness and devotedness, from the earth and his sight.

Taj Mahal rises in solemn grandeur and beauty, in the center of finely terraced grounds, on a slight eminence on the west bank of the Jumma, about three miles from the city, and is surrounded with twenty-five acres of land, laid out in immense gardens of indescribable richness and magnificence. Within its groves carol all the sweetest songsters of the air, springing fountains and silver streams leap up murmuringly at every hand, while the choicest and most beautiful flowers fill all the atmosphere with that rare fragrance of perfume which only oriental climes can boast. These grounds are surrounded by high, massive walls of brown stone, not unlike that used in the fronts of many of our Fifth avenue residences, the entrance thereto being through a grand gateway of immense proportions, overhung by an arch of eighty feet in height, composed of the same stone, and adorned with panelings of white marble. These panels are covered with texts from the Koran, the letters being most skillfully inlaid with black marble, each tablet, or panel, being surmounted with a delicate white marble minaret, the massiveness of the arch and its architectural embellishments being calculated to impress the beholder with that awe so peculiar in gazing upon the giant works of man in the majestic uprearing of the massive rocks.

We pass beneath this mighty arch and are treading the paved walks of variegated marbles, bordered with stone water trenches along which run curbing of richly carved marble, bordered with the rarest and loveliest flowers, while through the vista of waving cypress trees intersected with fountains, we behold the Taj, situated on an elevated square of thirty feet in height, which is paved with white and colored marble blocks, with a beautifully proportioned but slender white marble minaret rising at each corner of the platen full two hundred and seventy-five feet into the air. In the centre of this square, which is supported on its four sides by foundation walls of solid granite, stands the Taj, which is an octagonal structure of polished white marble, one hundred and fifty feet long at each point of the compass, which is surmounted by a huge dome seventy feet in diameter, which glistens in the sun like a burnished castle of silver, and which tapers from a globular into a spiral shape which terminates with a golden crescent. Four smaller domes of the same beautiful form crown the centre of the facades which rise two-thirds the height of the edifice over the four entrances or porches entering the tomb, a series of lesser arches being built in below them and extending inwards, upon and about which the entire chapters of the Koran are lettered in delicately inlaid black marble.

The Taj or tomb-palace is two hundred and forty-five feet in height, while the distance from the tesselalted pavement to the golden crescent is two hundred and seventy-five feet. But if we find the majesty of the outward view of this wonderful structure to baffle our description how can we hope to depict its matchless wealth of loveliness within, which rests rather than wearies our sight with grand visions, filling our souls with longing anticipations for the "house of many mansions, whose maker and builder is God"—a home of everlasting life instead of a mausoleum of the dead. Through the great kindness of the superintendent, Mr. Smith, we were permitted to see the exterior of the tomb by moon-light and the interior by lamp-light, both of which seems filled us with wonder and admiration and left an impression upon our minds never to be effaced.

Upon entering the tomb, beneath you, in the very centre of the structure, in a sunken circular chamber in the main floor, you behold the sarcophagi of Bunoo Begum and Shah Jehan. That of the Empress is in the centre of the chamber and that of the Emperor just by its side, both being constructed of spotless marble as white as the falling snow. But the glory of the building is embodied in its matchless dome of purest white marble, glittering with precious stones, through which a single delicate stream of light falls with mellowed softness on the tombs below.

"The floor of this dome-vaulted chamber is of polished marble and jasper, ornamented with wainscoting of sculptured marble tablets, inlaid with flowers formed of precious stones. Around are windows of screens of marble filigree, richly wrought in various patterns, which admit a faint and delicate illumination into the gorgeous apartment, all of which is of purest marble, so pierced and carved as to look like a high curtain of most exquisite lace-work, but is even far more refining, for every where along the panels are wreaths of flowers composed of lapis lazuli, jasper, chalcedony, cornelian, and other gems, so that to make one of the hundreds of these boquets a hundred different stones are required."

All this magnificence was executed for the empress, while Shah Jehan contemplated building a tomb as beautiful for himself on the other side of the river Jumna, designing to connect the two with a bridge of ivory. But giving

THE JUMMA MUSJID, DELHI.

up the latter project he decided to occupy the Taj with his Empress, and consequently applied the purest marbles and richest gems to the construction of her sarcophagus. Rev. Dr. Wm. Butler, who has the great honor of being the founder of our Methodism in India, in his very interesting book entitled "The Land of the Veda," thus describes her tomb:

"But her tomb how beautiful. The snow-white marble is inlaid with flowers of precious stones, so delicately formed that they look like embroidery on white satin, so exquisitely executed in the mosaic in cornelian, blood-stone, agate, jasper, turquoise, lapis lazuli and other gem stones."

On one side of her tomb, recorded in Arabic, the sacred language of the Mohammedans, each letter formed of gems, is the name of the empress, the date of her death, and a tribute to her virtuous qualities. The tomb of the emperor, though not as costly, has his name and the date of his death inscribed upon it, and is ornamented with flower work in brilliant gems. The great dome which rises above their last resting place is so constructed as to produce an echo which is unrivaled for its purity and sweetness. Seated on the marble floor beneath this great structure, with my dear family at my side, Supt. Smith said "sing something." Accordingly my son James struck up the hymn "My ain Countree," whose soft cadences were repeated by the echo with over powering and sublime sweetness, and whose melody passing from earth to heaven, seemed to be caught up by choir after choir in the ascent, and reuttered by millions of unseen vocalists of the air, and could only be compared to that which we all sometime hope to hear when the angel convoy of glory shall descend to earth to bear our ransomed spirits home. Says a brilliant author, in speaking of this most singular phenomenon:

"It is the very element of which sweet dreams are builded. It is the melancholy echo of the past, and the bright, delicate harping of the future. It is the atmosphere breathed by Ariel and playing about the fountains of Chindori. It is the spirit of Taj, the voice of inspired love, which called into being the peerless wonder of the world, and elaborated its symmetry, and composed its harmony, and eddying around its grand minarets and domes blended them without a line in the azure of immensity."

THE CITY OF DELHI.

Leaving Agra we came to the ancient sites and present city of Delhi, which is the most eminently historic in all India, and which, as it now stands, was commenced to be built in 1647. It is encircled by a massive wall of five and one-half miles in length, which is pierced with ten gates, the principal ones in use by the Europeans being the Cashmere, Cabul and Mora. The ruins of the former cities of that name which surround the present Delhi cover a territory of not less than forty-five square miles, those of principal interest extending ten miles to the south. Here it is asserted, that full a dozen proud cities have been built by Persian, Mohammedan and Brahmin, and conquered and razed in their turn. Following the lead of Sultan Mahmond in the eleventh century, who commenced the subjugation of northern India, Tamerlane in 1398 advanced on Delhi, which he occupied, and where he established the great Mogul Empire which Great Britain only succeeded in entirely suppressing in the period extending from 1803 to 1857. Towering two hundred and thirty-eight feet into the air and overlooking all these miles of ruins, is the famous Kootal Minor, which is claimed to be the highest pillar in the world, a massive circular column of fluted red sandstone and marble rising in five sections or stories, the base of each story being ornamented with a landing and balustrade, and all being wonderfully graduated from the base to the apex. Upon this pillar are carved texts from the Koran, in Arabic letters, while a circular iron staircase rises from the earth to its summit. For what purpose, or by whom this time-defying work of centuries, now thought to be fully three thousand years old, was built, is not known, while a cylindrical iron shaft, sixteen feet thick and sixty feet in length and thought to weigh seventeen tons, which stands upright in the earth quite near the pillar, is if anything of still greater antiquity. Here too, is seen the tomb of Humayuan, more massive and imposing than those at Agra, with its great dome of white marble resting on arcades of red sandstone inlaid with richly carved ornaments of the former material.

We were nicely entertained in Delhi at the missionary home of Rev. James Smith of the Baptist church, and my services were held in the English Institute building, a sort of English resort, clubroom and library. The whole city was in a flutter of expectancy and preparation for the coming of the Price of Wales, and therefore my simple service was not very well attended, although enough came in and listened to the singing to make it, to me at least, an occasion not to be forgotten, as in the adjacent newspaper room the people were talking so loudly of the coming event that I was obliged to personally request them to desist for a while that I might conclude my exercises. Oh, that these people might be as alert and active in preparation for the reception of the King of kings as they were at this time to welcome the heir presumptive of England's beloved Queen.

The day following was the Sabbath and in the morning we attended service in the Baptist chapel and listened to a good sermon from Bro. Smith, from the text "My peace I leave with you." The congregation was principally composed of English soldiers, while the estimiable wife of the pastor not only filled the position of organist but also led the singing, showing herself to be a helpmate to a missionary in foreign lands who was more priceless than gold. In

the evening I gave a song sermon service of praise and
Bible reading to a full house, and its novelty or some other
cause, held the audience in wrapt attention to its close. I
felt to thank God for this privilege of giving the gospel in
song in this old pagan city, whose dead grandeur fills the
soul with a strange awe which is only inspired by the
magnificence of its desolation.

My next service was my farewell, which was well attended and very pleasingly appreciated, and the following day being both bright and beautiful, we took advantage of the charming weather to visit several other places of interest, among which was the Jumma Musjid, the most famous as well as magnificent mosque on the earth. This wonderful structure is built on a rocky eminence, within the inclosure of the city walls, and extends from the Cashmere to the Delhi gate. It has three massive gateways of red sandstone, which are approached by three magnificent flights of steps, composed of the same material, all of which lead into an immense quadrangular court, in the center of which is located a spacious reservoir of water. On the west side of this court stands the mosque, two hundred and twenty feet long by twenty feet in width, which is surmounted with marble cupolas with gilded spires, while at each end of the structure are two beautiful minarets, composed of white and black marble, each rising to a height of one hundred and thirty feet. Here we saw the Mohammedans at their devotions, who, after washing at the basin, removed their sandals and knelt on the white marble squares with which the mosque was paved, each block or square being designed for the use of a single worshiper, the entire floor being surrounded with an inlaid border of black and white marble.

After a visit to the crumbling and thoroughly stripped palace of Shah Jehan, from which the British soldiers were driven in the great mutiny of 1857, and also to the heights which they then occupied and fortified, withstanding a six-months' siege, when, being reinforced, they descended therefrom and retook both the palace and the city, we made our way to our hospitable quarters. Here, too, the people were full of bustle and anxious preparation, looking forward to the coming of the prince, whom they were to entertain with a mock battle with blank cartridges, in which twenty thousand soldiers were to take part, and which was to be illustrative of the retaking of Delhi from the mutineers. Therefore, bidding this locality, so full of ancient and modern interest, adieu, we took the night train for

LUCKNOW, THE CAPITAL OF OUDE.

Arriving in the famous capital of the ancient Indian kingdom of Oude, which has become a sort of Methodist center in this empire, we were driven to the American Mission Home, which is presided over by Miss Thoburn, assisted by a noble band of lady associates, and which is doing a great and good work. My three services were held in the M. E. Church, which is undoubtedly the largest edifice of the denomination in northern India, and all of them were well attended and seemed to be generally appreciated. In addition to other branches of our denominational work in this city, is a sort of Methodist book house, and also a newspaper, established by Rev. J. M. Thoburn, and now edited by our Rev. J. M. Mudge, entitled "The Lucknow Witness," the advantage and influence of which is felt, not only in the city and vicinity, but throughout all northern India.

Lucknow is built on the south side of the Goomitee River, which is navigable downward through its whole course, to the confluence with the Ganges. It contains nearly half a million of inhabitants, and is divided into three distinct quarters, the first being the old native city, or "Chowk," spreading over considerable territory, but meanly built and very dirty; the second being the site of the palaces of the native king and the residences of his court, and the third consisting of palaces, religious edifices, and European residences. The great mutiny broke out at Lucknow, May 30, 1857, and continued until Sept. 25 of the same year. During this period the English kept up a constant siege, commencing the cannonade at daybreak, which continued for three hours, giving themselves a rest through the heat of mid-day, and again commencing the fire in the afternoon. With the fall of this city and the victory of the British troops, under the command of General Havelock, the backbone of this fearful rebellion was broken, and the distracted province was restored to peace.

Among our pleasant experiences here was a ride on an elephant kindly sent us by a rajah, for a day's enjoyment, in our seats upon whose back we were photographed by an accommodating artist, a Urasian gentleman being in our company. Riding through the native portion of the city, we were thus enabled to obtain a fine view, but the panorama of strange sights and the babel of strange sounds which came to our eyes and ears as we threaded the narrow avenues, crowded with native bazars, baffles all power of description.

THE GRAVE OF HAVELOCK.

We could not depart from this famous locality without driving some four miles in a gharry, in company with Mrs. Waugh, one of the noble ladies of the American Home, who kindly acted as our " friend, philosopher and guide," to several places of interest, prominent among which was the Residency, which was nearly rendered a mass of ruins in the Sepoy mutiny, and in the attack upon and siege of which by the insurgents the English residents and soldiery endured such horrible sufferings. Almost within the shadow of these ruins we came upon the quiet and peaceful spot in which repose the remains of the gallant Christian soldier, Sir Henry Havelock, whose life proved to be the ransom paid for the great victory gained in 1857. A large and beautiful tamarind tree overshadows his simple grave and monument, from which we plucked some dark green leaves in token of our visit, and bade a sad and reverential farewell to the silent sleeper beneath it.

After a glance at the home of Dr. Butler, while he was resident here, and a visit to a magnificent tomb of one of the ancient kings of the province, we came to a monkey temple whose grounds and surroundings, as well as its interior, fairly swarmed with troops of this curious and cunning animal, which here also are held in sacred veneration. As at the temple at Benares, they were left to wander where they pleased, and some of them jumped into our vehicle, mounted the backs of our horses, and indulged in other humorous familiarities.

During my stay at Lucknow I came in possession of a beautiful spread for my organ which was elegantly embroidered in gold, and was also shown a finely embroidered smoking cap ornamented with diamonds and valued at £12,000, which was to be presented to the Prince of Wales at his forthcoming visit to this city.

NORTH INDIA CONFERENCE AT CAWNPORE.

From Lucknow we went to Cawnpore to attend a session of the North India Conference. Here we were delightfully entertained at the splendid home of Arnold Beer, Esq., a prominent German citizen. This home seemed to be a sort of headquarters for missionaries and good people coming to the town, for it must be remembered that there are no hotels in the smaller towns in India, such being found only in the populous centers. In such localities, therefore strangers and visitors are entertained and cared for by the missionaries and their associate Christians, who seem to take delight in hospitably ministering to the temporal wants of American and European travelers as well as caring for the souls of men.

It was a blessed privilege to me to attend a Methodist conference in a heathen land and note the great and rapid progress of our church during the few short years since it had been planted here by our good Dr. Wm. Butler, as also to hear the sixty noble ministers and their working companions, devising methods and plans to give the gospel to the famishing millions of that far off land.

SUNDAY MORNING LOVE FEAST.

The Sunday morning love feast of this conference was one in which the spirit of God was grandly and sweetly manifest, and truly a repast of the richest spiritual things. All the members of the conference, and about one hundred visitors were present, while over sixty persons gave in their testimony for Jesus. It was a great pleasure to me to conduct the singing at this meeting, as well as that of the forenoon and evening, in which fine discourses were delivered by Rev. Mr. Hard, from the text, "Look unto me, and be ye saved, all the ends of the earth," and by Dr. Thoburn on the theme of "Entire consecration to Christ." I gave but one song service here, to a large congregation, rather desiring by my feeble services in the meeting of the conference to become filled with that spiritual rest which seemed to pervade this gathering of the dear Christian workers of Northern India.

Before leaving Cawnpore we visited one of the most intensely horrible scenes of the mutiny of 1857, where some two hundred women and children were ruthlessly butchered by the Sepoys, cast shrieking into a great well and left to die therein, an act of barbarity without parallel in the annals of history. Over this well the government has built a magnificent monument which is surrounded by a high iron fence, centers a spacious park of many acres, and on which is lettered an appropriate inscription recording the event.

A very pleasant incident during our stay here was our attendance upon a charming "tiffin" or garden party; which was held on very pleasant grounds some five miles distant from the town, at which a large number of the members of the conference with their wives were present.

Here I was handed by Rev. B. H. Badley, the secretary of the India M. E. Conference, a copy of the subjoined resolutions.

The following resolutions were adopted by a rising vote:

(1.)—That we hereby extend a most cordial welcome to our beloved brother, Philip Phillips, and rejoice that in the good providence of God, he has been brought to this distant land to labor for a time in the ministry of Sacred Song.

(2.)—That we tender him our sincere thanks for his services at different points in our field, and more particularly for his delightful singing during the present session of our Conference.

(3.)—That we commend our dear brother and sister Phillips with their children, to the watchful mercies of our Heavenly Father, and shall pray that they may be guided and guarded throughout their long journey and led in safety back to their native land.

J. M. THOBURN.
E. CUNNINGHAM.
C. P. HARD.

The following morning we again took the train to revisit Allahabad, and after a pleasant journey, soon found ourselves among the rank and file of the followers of the Lamb and soldiers of the cross in the salvation army of the Indian provinces.

PAGAN AND CHRISTIAN GATHERINGS.

Here now took place two gatherings of worshipers of the widest distinction. Relaying with horse, bullock and elephant conveyance, we went with a party of Christian gentlemen and ladies to look upon one of the great heathen fetes of the Hindoos, called "Mela," which was held annually at the mouth of the river Jumma where it rolls its waters into those of the Ganges. This is considered by the Hindoos to be the holiest spot on the sacred river, and hither the poor heathen make annual pilgrimage from hundreds of miles around, to bathe and make offerings, occupying temporary huts or booths in which they offer their wares and trinkets to purchasers. Here we saw a perfect army of blind, disfigured and disabled men and women asking alms, and hundreds of Fakirs, or holy men as they are called, with their faces begrimed with smoke, their bodies sprinkled with dirt and ashes, and their hair singed and matted, all busy with their idolatrous and blasphemous rites. So much heathenism in its vilest and most disgusting forms made our souls sick and our hearts ache.

We returned to the city to attend the other gathering, which was that of the first India Sunday-school Convention, to which I had come by special invitation to sing the sweet songs of Zion, and where were gathered the leading Sunday-school workers of all India. Oh what a contrast was here as we lifted our hearts to Jesus and counseled how we could best make known and glorify his name, to the pitiable scenes being enacted upon the banks of the Ganges by poor, deluded and misguided men and women.

We were housed and dined with the delegates to the convention in a large bungalo, which was our first experience in a native residence, and which will never let us forget Allahabad. Taking the night train, we arrived the following afternoon at Bombay, having been greatly interested on the route by the miles and miles of cob-cactus with which the railway was formidably and securely fenced in.

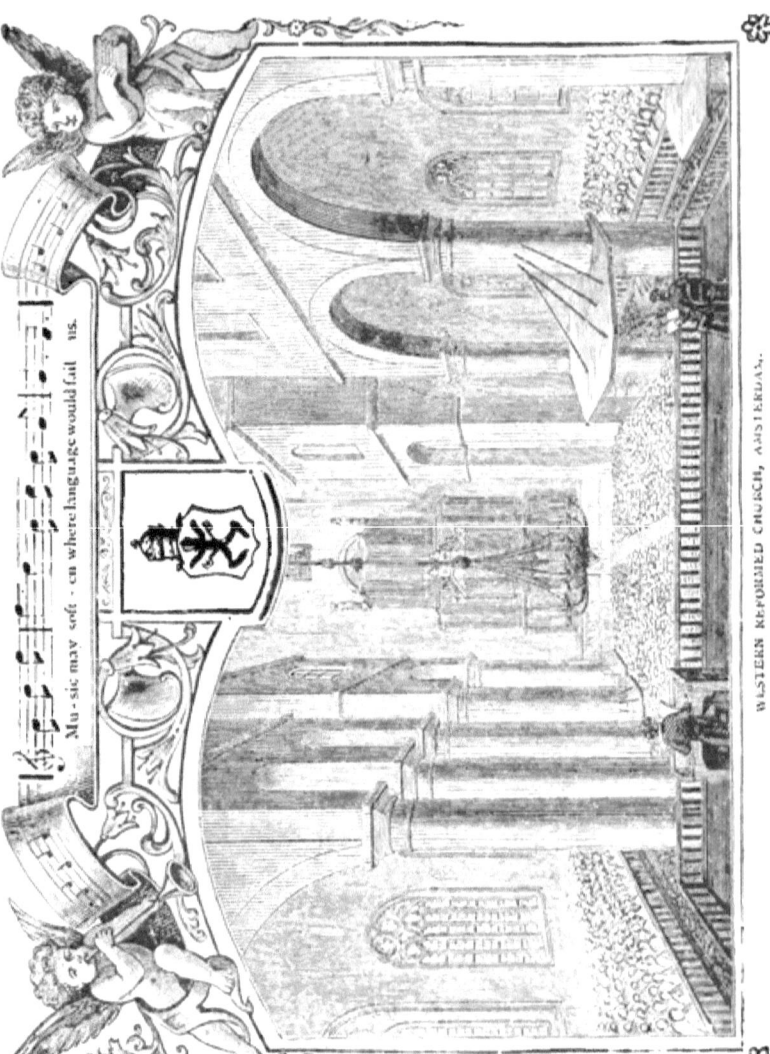

WESTERN REFORMED CHURCH, AMSTERDAM.

CHAPTER XXVI.

BOMBAY AND VICINITY.

BOMBAY is one of the greatest commercial centers, has the finest and most spacious harbor, and is really the golden gate of India. It is built on Bombay Island, which is connected with the island of Salsette, as also with the main land, by extensive causeways. It has a mixed population, of all nations, tongues and kindred, its most distinguished, prosperous, intelligent and public-spirited citizens being the Parsees, descendants from the ancient Persian worshipers of fire, who are also noted for their commercial and business qualifications and for their great wealth, and are in charge of most of the government works of the city.

We took up our quarters for a few days at the Esplanade Hotel, a massive structure, seven stories in height. In fact, most of the government and mercantile buildings of this great city are noteworthy, spacious and imposing. Then, too, unlike in other Indian cities, it is difficult to designate the streets and dwellings more exclusively occupied by the English, from those of the natives, as all are of quite modest and modern construction, and embowered in the shade of the favorite cocoanut palm, planted in the streets, yards and gardens by the thousand. Here, also, as in Calcutta, are miles on miles of native bazaars, in which all castes, sects and colors sell their fruits and wares, while, as the crowds pass along the streets, the eye is relieved, not only by the appearance of those clad in garments of European fashion and fabric, but by the awkward, funneled-shaped hats worn by the Parsee men, as also by the bright-colored silk dresses and turbans of their wives and daughters.

Here I gave several of my services, and in no city of the East did I receive a more hearty reception than in Bombay, for not only was I warmly welcomed by the Baptist, Methodist, Presbyterian and Wesleyan Missions, but the Church of England people met me with great cordiality. Here I met that good man, Rev. George Bowen, editor of the "Bombay Guardian," Mr. Henry Conder, one of the managers of the great India Railway, and several of the converts of the Rev. Wm. Taylor, who, here, as well as in Australia, has been the means, under God, of greatly augmenting the churches, and who are doing most noble work for the Master. While singing here, the "Bombay Gazette" did me the great honor of publishing a sketch of my life, speaking in highest compliment and with much enthusiasm of my singing services in the connection, for all of which I felt thankful, for the sake of the cause in which I was engaged, as well as for myself. I also attended a large tea meeting, held by the city merchants, where I met quite a number of distinguished Parsees.

THE WORSHIPERS OF THE SUN.

The Parsees are of Persian origin, and are disciples of Zoroaster, who is supposed to have brought his sacred fire from heaven. That portion of this race which wandered from Persia to India after they had been conquered by the Mohammedans, and who were taken under protection by the rajah of Guzerat, claim to have brought this sacred fire, which has never been extinguished, hither with them, and which their priests keep burning in their temples, feeding it with the choicest woods and spices. They recognize one omnipresent, omnipotent and invisible God, without form, the creator, ruler, and preserver of the universe, and the last judge, whom they call Ormazd. They believe in astrology, and that the stars have a beneficent influence upon the affairs of men, and to those who can understand them, can reveal the secrets of the future. While they abominate idols, they reverence fire and the sun as emblems of the supreme deity, the sun being recognized as the eye of Ormazd, their God. Their religion enjoins prayer, obedience, industry, honesty, hospitality, charity, chastity and truthfulness, while envy, hatred, anger, revenge and polygamy are strictly forbidden. They have borrowed somewhat the fashion of priesthood and caste from the Hindoos, and their funeral rites and the disposal of their dead are very strange. Their cemeteries are erected on a high eminence, and are in the form of a circle, being smoothly paved with stone and surrounded with high walls, which rise even above the tops of tall trees which are found within the inclosure. Upon a tall stone tower, built in the center of the inclosure, upon the summit of which is an open iron grating, they lay the naked bodies of their dead, to be stripped of flesh by birds of prey, the bones falling through the grating into a pit or common receptacle beneath, which, when filled, are secretly removed through subterranean passages. The males have worn the same ungainly and peculiar shaped hat for ages, and the number of this people resident in India and its adjacent islands is estimated at about 125,000.

MISSIONARY HOUSE AT BYCULLA.

Completing my arrangements for a trip to Madras, for an absence of two weeks, I accepted the kind invitation of Miss Butts to leave my family at the Church of England Mission Home, located in Byculla, a charming little suburb of Bombay. While there my dear wife gained additional insight into the methods of this most important branch of the India mission work, which is so vitally aided by the English and American lady physicians, whose skill is greatly prized by the native idolaters of all castes, and into whose homes they soon gain access to attend to the medical wants of the women and children, and in so doing often pave the way for the admittance of the Zenana teachers.

A few of the pupils at this church home boarded there, and were instructed in the English and Mahratti languages, by both English and native pundits. My wife, in company with Miss Butts, visited the Alexandria Institute, presided over by a Parsee gentleman. The school was composed of the daughters of well-to-do Parsees, who were here taught to draw and embroider, and the elementary branches of study. There were about fifty in attendance, all wearing bright little turbans handsomely embroidered on silk, with beads and precious stones. They were robed in the brightest colored silk trowsers, with silk or lace tunics, all of which were beautifully embroidered. Their shoes, which were cut high, seemed to represent the hues of the rainbow. Accompanying Miss Butts, they called upon a Hindoo lady of high caste, who spoke English and seemed much inclined to our religion. In another family, where she was teaching the children embroidery and needlework, it was very interesting to see the little, eager, dark-faced group gathered about her. Here she had but recently gained admission, and must not force or urge her religious ideas upon the children, but first gain their attention by teaching them some pretty needlework, or showing them some bright picture, or telling some interesting story.

She commenced this day by asking these little ones if they ever knew any little boy who never did anything wrong, never told lies, never struck his little friends, and always loved and minded his parents.

Of course, they replied, they never knew one so good,

and she said she would tell them of one such good boy. Then gradually she told them in simple, earnest words of the childhood of Jesus, never mentioning his name in the connection, but reserving it for future lessons, when as she has gained their full love and confidence she will gradually unfold the dear

"Old, old story of Jesus and his love."

We shall ever remember gratefully the kind attentions of the ladies at this "home," and the religious exercises therein, at which teachers, pupils, visitors and servants, participated, and which were truly "blessed hours."

FRAGMENTARY FACTS.

A few facts gathered from authentic sources relative to the missionary work in India, may not here come amiss. "The Danes first carried the gospel to the races of India. In the year 1705, two young men, Ziegenbalg and Plutschan, were sent thither as missionaries from Denmark, and a little more than two years later the former commenced the translation of the Bible into the Tamil language. The first medical missionary arrived here in 1730, and in 1736 the first native pastors were ordained. Schwartz, a Danish missionary, died here in 1798, after spending forty-eight years in uninterrupted work in this field. During the eighteenth century, fifty thousand natives of India abandoned heathenism and embraced Christianity, but the permission to retain their caste, customs and prejudices throws considerable suspicion on the spiritual work accomplished during that period. Rev. Mr. Carey, a Baptist, came from England to India in 1793, hoping to till the land for his own sustenance and to instruct the people. But his means soon being exhausted, and having taken up his residence in a scantily populated tract of country, noted for its unhealthiness and the fierceness of the wild beasts, he endured great privation and suffering. Finally, being convinced of the uselessness of prosecuting missionary work under such adverse circumstances, he accepted the position of superintendent of a factory, and during the five years which he held this position, translated the New Testament into the Bengali language.

In 1797 the church of England sent its first missionary to India, Rev. Mr. Clark, who in 1800 commenced printing the Bengali Bible. In 1830, Rev. Dr. Duff was sent to India by the Church of Scotland, as its first missionary, who was eight months in making the voyage, being twice shipwrecked in the passage, and who is accredited as being the champion of India education.

For many years the English Church Missionary Society were unable to supply this field with their own ministers, who did not like to come here in the humble capacity of missionaries, and therefore the church, in their great necessity, supplied the want by securing the service of Lutheran ministers, who were willing to undergo the hardships and practice the self-denial concomitant upon this labor. But after a season, the latter, thinking as much of their own orders as churchmen, as the Church of England did of theirs, for a time there was a sad controversy between them.

The question of caste has at all times been a troublesome one to our missionaries in their attempts to Christianize India—in fact it has been the great ban in the way of bringing the natives to the knowedge and acceptance of Christ. The first missionaries did not interfere with caste, and the Leipzic missionaries still continue to let it alone, but in so doing have committed a grievous error, which makes their evangelical work one of doubtful fruitage, and hinders that of other missionaries. In this connection we read of one remarkable English minister, Rev. Dr. John, who in 1805, found his people contending for separate cups at the communion table, in fact found them occupying separate places with separate cups. Not being able to brook this anti-Christian custom, he told them if they did not put an end to these odious distinctions at the Lord's table, that he would. Not heeding his admonitions, he melted the two cups into one, and thus effectually settled the matter.

The following are some of the points subscribed to by those wishing to to renounce heathenism: We promise most faithfully to abandon idolatry and worship the true God. We promise to observe the Sabbath and abstain from all secular work. We promise to abstain from the use of flesh that has died of itself. They are also required to abstain from intoxicating drink and to abandon caste, as also to remove the Kudumi, or tuft of hair from the crown of the head, which is a strong link in the chain of caste feeling."

CHAPTER XXVII.

MADRAS AND LEAVING BOMBAY.

TAKING the train for Madras, seven hundred miles distant, I make my first halt at Poonah, where I found our good brother, Rev. D. O. Fox, working for the Master of souls for souls. Here I sang in the Scotch Presbyterian Church to a great audience, who seemed to be in closest sympathy with my work of singing the dear old gospel, not only in psalms, but in hymns and spiritual songs. I was at this place the guest of the estimable Dr. Frazer, who gave me thirty rupees for my mission hall fund, to which an English general added enough more to make me a British India brick. My second service here was held in the M. E. Church, and was fully attended and thoroughly enjoyed.

From Poonah I went forward to Secunderbad, in the Decan district, where, in connection with our most zealous worker, Rev. J. E. Robinson, I held several excellently attended services, which were blessed of God to the salvation of many present. Bro. Robinson is a most thoroughly active Christian, is an excellent singer and Sunday-school worker, as well as preacher, and possessing the love and respect of all with whom he comes in contact, is as a consequence doing a great and good work in his locality. Presenting his people with several hundred singing books I bade them good-bye, even as they were voicing hymns of praise.

PANDAL (NATIVE MEETING HOUSE), MADRAS.

Stopping at Shahabad, I sang my songs to a few who had gathered at the railway depot, in a room without chairs or benches, with the hope that they might in turn learn to sing Christ's praises, and continued on my journey to Bellary, where I was joined by good brother C. P. Hard. Here I held a service in a large government school house, which was filled with people, who were so enthusiastic, that at the close several contributed very liberally towards building a new Methodist Chapel, an amount thus being raised nearly sufficient to complete the structure, which was subsequently done, and where the gospel is now preached. I also gave one other service at this town, which seemed to be a kind of military station or government barracks, and where we were kindly cared for by Mr. Froist, a man of authority among men, who reminded me of the centurion of old, but an intelligent and earnest Christian. At the close of this service, Bro. Hard and myself took an all night's ride by rail, and arrived at Madras, his field of labor, in the early morning.

My first appointments in Madras were in connection with Rev. James Gelling, a most successful Wesleyan Missionary who has been stationed here for many years, and although my first service was not largely attended, I never felt more thoroughly the presence of the Holy Spirit. My second service was to the children, and some four hundred being present, we had a most delightful and refreshing meeting, which fully repaid me for the discomforts of the journey hither.

Madras borders the open sea-coast for a distance of several miles, and is especially noted as the first place where the English commenced the subjugation of India. It is a beautiful city, its spacious districts being separated by fine groves and gardens, while its principal objects of interest are its magnificent government buildings and the great Fort of St. George, whose esplanade is protected from the sea by a great wall of heavy masonry.

On Sabbath evening I sang at the church of Bro. Hard to a large congregation, and at the close of the service over two thousand rupees were contributed towards building a new chapel, which has since been completed and dedicated. On Monday morning at eight o'clock, I sang to a fine gathering in the large Pandal, and in the afternoon before Dr. Duff's Scottish School, composed of four hundred young native students of all ranks and castes. That evening I gave my farewell service in the large Memorial Hall and Bible Depository of the East, which was before another excellent house. On coming out of the hall into the street, my eyes rested upon the curious procession of Mahommedans called the Marhovrim, a company of nude men besmeared with filth and mud, who were marching to the beat of native drums.

The next morning, after two weeks of intense and interesting labor, I took train towards Bombay, making my first halt at Bangalore, where in company with Bros. Hard and Newland, I gave a service of an hour and a half in length to a very appreciative audience. We all stopped for the night with Rev. James Shaw, the resident missionary, where I dined on the only strawberries and raspberries which I saw while in India.

Our very zealous Bro. Fisher having telegraphed me I must stop over a train and give a service at Aconium, and it being my mission to sing as I go, I therefore complied with his request and sang for an hour in the railway station to a very attentive assemblage. While my train stopped for a moment at Poonah, good Brother Fox was on hand at the depot with a hot cup of tea and a " God bless you " to speed me on the way.

BACK TO BOMBAY.

I was delighted to get back to my dear ones, and found that it had been planned that I give an evening of song in the large parlors of the Missionary Home, but the surroundings being new to me and being somewhat fatigued, I fear I did not sing with my usual freedom. The next morning I awoke quite rested and refreshed, and gave my last and farewell song service in India at the great hall, where I was greeted with a fine audience of English speaking people. At my song sermon in the hall of the M. E. Church, the same evening, there was a large attendance, and at the close of the exercises many came forward for prayers. Being much fatigued, dear Bro. George Bowen said to me, " You rest and I will pray for these mourners," and thus I left him on his knees pouring out his soul to God for the salvation and redemption of these poor sinners. Thus ended my ever to be cherished song labors among the Christian and pagan people of the great Eastern Empire.

CHAPTER XXVIII.

EN ROUTE TO PALESTINE.

WE were accompanied by several friends to the steamer "India," of the Italian line, the next forenoon, and after a sweet season of prayer in our cabin, committing each other to the care of Him who is "Mighty to save," our farewells said, and our friends having taken boat for shore, our anchors were raised, and we glided from the harbor, soon losing sight of the shores of old India. We had for fellow passengers, Rev. Mr. Burton and family, of Madras, and Rev. Mr. Clark, of Punjab, and Miss Le Fevre, an American lady who was returning home from her mission work in Burmah. The eight days' passage to Aden, the celebrated ostrich feather sea-port, was calm, and we passed them in conversation, reading and in looking upon the Arabian sea and the wonders therein, whose waters were so clear that we could see the reflection of our steamer, the prow looking like some great alligator or other living monster moving along in the water, and as we came nearer shore we could see hundreds of jelly fish, pretty, little, pink creatures, with their soft little umbrellas spread. At night these waters were beautifully illuminated with phosphorescent light.

On entering the Red Sea through the straits, from the gulf of Aden, we encountered head winds, which continued almost the entire passage up its long and narrow channel.

In six days more we entered the Gulf of Suez, with

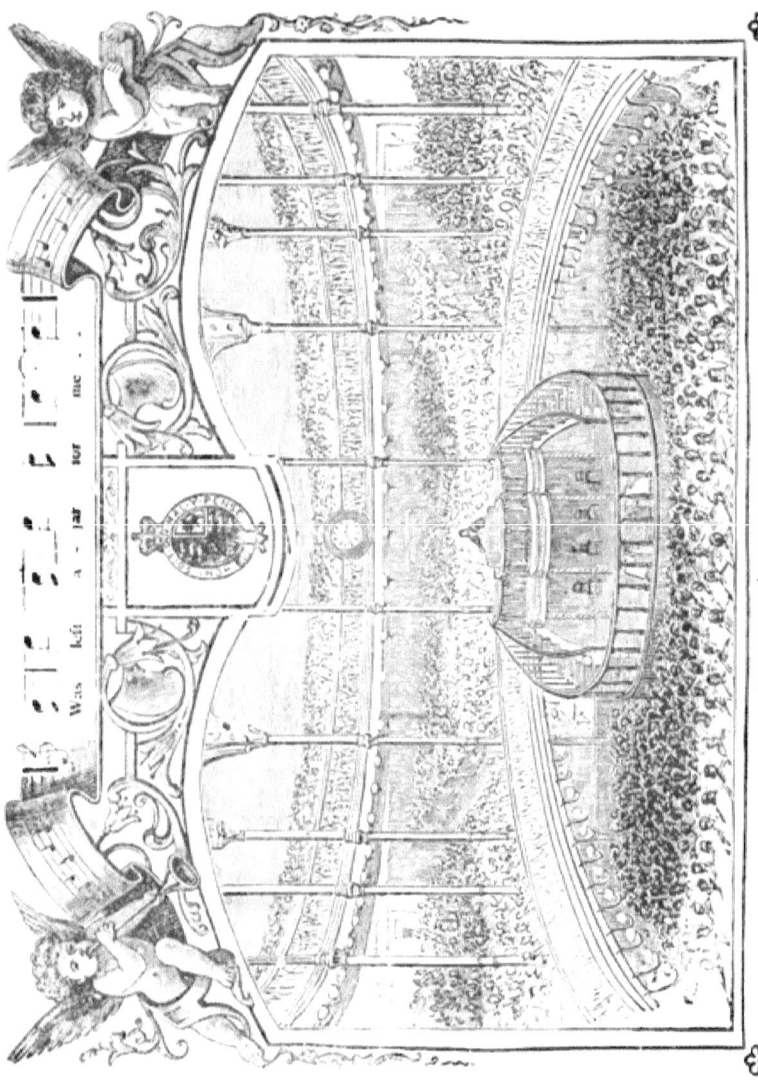

C. H. SPURGEON'S TABERNACLE, LONDON.

Egypt on the one hand and Arabia on the other, and were able to discern the Mt. Sinai range in the distance. As we were gazing for the first time upon these scenes, rendered so interesting because of Bible history, my little son Philip crept up into my lap with this enquiry, "Papa, why is not the water in this sea *red!*" I tried to explain, and this led to many other questions in regard to Bible countries, and he seemed so astonished to know that scenes of Bible stories took place upon *our earth*, instead, as he had imagined, in some far off country of which we had no definite or particular knowledge. This little incident so characteristic of childhood inquiry, seemed to say to me, do not we Christians and Sunday-school teachers mystify and darken the minds of our youth by speaking of Biblical scenes and events as so *long* gone by, and so *far* away, while even as we teach and exhort, the crucified and risen Savior, with the marks of the thorns and spears of Judea, is ever present with us, and who has said so emphatically, "Where two or three are gathered together in my name there am I in the midst of them."

Coming up to Suez, a lonely place, situated near the sea, on the sand, we entered the famous

SUEZ CANAL,

Just before sunset, and our steamer was tied up to posts, like an ox, for the night. It was a strange sensation that crept over us as here, with a wilderness of desert on each side, we could hear no sound of living or animate thing except that produced by ourselves and companions, while even the noise of the sea would have been music to our ears in this solitude of solitudes. The Suez Canal is a channel cut from Suez to Port Said, connecting the Arabian and Red Sea with the Mediterranean, and is one hundred miles in length and three hundred feet in width. No vessel is allowed to enter either of its mouths after sunset, or before sunrise, and all vessels sailing therein are compelled to stop and tie up to posts on the banks during the night, in order to prevent accident from collision. There is a telegraph station every five miles along its banks, which regulates the passage of vessels, as trains are regulated by the same method on railroads. At each of these stations can be seen a bit of green sward, all the rest of the land through which this great thoroughfare is constructed, being a barren stretch of desert sand. At six o'clock in the morning the steamer left her mooring, passing Ishmalia about three hours later, where we discharged several passengers, reaching Port Said on the Mediterranean Sea, where is situated the great electric light house of the canal, at four o'clock in the afternoon, where, on coming to anchor, we were at once surrounded with little crafts most prettily cushioned with bright chintz, whose pilots were clamorous to take passengers ashore, while coolies swarmed the banks, some of whom took our luggage on their backs and heads to the "Hotel de France," they being accustomed to bear the heaviest burdens in this manner, and of such strength and muscle that we did not so much wonder, after all, that the pyramids reared their massive forms in this land.

It is always a relief to get on land after a long sea voyage, even if it be the miserable land of the Arabs. We remained at Port Said for two days waiting for a steamer during which time it rained incessantly, when on Saturday, wet and dripping, we boarded, from a little boat, the steamer "Aurora," bound for

JOPPA, AND THE HOLY LAND.

The storm continued after we reached the vessel to such an extent that we did not move out of the harbor until Monday morning, as passengers could not be landed at Joppa in such a boisterous sea.

We found on board the steamer several Americans who

were bound for Palestine, and although they were strangers we were glad to meet our countrymen. There was a large company of pilgrims going to "Mecca," and a lot of the most filthy and hideous looking second-class passengers we ever looked upon. There were twenty-six nationalities represented on our passenger list. Notwithstanding the storm and delay, we had a blessed service on board the steamer, in which we sang of Jesus, and Rev. Mr. Clark preached a most affecting discourse from the words, "And they crucified Him."

How appropriate this theme, as we were about to set foot on the land where our Savior had lived and died that we "might ransomed be."

Anchoring off Joppa on Tuesday morning, a distance of one mile from shore, we took a small boat and sailed in between the huge old rocks lining the dangerous channel. Our landing was effected safely, but not without considerable fear on our part. Oh, what emotions fill the soul at the first sight of Palestine as caught from the hill of Joppa, "The watch-tower of joy and beauty." At last we behold the Christ land with our own eyes, but how sad it seems, as we touch its sacred soil, to look upon the filth and squalor on every side. At the wharf we are met by a dragoman, who takes us through this queer old place of narrow and muddy streets, to the "Jerusalem Hotel," which is situated in the German quarter of the city. After visiting the house of Simon, the tanner, and calling to mind as I looked out upon the sea, that it was here from whence Jonah sailed on his intended voyage to Tarshish, in which his plans were so suddenly changed by the Almighty, we called at the mission and one of its schools, soon after which we took horses for Jerusalem, and made our first stay at Ramleh. Near Joppa we were much attracted by the large orchards of orange trees, which were literally loaded down with luscious, seedless fruit, which at this season of the year was at its prime. But as the soil is not cultivated to any extent except in the immediate vicinity of the towns and cities of Palestine, we soon left these scenes behind us, and after twelve miles ride, came to the quiet old city of Ramleh, situated in the midst of a fertile valley. Having ridden with my little Phillie in front, I was glad to dismount from my hard Arabian saddle, and rest. There we stopped for the night at a curiously constructed old Latin convent, where we were hospitably entertained, our stone-paved bed-rooms opening into a large court, and which were lighted from the top instead of sides. Amid the ruins of old towers, walls, and vaults, we slept soundly on this our first night in the Holy Land, on much softer beds, if they were hard and damp, than that at Bethlehem on which our infant Redeemer was laid in this, the land of his birth.

ONWARD TO JERUSALEM.

We resumed our journey in the early morning, and passing over the Plains of Esdrælon, we came into a mountainous country. abounding in wooded ravines, and flowers of various hues adorning the way, our every view becoming more and more interesting as we ascended the hills leading up to Jerusalem.

Some five miles out of the city we were met by our good counsul, Dr. De Hass, who was mounted on a fine white horse, and who escorted us thither, pointing out the many places of interest on the way, among which was the tomb of Samuel, Mt. Olivet, Mt. Moriah and Mt. Zion. We entered the Joppa gate into the city, and took up our quarters in the Mediterranean Hotel.

Though thoroughly fatigued, such had been our emotions at the sight of so many scenes and objects with which our Bible had made us familiar, that it was long before sleep would come to us, situated as we were, with the windows of our apartments looking out over and upon the pool of Hezekiah.

We could hardly understand, the next morning, that we had come into the realization of our hopes, and were, indeed, beholding the sun rise in the land of the prophets and disciples, so filled with the scenes and events of sacred story which foretold the coming of the Savior, and witnessed his birth, crucifixion, resurrection and transfiguration. After breakfast we took a stroll in the narrow, ill-paved streets, which were dark and filthy, and crowded with a motley assemblage of people, and purchased some souvenirs of our visit. During the forenoon we changed our quarters to the Cazenovia or Latin Convent, where we found pleasant apartments, and, after a call at the Consuls, in the afternoon, with a small party, we visited the Mosque of Omar, built over the ruins of King Solomon's temple, and enclosing the ground where God tested the faith of Abraham to the point of offering his only son for sacrifice.

The Mosque is a beautiful structure, and with its grounds occupies nearly one-fifth the area of the city; but its intense interest to us, was because of its hallowed associations.

Near the golden gate we mounted the walls of the city from which we could see more prominently that Jerusalem was situated on, an elevation with the higher peaks of Judea rising in the distance, while we fixed our earnest gaze down the valley of Jehoshaphat, to the garden of Gethsemane, and onward to the Mount of Olives.

Then the old hymn came whispering to me on these turreted battlements, breathing of the new Jerusalem, a city not made with hands, eternal in the heavens:

> "Jerusalem, my happy home,
> Name ever dear to me
> When shall my labors have an end
> In joy and peace in thee.

In the course of the day I was introduced to the Reverend Bishop Bogart, who kindly invited me to give one of my services in St. Paul's Church, which made me glad to have the way opened to sing in the city of David, himself the sweet singer of old Israel.

I had a good attendance on this occasion, and at its close one of the audience, a very intelligent looking young German resident, came to me and said that my singing had then and there been the means of bringing him to Christ, which filled my heart with rejoicing as I left the edifice.

The next day our party took their way outside the city walls, leaving by the Damascus gate to visit the quarries from which the immense stones used in the erection of Solomon's temple were obtained.

Returning, we stopped at the Church of the Holy Sepulchre, certain parts of which are common property, all sects—Latin, Greek, Armenian and Coptic, having free access to them. Rev. J. L. Porter, in his "Giant Cities of Bashan," thus graphically describes the Sepulchre:

"The principal part of the building is the Rotunda, which has a dome open at the top, like the Pantheon. Beneath the dome stands the Holy Sepulchre, a little structure, like a church in miniature, encased in white stone profusely ornamented, and surmounted by a crown shaped cupola. It contains two small chambers—the first called the "Chapel of the Angel," and said to be the place where the Angel sat after he had rolled away the stone from the door of the sepulchre.

The stone itself is there too!

Through this we pass, and enter the Sepulchre by a very low door. It is a vault, measuring six feet by seven. The tomb—a raised couch covered with a slab of white marble—occupies the whole of the right side. Over it hang forty lamps of gold and silver, kept constantly burning.

I lingered long here—solemnized, almost awe-stricken—looking at pilgrim after pilgrim, in endless succession, crawling in on bended knees, putting lips, forehead and cheeks to the cold marble, bathing it with tears, then drag-

DAMASCUS.

ging himself away backwards, still in the attitude of devotion, until the threshhold is again crossed."

It was a sad sight to see this locality, hallowed by the death and presence of our Savior, under guard of the Mohammedan soldiers and police to prevent pilgrims of rival religious beliefs from fighting, as to who should have the first opportunity to put their lips to these cold rocks and stones, and even with these precautions, to witness the exchange of blows and angry epithets.

Of course, as we looked upon these reputed relics of the presence of Jesus upon this spot, being shown the stone of unction, Golgotha and many other objects which these poor pilgrims worship instead of the true and living God, we felt no spirit of either accepting or rejecting them in a literal sense, satisfied as we were to breath the air of Jerusalem and Judea made sacred by His presence, to gaze upon the hills over which His footsteps had fallen, and to have the same sunshine fall upon our faces, which bathed him in its glory, from the inception at Bethlehem to the transfiguration on the mount.

Thence we proceeded to the inhabited part of the old city, to the Jews' "wailing place," where every Friday, these poor creatures assemble to bewail because of the long catalogue of woes that have fallen upon Jerusalem, chanting the prophetic words of their own Psalmist,—"O God, the heathen are come into thine inheritance, thy holy temple have they defiled."

Having engaged a dragoman, and completed our arrangements on Saturday for a trip to the river Jordan on Monday, we tried our horses in a short excursion through Damascus gate, around the city, across the valley of Jehoshaphat, and up the Mount of Olives, where we drank in the grand view over Judea. Some twenty-five miles away to the east, we beheld the mountains of Moab, and the Dead Sea, while we could trace the winding course of the Jordan by the deeper green of the verdure along its banks. Below us stands the sacred city encircled with its belt of walls, with its high domes, minarets and towers, imposing even in their decay.

To the north lies the wilderness of Judea, and to the south we see the hills which surround Bethlehem. Here, too, we look down upon the pathways that lead from Jerusalem to the solitudes of Bethany, to Jericho, to Gethsemane—paths that have been trodden by Him "Who lived as never man lived, and spake as never man spake."

Returning to Jerusalem, we attended the English church on the Sabbath, where Rev. Mr. Walton gave an excellent discourse from the text, "I am the light of the world."

OUR TRIP TO THE JORDAN.

Leaving Jerusalem, at an early hour, through the Joppa gate, we rode past the tomb of Rachel, to the pools of Solomon, partly excavated from the rock, and partly constructed of masonry. There are three of these reservoirs, placed one above the other on the slope, but not in a direct line. They are so arranged that the bottom of the second is higher than the surface of the lowest, and that of the third higher than the surface of the second. Flights of steps lead down to the water. Taken all together they are about thirteen hundred feet long and two hundred and fifty wide, and, it is said, the supply of water is from a concealed fountain. His gardens are supposed to be near here, which he so often frequented, and where he wrote the beautiful and soul-inspiring "Proverbs."

Onward we go, passing over the plains where David fed his sheep, where Ruth gleaned, where the shepherds were watching their flocks when they saw the "Star in the east," to Bethlehem, travelers not from the near east, as of old, but from the far, *far* west, though also to see, as they who fed their flocks upon the "nightly plains," "the place where

GERMAN ASSEMBLY ROOMS, JERUSALEM

the young child lay." Arriving at this city of the plain, we visited the "Church of the Nativity," alleged to be built over the spot where the Savior was born. In the interior the visitor is led to a place called the "Grotto of the Nativity," a semi-circular space covered with marble, in the centre of which was a silver star, over which sixteen lamps are kept burning night and day. Around the star is the Latin inscription: "Here Jesus Christ was born of the Virgin Mary." We descended into the cave by a dark flight of stone steps to the reputed manger. Finding a small melodeon in a niche in the wall, as we approached, I opened it and sang, "I will sing for Jesus," remembering that it was assuredly somewhere *near* this spot where Jesus was born; who could fail to utter praises both in song and in prayer in such a spot, exalted of all the earth as the birthplace of our Savior-King.

In the afternoon we wended our way into one of the wildest, most remote and silent spots in all Palestine, where the grim old convent of Marsaba is located in a lonely gorge. The assistants of our dragoman, guard, guide and commissary, had preceded us, and, as we came in sight of its walls, we saw our tents all pitched in the valley below, with the American flag furled in front, and, on our arrival, found our dinner awaiting us. After a night of sweet, refreshing sleep, undisturbed from hardly a sound from nature or beast or bird, we were in our saddles at sunrise and soon emerged from a wild mass of rock and ravine, into the cheerless desert or plain, occasionally catching sight of a solitary Bedouin, with the same striped blanket dependent from the shoulder, and the same murderous looking gun in hand. Coming to the Dead Sea about noon, we dismounted, a few of our party trying a bath, who came out of the heavy waters refreshed, salted, and undryable, with their tongues agonized with bitterness. They tested the fact that the human body would not sink in its waters owing to

its specific gravity, composed as it is of twenty-six parts
salt, while ordinary sea water is but four, and fully satisfied
that only the lowest species of animal life could exist
therein, and ready to accept the fact in the fullest sense
that the Dead Sea is both a physical and historical
wonder. Taking our departure from this famous locality,
we passed over great alkaline beds or deposits, until we
came to the Jordan, with its muddy stream, swift current
and willowy banks, stopping at the point where the waters
were so miraculously parted for the safe passage of God's
people, and where the dove descended upon the head of
Jesus as he was baptized. Washing our faces in this historic stream, and bottling some of its waters for keepsakes,
and lunching upon its banks, we kept on toward Jericho,
and found this once renowned of the ancient Israelitish cities,
a collection of miserable huts, roofed with the stalks of
plants and thorn-bushes; and, close by a mound of ruins,
among which a tower rises, reputed to be a portion of the
house in which Zaccheus lived. In the evening our pleasant
little party assembled in one tent, and together read of the
early history of this place, ranking as it does among the
most profound in the Bible, for it is the *wonders* which God
wrought which awes one here! After thanking God for the
privilege of seeing this land, and for the Bible which gives
us so correct a history of the same, we sought our couches
for needed rest, and, after an early breakfast, left our tents
and repaired to a fountain near the town, said to be the
"pool of Elisha," from which we drank of its pure, sweet
waters, and from near the source of which I cut me a staff
of thorn. Again mounting our horses, we rode along,
twice crossing the "Brook Cherith," where Elisha was fed
by the ravens, and of which region some one has said:
"The gorge of the brook Cherith is very magnificent. I
have seen none in Alpine history to equal it for wild and
desolate beauty."

Taking our lunch in a cave cut from the solid rock, we then ascended the steep hills; stopping for a short time at Bethany, to see the tomb of Lazarus and the house of Martha and Mary, we passed on, over Mt. Olivet and into Jerusalem by the gate of St. Stephen. Our few remaining days in Palestine were spent with our friends, Rev. Mr. Clark, Miss Le Fevre and others, in sight-seeing in the city and vicinity. At the Church of the Holy Sepulchre we secured a seat just in front of the Patriarch, who sat on an elegant throne, and who was gorgeously dressed in velvets and jewels. The service was conducted in Greek, was very lengthy, very imposing and exceedingly disgusting. Among other ceremonies the ark of the covenant, the seven golden candlesticks, and the shew-bread was brought out, while censors of insense were continually kept burning and swinging, which filled the old building with perfume. The audience was chiefly composed of the poorest and most degraded looking humanity, every one of them bringing a candle to aid in the illumination of the altar. Oh, that instead of this mummery, they might learn the simple way of faith, and receive Jesus into their hearts.

Visiting the Armenian Church, through the influence of Dr. De Hass we we were shown the jewels worn by their Patriarchs at festivals or services, costing millions of money, and all expended for pomp and show, instead of being used to educate and elevate these miserable beings, dazzled into false worship by their magnificence.

The following evening I gave my second service in Jerusalem, at the Evangelical Room of the German Assembly, which consisted of singing and responsive Bible-readings in which the audience readily participated.

Reserving Gethsemane for my final visit in this vicinity, in company with my little family, we went out by the Joppa gate, past the tombs of Absalom and Hezekiah, over the same pathway " the Son of Man " had often passed, to the garden, one of the most interesting spots the traveler can visit, and its position as little questionable. This enclosure comprises about one acre, and is surrounded by a stone wall ten feet high. As the old monk opened the gate to admit us, the perfume of the lavender and a great variety of other flowers extensively cultivated here, fell upon our senses most gratefully, while our attention was greatly attracted to eight large old olive trees, upon whose trunks were the marks of centuries, almost leading us in our imagination to the thought that beneath their gnarled branches our Savior agonized. Leaving my dear ones here, I walked over Olivet to Bethany, meditating on the sacred scenes with which we were surrounded, and returning in the fading twilight, we silently bent our steps towards St. Stephen's gate, and to our lodgings.

DEPARTURE FROM JERUSALEM.

On Monday morning, March 20, we turned our faces seaward and our backs upon these sacred spots, making our exit through the Joppa gate; and, when about three miles away from the old city, we turned our eyes once more toward "Olivet," bidding a long "good bye" to the places so dear to us, because once the home of Him who did so much for us. We arrived at Ramleh just in the gloaming, and found the Convent full of tourists. Resuming the journey at day break, we reached Joppa in time to take passage for Egypt. A pleasant sail, and we were at Alexandria on the 22d of March, and, after going through the ordeal of the customs, and being besieged by boatmen, we reached the "Hotel Europe," situated on a large and pleasant square, and found the city, contrary to our expectations, to be very fine and spacious.

CHAPTER XXIX.

EGYPT AND CROSSING THE MEDITERRANEAN SEA.

THE next morning we took the cars for Cairo, arriving in the afternoon, and taking up our quarters at the Hotel de 'Orento. The route thither was through a beautiful green valley along the banks of the Nile, but the mud huts of the natives resembled those of Syria, while their children who surrounded us at the stations, were filthily clad, sore eyed, and covered with flies which they did not make the least effort to rid themselves of.

The morning after my arrival, Rev. Dr. Lansing called, and arranged for a "service of song" to be held in the mission church. This was one of the most singularly constructed edifices I ever sang in, having a high ceiling and being furnished with neither seats or lights, excepting a few dozen candles with which to make a slight impression on the Egyptian darkness. I sang to some two hundred persons, composed of many nationalities. The exercises were so much appreciated and enjoyed that I was then and there invited to give a second service, which I did in the same church, and at its close a most cordial vote of thanks was tendered me.

SIGHTS IN AND ABOUT CAIRO.

Visiting the bazaars and walking the streets, we found the Egyptians to be a very common looking, in fact, homely people, as far as the males are concerned, the women's faces being concealed, excepting their eyes, and who carry their infants astride the left shoulder. Nearly every male, great and small, rich or poor, is clad in Turkish trousers and vest, and wears upon his head the red fez or felt cap, to which depends a black tassel, and if he is not afflicted with opthalmia or sore eyes the fact is an exception to the general rule.

Donkeys are for hire on every corner, and have been called the "omnibus of Egypt." The boy attendant runs along beside the animal and assists you to *embark* or *disembark* with great convenience. After visiting some of the mission schools, among which was a very flourishing one taught by Miss Whately of England, and under the charge of Miss Johnson, an American, meeting with great success in her noble efforts here, we visited the Mosque of alabaster marble, in which repose the remains of Mahomet Ali, and also several other points of interest.

A DAY AT THE PYRAMIDS.

We were driven seven miles thither, through a lovely green valley, over a fine road planted on either side with Acassia trees, bordering great stretches of magnificent fields of white and red clover in full bloom. On the way out we met great numbers of camels and donkeys loaded with bales of this sweet red clover, the blossoms hanging from either side of their panniers, making an exceedingly pretty sight. Little bunches of this clover are always seen in the front of all vehicles, the drivers feeding their horses from it with their hands, when making a halt, or while waiting for their passengers.

The approach to the pyramids is truly calculated to strike the beholder with awe, rising as they do in terrace above terrace of massive limestone blocks, against the eastern heavens. With two dirty Arabs to pull or lift on your arms and one to push or hoist from behind, after several rests, we reached the summit, and were more than compensated for our trouble, by the fine view we obtained from the lofty eminence. Standing here as they have for thousands of years, probably from this same massive monument Abraham and Moses and Joseph have looked out over the fertile valley of the ancient Nile, but, possibly, unlike us, with the knowledge of how these great rocks were piled on high, and what great machinery or power had been impressed by the Egyptian architect and builder to rear these monuments as a wonder for ages to come, perhaps not to crumble or *fall* until that time when the earth shall be consumed with fervent heat, and the heavens rolled together like a scroll. Descending, we stood before the great Sphinx with its stony, far-off gaze which seems to pierce the veil of the Infinite, and fills us with mingled awe and wonder. To us this wonderful creation of unknown conception and build, is a symbol of the grave, the unknown country of the dead from which "no traveler hath returned." The day following we went over to old Cairo, the very nest of Paganism, where we saw the howling and whirling Dervishes, in their disgusting devotions. The "howlers" sitting in a circle, would simultaneously bow their faces to the floor, each uttering a fearful groan, then rising to their feet, would sway their bodies backward and forward, their long hair sweeping over their faces at each movement, all the time uttering a most doleful guttural sound which gradually increased in violence to a prolonged *howl*. The "whirlers" were habited in mud-colored, high peaked felt hats, with gored skirts, having weights in the hem for ballast, and in their dance accompanied by a dull sound, would whirl round and round, with their hands and heads in one position, while, by the celerity of the movement, their skirts would expand and remain in the shape of a bell. The sum total of the "religion" of these enthusiasts is to endeavor to propitiate divine favor by their antics and macerations and to make their "piety" so wonderfully prominent as to lead the ignorant to pay them bountifully for their pretended intercessions with Deity. Superstition has its quack puddings as well as Bartholomew's fair, and this is one of them.

We spent but one Sabbath in Cairo, going out in the afternoon to hear Rev. Mr. Lansing, the pastor of the American Presbyterian Church. This earnest missionary took his text from Daniel 9: 25—"And the streets shall be built again, and the wall even in troublous times." I had of late been seeing so much heathenism, idolatry, and wretchedness, that it was only that morning I had said, "one is sometimes disposed to question whether or not the world is becoming better," and I felt that discourse so prophetic of the millennium, and illustrative of the faithfulness with which the Lord had fulfilled his promises all along down the pathway of the past to the present, was just what my soul needed, and I was enabled with greater faith, to sing

"Jesus shall reign where e'er the sun
Doth his successive journeys run."

BACK TO ALEXANDRIA.

On Monday morning, we returned to Alexandria, where I was booked for three services, in connection with the noble missionary, Rev. Dr. Yule. Judge Barring, an English barrister, took much interest in these services, which were held in the large Scotch Presbyterian Church, which had recently been built, and where the exercises were received with even more than usual interest. The following morning I sang before a school of young ladies, and they in turn sang some pieces in Arabic for me, and at its close gave me a little collection for my mission hall fund, as a testimonial of their appreciation of my songs.

STREET SCENE IN ALEXANDRIA.

In the older portions of the city, the streets are very dingy and narrow, but in the newer part the houses are very good, the streets nicely paved, while there are large avenues studded with fine commercial structures, which under gas-light gives one a sort of reminiscence of Paris. A visit to Pompey's pillar, Cleopatra's needle, the Kedive's palace, and other points of interest, terminated our stay in this old city, which by the hand of man and the process of irrigation has been built upon the desert sands.

CHAPTER XXX.

ITALY AND AUSTRIA.

ON the afternoon of April 7, we find ourselves again on board the steamer India, it being the same in which we had sailed from Bombay to Port Said, and it was very pleasant to meet our old Italian Captain, and his officers; although we could hardly exchange a word with them in their language, yet there was a general hand shaking and pleasant greeting.

We remained on deck for a long time, as the Egyptian shores receded, and until only a long white line of sandy shore was visible. On Sabbath we had no public service on board the ship, as the most of the passengers were Catholics, among whom were several Italian theatrical and operatic troupes on the homeward voyage.

Late in the afternoon of Monday, we passed quite near Candia Island, being able to see the snow-capped peaks quite plainly, and although the sunset was glorious, looking, as my little boy said, "like a city burning up," the night proved very stormy. The wind gradually became very high, causing the steamer to roll, and plunge considerably, but there was really nothing terrifying except to very nervous persons. Some of our passengers became much frightened, while two or three women were so thoroughly unnerved as to commence running through the saloon at midnight, arousing every body with their most piteous cries of fear.

The next day was calm and cloudless, while the water had assumed the color of a deep, rich, and beautiful green. My boys caught a little land-bird on the deck, and brought the little wanderer into the saloon while we were at dinner, where he found ever so many welcomes from the passengers as he passed from hand to hand. We saw in the distance, islands belonging to Greece. We anchored off Messina, on the Island of Sicily, at midnight, having before sunset caught a glimpse of Mt. Etna, and the island mountain ranges.

In the morning the air was fragrant with the perfume of the orange blossoms, heliotrope, and other flowers, and after purchasing a basket of strawberries, my wife and myself, with Miss Le Fevre and a few others, disembarked to visit some places of interest, among which was a beautiful cathedral.

Leaving at noon we sailed up through the straits of Messina, with Sicily on the one side, and Italy on the other, passing Mount Stromboli, whose rocky cone rises sheer out of the sea, and now being in a state of eruption was belching forth great clouds of fire and smoke.

THE QUEEN CITY BY THE SEA.

The next morning, from the quarter-deck, we caught our first view of the charming Bay of Naples and its surroundings. To the left was the famed Mount Vesuvius, so different from the ideal treasured up in my mind from school-day hours up to the very moment my vision rested upon it. On the right nestled the island of Capri, surrounded by others of equal size and beauty, bathed in the beams of the rising sun, while seaward the resplendent waters of the bay shone like burnished silver. Turning thence, our eyes were filled with delight as we looked on the palaces and villas of this exquisite city, resting on its half-amphitheatre stone-front, with its hill slopes in the background, rendered so famous to the world by the pen of the historian and tourist, as well as by minstrel and poet in song and verse.

My experience in getting my baggage through the customs was quite humorous, of which my organ seemed to be the perplexing mystery to the officials, who were only convinced of its non-warlike and inoffensive character by my opening it and playing a tune, after which, themselves laughing at the ridiculousness of the affair, they permitted us to seek our quarters at the Hotel Washington.

POMPEII AND VESUVIUS.

After a visit to the museum, where were gathered many Egyptian curiosities, relics from Pompeii, paintings by ancient and modern masters, statuary and bronzes; as also a call at the Aquarium, which proved to be very interesting, and where we witnessed the feeding of a huge devil-fish, in company with several friends, we took carriage the morning following, and were driven to the excavations at Pompeii. It had always seemed to me that in order to visit the ruins of this buried city, it would be necessary to descend below the surface of the earth with torches in hand as into a cave, and I was surprised to find a large portion of it thoroughly exhumed, and surrounded by an enclosure, to gain admission to which we were charged one franc each, which sum also furnished us with a guide. About one-half of the city still remains in sepulchre, while the exhumed portion consists of long rows of hundreds of solidly built but roofless houses, bordering a tangled maze of narrow streets, in the intricate windings and crossings of which it would be an easy matter to become lost without a monitor. Here we looked in upon temples, halls, baths, bake-shops, theatres and amphitheatres, as also at some Mosaics, which were just as bright as when that fearful night of destruction swept down upon and drowned this city in a lake of

liquid mud and ashes, full eighteen hundred years ago. One
is continually wondering amid these ruins how old this city
could have been before it met with its terrible fate,
while the curiosity is heightened in gazing upon doorsteps
of full two feet in thickness almost worn through in the
centre by the feet of its luckless inhabitants, as also by the
deep ruts or lines worn in the solid stone pavements by
their vehicles. Gathering some flowers and maiden's hair
fern which were growing on the ruins, we partook of our
luncheon near the entrance and then drove on to Hercula-
neum, a part of which can only be viewed by descending
beneath the surface with torches in hand, which though as
suddenly entombed as Pompeii, was swallowed up in a
molten sea of scoria.

MOUNT VESUVIUS.

A few mornings afterward our party drove four miles to
the city's boundary limits, riding in carriages up and beyond
the cultivated side of Vesuvius, to and over the black,
gnarled old lava flow, an inky ocean tumbled into a thousand fantastic shapes, and reaching the Hermitage, some
1,800 feet above the level of the sea, left our conveyance.
From this point the journey to the summit must be conducted on foot, and any number of guides, with climbing-
stock in hand, stand ready to assist you. Myself and wife
not desiring to go higher, walked leisurely on until we
reached the base of the principal cone, and here had a fine
opportunity of studying the panoramic natural picture presented to our view. At our feet, upon one side, lay the
clear blue sea, with its charming island clusters; on the
other, or land side, a carpet of living green verdure stretched
far away into the distance, while at our front the olden city
of Naples nestled quietly and peacefully at the feet of the
headlands of its beautiful bay. Others of our party, however, including my son, James, reached the sides of the

crater and looked down into its seething, sulphurous caldron, but their view outward from these volcanic heights, was much curtailed by mingled cloud and smoke which enveloped the summit as with a thick mantle.

I had been very cordially invited to give several services at Naples in connection with the Scotch Church, and it was a great gratification to meet its warm-hearted pastor and missionary, Rev. T. W. S. Jones, while my five song sermons in that beautiful edifice, were richly blessed of God in spiritual results. At their close, a collection was taken up for the benefit of my Mission Hall Fund, which, though not amounting to a large sum, was thoroughly appreciated. I also had the great pleasure of introducing Hon. Advocate Eaton, of Ceylon, to the Christian people here, who spoke most eloquently for the Master, prefacing his discourse by remarking that it was a great gratification to tell this congregation that through the instrumentality of the song services which I had given in his island several months ago, quite a number had found Christ precious to their souls. According to previous arrangement we left Naples on the following Friday for

ROME, THE ETERNAL CITY,

Where we were kindly met at the Depot by our old friend Rev. Dr. L. M. Vernon, and took up our quarters at the Hotel de Europe. By previous appointment, I gave two services in our M. E Church, Dr. Vernon's Italian mission exclusively, as also two in Rev. Mr. Van Meter's American Union Church, whose pastor has ever seemed to be a persecuted Paul, but has always proved to be master of the situation. On all these occasions I sang my songs in my native tongue, which were faithfully translated to my audiences by Rev. Dr. Leuna, and thus they received the gospel of song through the instrumentality of a converted Italian priest of much more than ordinary ability.

In our rambles in and about the city, we visited St. Paul's Church, a modern-built edifice, most elegantly constructed; its delicately-stained windows producing a rich and softening effect upon its interior, where we were shown some fine malachite altars and twelve pillars, which are said to have been brought from Solomon's temple. Thence we repaired to the Pantheon, entering it on a level from the ground, though recent excavations have brought to light the fact that its portico, the bronze on whose pillars has been taken to cover the high altar at St. Peter's, was once reached by a colossal flight of broad steps. Here, among many other objects of interest, we looked upon the tomb of Raphael, with his last "sketch" inscribed above it upon a tablet. After a short visit to the old Roman Forum, we repaired to the ruins of the palace of the Cæsars and wandered wonderingly among its old vine-covered walls and decaying, crumbling arches and apartments. A short distance further on we come upon the ruins of the mighty Coliseum, so symbolic of the power and grandeur of the ancient Roman Empire, and, picking our way downward into its magnificent amphitheatre, could hear nothing to break the great silence except the twittering of a few birds who were circling above our heads, where once the proud shouts of thousands on thousands, assembled to witness the most terrible scenes of barbarity, rang out and were echoed and re-echoed by its massive walls.

On Sunday we attended the American Chapel and listened to a good sermon from Rev. Mr. Langley, from the words: " And they were all with one accord in one place," and spent the remainder of the day with Dr. Vernon and his wife, talking of his mission work, in which we felt a most lively interest. He had but just completed a neat little M. E. church, which was situated in a pleasant locality in the very centre of the city, in whose services his amiable wife led the singing in Italian, having thoroughly mastered the language in their four years' residence, and whose success during that time, is second to none other in Rome.

On Monday, with Dr. Vernon as our chaperon, we visited St. Peters, the largest church in the world, looking with especial curiosity upon its magnificent altars and its rich pictures in Mosaic, the pieces in some of which were so diminutive as to be hardly discernable with the naked eye. Here we were shown the reputed tomb and the chair of St. Peter, whose disciple life has such peculiar interest to the Christian believer as it is delineated in sacred page. From thence we proceeded to the Vatican hall of statuary, where we were more particularly interested in the representation in marble of the "Dying Gladiator," with Raphael's paintings of the "Madonna," the "Transfiguration," and "Jerome's Last Supper." From Rome we depart for

FLORENCE, THE CITY OF ART,

Where we put up at the Hotel de Paix, situated on the banks of the Arno, the falling waters from a great dam just opposite giving me reminiscence of one other night in which I tried in vain to sleep in the vicinity of the great cataract of Niagara. I gave three services here, two of which were in connection with the church of Rev. Dr. Kittredge, and one with the Scotch Presbyterian Church, all being most cordially received.

Our route thither was through a most highly cultivated country, its broad and fertile fields being as choicely kept as a flower-garden, and those accustomed only to seeing our farms in America can have but a faint idea from the description of any pen, of its transcendent natural and agricultural beauty. While in Florence we paid a visit to the famous church, Santa Maria Novello, the pride of the great artist, architect and builder, Michael Angelo, and which he called "his bride." Thence we wended our way to the National Museum, where among the thousands of rich and rare curiosities, we more particularly noticed a great collection of antique and ancient weapons and armor. Furniture manufactured in the year 1600, majolicas from the famed manufactories of Urbino and Grabbio, as also "the mask of a satyr," the first work of Michael Angelo, when but fifteen years of age. During our stay here we also visited the celebrated Uffizi galleries, containing without doubt the richest and most celebrated collection of paintings and statuary on either hemisphere, among which is the "Venus de Medici" and other works of Raphael, as well as thirty-seven original drawings by this great master, and twenty-one by Michael Angelo. Here we wandered for hours feasting our eyes on the sublime achievements of the pencil, brush and chisel, and amid a perfect mine of bronzes and engraved precious stones and gems, feeling our inability to indelibly impress upon our memory even a tithe of the rarest and most beautiful objects which met our vision.

Our last afternoon in this entrancing city was spent in visiting the churches of Santa Croce, in which are the tombs of Dante, Gallio and Michael Angelo; San Lorenzo, where the Medici are entombed in the wonderful sacristy erected by Michael Angelo, and within whose walls are the famous statues of day and night, and by a call on an Italian Methodist minister who wedded a wife in Delaware, Ohio, in whose company we visited a cemetery adjacent or near his residence, in which we looked upon the silent mounds where rest the remains of Mrs. E. B. Browning, Hiram Powers and Theodore Parker.

THE CITY OF TURIN.

Climbing the Apennines by rail, we pass through the gloomy cavern of the Mt. Cenis tunnel to find ourselves in this charming city, which is the capital of Piedmont, is situated on the left bank of the River Po, and is in full view of Monte Rosa and the Alps. Here we spent the Sabbath, and on the following evening I gave a song service in connection with one of Dr. Vernon's ministers, to a fine audience. Taking train we came on to

GENOA, THE TALL CITY OF MARBLE.

And which I call the " step-stone city " of all Europe, it being one of the chief ports of Italy. The ground on which it is built is very rolling and uneven, a noble succession of large and ancient-looking white marble palaces are situated upon its three principal streets, while beautiful villas and gardens cover the hills in its back-ground, presenting a beautiful sight from the sea. Here I was made to feel thoroughly at home by our most excellent consul, O. M. Spencer, who is not only an eloquent speaker and able writer, but a noble Christian as well. My services, which seemed to be greatly enjoyed, were given in the Scotch Church, whose pastor was Rev. Donald Miller, D. D., an able and esteemed clergyman.

During my stay in Genoa, I visited its famous cemetery, about two miles from the city, and which with its carved cloisters and sculptured tombs embraces an area of nearly four acres. As I passed its gates it seemed as though I was entering a hall of exquisite statuary, rather than a silent city of the dead, for on every hand these finely executed human forms in stone rose up on pedestal after pedestal to mark the spot where silent sleepers lay, in the centre of which dumb monuments was a circular plot or area in which the poorer people were interred. In this city I also visited the celebrated cathedral of San Lorenzo, which is both in exterior and interior one of the most gorgeous in the world, the chapel of St. John, which is located therein, being literally decked with gold and precious stones.

THE CITY OF MILAN.

Arriving in this city, I sang to a small audience in Evangelical Hall, where Rev. J. C. Ivill was preaching, but so few comprehended or understood the words of my songs, that I felt but very little good was accomplished by the service. I did not feel interested to visit any locality of interest in this city but the great Domo Cathedral, which is modeled after St. Peter's at Rome; is considered the second largest structure of its character in Europe, and the greatest work of Michael Angelo. This edifice is built entirely of white marble and is of the richest and most massive architecture. From its roof rise into the air a forest of domes or spires to the number of one hundred and thirty-five, while its facades and eaves are decorated with nineteen hundred and twenty-three marble statues, and its interior embellished with six hundred and seventy-nine. The massiveness of this great building without is fully equalled by the richness of its ornamentation and decoration within, the Virgin's Chapel being most beautifully constructed and adorned, while its stained windows are said to surpass all similar workmanship on either continent.

VIENNA, THE CAPITAL OF AUSTRIA.

From Italy I went forward to Vienna, the capital of Austria, which proved the most difficult place to sing in all my travels. Calling upon Mr. E. Millard, Bible Agent, and Mr. Priggen, Religious Tract Agent, from them I learned that it was necessary to apply to the police-headquarters for permission to hold *all kinds* of Protestant religious services. Going out in a rain-storm, I visited the station to find that they took three or four days to consider an application for service of song, and, having but a few days at my disposal, I returned to Mr. Priggen and told him I could not wait the action of the authorities. Together with Mr. Millard he managed to give me an opportunity of holding a service in place of a date set aside for regular preaching, at which one or two spies of the police force were present to see if I did or said anything against the Romish church, who, at its close, announced themselves to me, as well as their fruitless errand, and gave me liberty to sing as often and as much as I pleased. It is poor policy always and everywhere to denounce other sects or religions, so long as their services consist in preaching or singing of Jesus and the dear old gospel. This, my only Vienna service, was held in Evangelical Hall, a beautiful room capable of seating four hundred persons, wherein a goodly number were assembled. Mr. Millard was appointed chairman, and, besides introducing me to my audience, translated whatever I had to say or sing, giving a good idea of the sentiment of my songs, the occasion giving me much enjoyment.

The following evening I attended the Emperor's opera, where I think I listened to the finest music and singing I have ever been permitted to hear, but, having previously heard much of the best talent in classical music in other great cities of Europe, which was beyond the power of pen to describe, I will not here undertake to give an idea to the reader of what, in this especial field of musical culture, far excelled all I had ever before heard evoked from musical instruments or mortal lips.

Vienna has rising of 1,100,000 population as well as many places of interest to amuse the traveler. During my stay at the Hotel Imperial, which was once the palace of the Duke of Wurtemburg, I went out to view the Prater, or Hyde Park of the city, containing four English square miles and beautifully studded with lime and chestnut trees, in which was held the International Exhibition of 1873, as also the Sladtpark, or Imperial Garden, besides visiting the Cathedral of St. Stephens, the churches of St. Augustin and the Capuchine, with their celebrated tombs in which so many royal dead are sepulchered. My next stop was at the

QUAINT OLD CITY OF PRAGUE,

Where my service had already been arranged by that most energetic missionary brother, Rev. Andrew Moody, who kindly met me at the railway station and escorted me to my delightful lodgings. Here I received a most hearty welcome from a fine audience, who manifested much enthusiasm over my service, and I was sorry that my visit here had to be curtailed because of previous arrangements. Before my departure, however, I was handed a little memento of appreciation and esteem from the good people of Prague, in the shape of a sum representing an Austrian brick for my Mission Hall.

The population of this ancient city is about 200,000, of whom full two-thirds are Jews. It was the seat of learning in the Austrian Empire until John Huss, in the attempt to exclude foreign students from attendance upon its great University, which was founded in 1348, and had two hundred Professors and thirty thousand pupils, led to its destruction by twenty-five thousand of the latter, to found the Universities at Heidelberg, Leipsig and Cracow. From Prague I proceeded to Dresden, the tourist's Paradise.

CHAPTER XXXI.

GERMANY AND HOLLAND.

AT Dresden I spent several days including the Sabbath. This is a most delightful city, and is much admired by both English and American tourists, who are consequently to be found assembled here in large numbers, being especially delighted with its cheap living, excellent music and rare works of art. Here the eye is delighted with beautiful paintings, sculpture and rare china and other wares, and the ear entranced by the grand music of the brass bands in their open-air concerts. I gave my first service of song on the evening of my arrival to a large audience, composed mostly of English and American visitors, who seemed much pleased with the songs of homeland, and a song-sermon the Sabbath evening following in Rev. Mr. Fogo's church, in which the spirit of the Master was truly manifest, and from which the audience seemed to depart reluctantly. My next visit was to

LEIPSIC, THE PUBLISHING CITY.

And musical centre of the Empire. I confess to a feeling of trepidation at the thought of singing beneath the very eaves of the great musical college of Europe, but when I came to consider that my singing was rather a service than a musical fete, new courage came to me. My service here had been nicely planned by the Rev. Mr. Curtiss, a young man who was studying for the ministry, and also preaching in the American Church, and was well attended. Several of the students from the musical college were present, and I sang with even more than my wonted zeal, praying and hoping that some one of them might be induced to give their talents also to singing God's praises. I could not but help feeling on this occasion what a mighty power it would be for good in the world if all singers would dedicate their voice to singing Gospel truth and Christian sentiment not only in simple melody but in classical strains.

Here also is the great German Bookseller's Exchange, the city having over three hundred booksellers and publishers, one hundred steam and two hundred hand-presses constantly engaged in printing works in all languages, it being the great metropolis of the German book trade. Near the site of Prague, Napoleon was defeated by the Allies in 1813, while here is also to be seen a fine monument to Hahneman, the inventor of homeopathy. Through the kindness of the London Sabbath-school mission I was next at the

CITY OF BERLIN,

By their agent, Dr. G. D. Prochnow, who treated me with the warmest hospitality. At the outset I experienced a little difficulty, owing to some ill-reports concerning an American Christian brother who had preceded me, but Dr. Prochnow overcame them and a service was arranged for me at the Moravian Church, where several hundred people listened with strange interest to my entire programme. At their urgent request I repeated the service on the following evening, when at least half of my audience were German-speaking people, who listened with deep attention, after the verses, previous to their singing, had been translated to them.

Berlin, the capital of the Prussian and German Empire, has fully 1,000,000 inhabitants, is finely situated on the

River Spree, has five hundred streets and fifty-eight squares, is twelve miles in circumference, and is one of the largest and handsomest cities of the old world. Here are to be found some of the very finest hotels on the Continent, with many public and private structures of great magnificence, charming zoological and botanical gardens, and many fine equestrian and other statues in marble and bronze. The old and new museums are filled with the finest paintings and bronzes, while the royal library of seven hundred thousand volumes and fifteen hundred manuscripts, contains the Gutenberg Bible, the first book printed with movable types. I also visited several other localities of much interest, and while passing the Royal Palace caught a glimpse of Emperor William sitting at one of the windows. From Berlin I journeyed on to the

BEAUTIFUL CITY OF HAMBURG,

Which in my estimation, outside of Paris, is the handsomest city in Europe. Here I remained over the Sabbath and gave three services, two of which were held in Rev. James Edward's Scotch Church and one in Sacristan Hall. Although these audiences were composed mainly of Germans, and but few understood the words of my songs, yet they attentively listened to me.

Hamburg, with its environs, has a population of 300,000 souls, and is situated on the north bank of the River Elbe, and about seventy miles from its mouth. A magnificent view of the city and its suburbs was obtained by me from the tower of St. Michael's Church, which rises four hundred and fifty-six feet into the air, while the botanical and zoological gardens, which are very extensive, claimed considerable of my attention. It being the chief commercial port of the transit trade of Germany, of course it bustled with business, and a glance at its merchants assembled in their spacious exchange, gave me a thought of the busy throngs in my own home city of New York. Thence I came on to the

CITY OF BREMEN,

Which is the German head-quarters of our M. E. Church, where I gave three services in Rev. H. Rosenthall's church, and many of my songs being published here in the German language, I felt thoroughly at home in singing to my brother German audiences. I found this an active little commercial city, situated on the river Weser, having intimate trade relations with the United States, beautiful public gardens, with running water, and sheltered walks, laid out in the English style, which were located on a site formerly occupied by grim fortifications, showing that the reign of peace within its borders had verily "turned the swords into ploughshares and the spears into pruning hooks."

THE CITY OF AMSTERDAM.

The next stage of my journey brought me to Amsterdam in old Holland, and in no section in Europe did I find myself better known, or was I welcomed with such heartiness as by the good old Knickerbocker Dutch. Here Pastear Adama Von Scheltama for a number of years had been engaged in translating my songs into the Holland Dutch, and, in fact, had completed my entire song ministry in that language. Not only did I find my songs in use in the Sunday-schools, but also in many of the day schools and charitable and benevolent institutions of the Faderland, and general favorites everywhere with both young and old. Mr. Von Scheltama having arranged a series of song services for me in the Williams House, and in several of the churches, with this esteemed clergyman and friend at my side translating my songs and giving a sort of prelude to each, they were received with evident pleasure by our congregations, an eloquent teacher and scholar in one of which made me a pleasant address of welcome.

There are nearly 300,000 inhabitants in this famous old city, which is fully nine miles in circumference. Its foundations are reared upon spiles driven into the shifting sands, upon land snatched from the embrace of the sea, the city proper being ribboned with a perfect net-work of canals which are crossed by more than three hundred bridges. Besides its immense commercial importance, having deal with all nations, it is very famous for its diamond cutting skill and industry, which employs ten thousand men, and where the most precious stones in the world received their finish, including the celebrated Kohinoor. This, too, was the home of most of the renowned Dutch painters, who have passed from earth, an elegant monument to the great Rembrant being erected in Oude Kirk, or Church. From thence I proceeded, in company with Mr. Von Scheltma, to

THE HAGUE, OR CAPITAL,

Of Holland, where we were most kindly entertained by a good Baron, a grand type of Dutch nobility and hospitality. At his own expense this nobleman had engaged the elegant Opera Hall for my service, and had so arranged as to present me to a fine audience. The Hague, having nearly 100,000 population, is the residence of the Court and the seat of government, being fourteen miles from Rotterdam and five from the sea. Five bronze statues of William, Prince of Orange, and William, King of the Netherlands, adorn the ground of the Parliament House, and the Museum, in which latter is a fine collection of paintings by the old Dutch masters, including Rembrant's "Anatomical Lesson" and Vandyek's portrait of "Simon, the Painter." This city had further interest to me from the fact of its being the birth-place of Huggens, the inventor of the pendulum clock, now in use in every portion of the habitable globe. I next visited the

CITY OF ROTTERDAM,

The second in size and importance in Holland, situated on the river Maas, and though twenty miles distant from the sea, greatly resembles at this point an arm thereof. It has a population of 130,000, and is also threaded with canals spanned by many bridges, and bordered with luxuriant shade trees. It is also a port of great commercial wealth and importance, the home of opulent and thriving merchants and ship owners, the largest steamers and sail vessels landing passengers and the products of all countries upon its massive quays.

I was most hospitably entertained here at the fine old home of William Gregory Herklotz, (since deceased), a gentleman of great wealth and mental attainment, who made it especial delight to entertain all strangers bearing the name of Christians. My services had been nicely planned by Philip G. Ittman, Esq., a most earnest man, diligent in business and serving the Lord, and called out a good attendance. Two of these were held in churches and one in a spacious Hall, and were my last public song services on the continent. Visiting the "Old Ladies' Home," which Mr. Ittman, with his great wealth and liberality, manages and supports, and trying to comfort its feeble and once homeless inmates by singing to them my "Home of the Soul," after bidding my many new and dear friends farewell, I took steamer for London. Subsequently I received a letter at the latter city from this dear brother and his wife, inclosing a telegraphic despatch to be forwarded to the United States if I thought best, desiring if possible to adopt as their own, the orphaned children of P. P. Bliss and wife, of whose sad death they had just learned.

---

*Sixty pages are here added to correct omission in paging the illustrations.

CHAPTER XXXII.

BRIEF ACCOUNT OF THE THIRD ENGLISH TOUR.

REALIZING that our present stay in this vast old city would probably continue for a year, we secured pleasant apartments which my dear wife cozily prepared for our convenience and comfort, and we immediately commenced searching for suitable schools in which to place our two boys. Very fortunately we were led to Mrs. Scott's private school, situated quite near our lodgings, which proved to be of superior excellence, and here our little Philip, in our country's centennial year, received his first educational instruction, outside his home. For his encouragement in future study and in the arduous pursuits of life which may be in store for him, it pleases me to note that he never missed a day's attendance upon this school for a year, and at its close received the first prize for conduct and the second prize for scholarship. Our eldest son, James, entered the "Grove House School," and also began his lessons in music with Mr. West, a graduate of the London Royal Music Society, making much proficiency therein and acquiring a taste which we trust will prove of lasting and beneficial service to him in the future.

While the preliminary preparations were being made and perfected for my giving another one hundred nights of song in behalf of the English Sunday-school interest, the

London Sabbath-school Union Committee, with commendable forethought, arranged for me a gathering which may be appropriately termed a greeting of welcome or send-off to my work which served a great inspiration to me during my whole tour throughout the United Kingdom. This meeting was appointed for the 13th day of July, and a beautiful ticket of invitation was engraved and sent out to full one thousand Christian and Sabbath-school workers, bidding them to attend thereon. This card of invitation was worded as follows:

SUNDAY-SCHOOL UNION
Welcome to Philip Phillips.

Mr. Phillips having arrived in England in completion of his journey round the world, a meeting will be held to welcome him, on Thursday evening, July 13, 1876.

Col. Sir H. M. Havelock, Bart: V.C., C.B., M.P., President of the Union, has kindly consented to preside.

Tea and coffee will be served in the Library at six o'clock. Meeting in the Lecture Hall at seven.

ADMIT ONE. } W. GROSER, F. J. HARTLEY,
Hon. Sec's. } A. BENHAM, J. E. TRESSIDER.

The hour of my third welcome in London had arrived, and on being conducted into Jubilee Hall, I found it filled with the *elite* of the London Sabbath-school laborers. Sir Henry Havelock was to have presided, but was unavoidably detained at the House of Commons, and the ever genial Sir Charles Reed was chosen in his stead, while upon the platform were Messrs. Hartley and Shrimpton of the Committee, to speak on behalf of English Sabbath-school work; Hon. J. H. Eaton, of Ceylon, to discourse of my services in that famous island; Rev. J. F. Horsley, of Australia, to give an account of my work in those distant colonies; Dr. Alexander Clark, of Pittsburg, to say a word of my song services in my own land; Mr. Richards, the worthy secretary of the meeting, to give some most appropriate remarks, and, last of all, myself, to sandwich in the songs of the evening. The exercises opened by singing in concert:

> "And are we yet alive
> And see each other's face,
> Glory and praise to Jesus give,
> For his redeeming grace."

After prayer by Rev. Dr. Bliss, of Syria, Sir Charles Reed, in a few well chosen words, illustrated the object of the gathering and in turn most appropriately introduced each speaker to the assemblage. The exercises in all their features, were most interesting and enjoyable to me, with the exception of some personal allusions, yet these were all spoken in a spirit of love and in a manner designed to especially aid me in the arduous engagement upon which I was just about to enter. At the close of his speech Mr. Richards gave me the places and dates where it had been arranged I should sing for one hundred consecutive evenings, and, after singing from Song Life, "Sweet By and By," the audience dispersed to their homes, and I to mine, wondering and praying if I might have strength to perform the work which had been allotted me.

The day for setting out on my song-journey soon came and accompanied by my ever faithful friend, Richards, and my dear family, I went to the station where they bade me God-speed. My first engagement was at Colchester, distant some sixty miles from London, and having a population of about 20,000 people. I was kindly received at the station on my arrival and conducted to the pleasant English home of Mr. Daniels, and in his company visited several noted mines and places of historic interest during the afternoon. I held my first service, August 7, in the Baptist church, and was cordially greeted by a good audience, singing as usual for an hour and a half, experiencing a feeling of great earnestness for my work, now that, to use a common phrase, "the ice had been broken."

Having described most of the towns visited in England, and instances connected therewith, in my previous sketches, I shall only refer to a few in my present tour which I did not before mention. At Louth I was entertained at the model home of Alderman C. Smith, Esq., which, though furnished with all the surroundings of wealth and culture, was thoroughly adorned by those sweet Christian graces and influences which far outshine all other gifts vouchsafed to the human family by the divine hand. In the evening Mr. Smith, as chairman, felicitously introduced me to an audience of one thousand persons assembled in the Town Hall, and the dear Lord helped me sing to His praise and glory to them, as also onward at Boston, Newark, Retford, Peterboro, Nottingham and Loughborough.

At Derby a service had been arranged for me by Mr. W. Wilson, in Temperance Hall, which was filled to overflowing, and where I sung with much satisfaction. I was hospitably cared for here at the home of Mr. Carp, who had a family of twelve interesting children, whose bright cheery faces and winning ways, as they gathered with us at the family board, have a reserved corner in my remembrance. There is no pleasanter sight on the broad earth than a large family of children gathered together around the hearthstone of home, in all the innocence and life of childhood's happy hours.

From here I passed on, singing at Chesterfield, Manchester, Dewsbury, to Leeds, where I have ever had a right royal welcome, and where, as previously, I was the guest of Robert Slades, Esq., whose enthusiasm in the Sabbath-school work knows no boundaries, and which will always insure a full house when he has a service for its benefit in charge. My song service on this occasion, was held in the great Town Hall, which was filled with people even to the end gallery, and a more enthusiastic audience I have seldom, if ever, met.

My next stop was at Staningly, where I gave a song sermon on the Sabbath, in the large Baptist church, to at least an audience of three thousand persons, who manifested the greatest enjoyment, and, at its close, presented me £12 on behalf of the Sunday-school, for my Mission Hall fund. Proceeding to Harrogate, the great English watering place, I was entertained by Dr. J. T. Armstrong, and sung to a full house in the Primitive Methodist Church. Thence I went on to Scarboro, another watering place of great notoriety, where I was again greeted with an audience of at least one thousand persons. Middleboro, Darlington, Thirsk, East and West Hartlepool and Sunderland, were the scene of my next services. At the latter place thirty-two hundred tickets had been sold, and my faithful associate, Mr. Thomas Sutherland, sold over £25 worth of my Song Ministry. The occasion was the most successful one held in the country during the tour. All seemed thoroughly delighted with the service, the great hall was filled with attentive listeners, the building was well ventilated and very easy to sing in, I felt in the best of spirits and voice, and thanked God and took courage.

My next service was at Jarrow, and the following at Newcastle, where I had a full house, singing in the Central Hall, in which Bro. Moody's prayer meeting, organized two years previous to my visit, was still in progress. Here I was greeted by a bright, earnest convert, who attributed his coming to Christ and his awakening from sin, from hearing me sing in Newcastle four years previous. Such evidence as this that I am a humble instrument of the Master for the salvation of souls, ever stimulates me to renewed zeal in the services of sacred song.

I next gave services in Edinburgh, Lancaster, Holden, Bary, Blackburn, Burnley, Middleton, Hollingwood, Stock-

port, Mexboro, Southport, and Liverpool, and thence proceeded to Belfast, Ireland. Belfast is one of my pet cities, for many reasons, perhaps the foremost of which is that its inhabitants appreciate me better than I deserve. Another of these reasons for my preference is, that this old city is the home of Rev. Dr. Robert Knox, which has become emphatically my home in Ireland, for here I once stopped with my dear family two weeks in the Christian society of the good Mrs. Knox and her eloquent husband, experiencing a rare contentment which is only peculiar to the precincts of the home we have personally secured and which shelters those we love. I have sung in my visits to Ireland, eight nights in the city of Belfast, and always to full houses, rain or shine. On one occasion I was invited to visit one of the prisons, and, accepting, found that the warden had made quite elaborate preparations for receiving me. Mottoes of welcome were hung about the prison walls, and, as I entered the corridors, I was greeted by a sort of welcome salute from a number of the inmates to whom I was introduced, and invited to make a speech. Feeling thoroughly embarassed, but realizing that I must say something, I commenced with "Gentlemen, I'm glad to see so many of you here." Just at this point my wife touching my toes and whispering "This is a prison and not a Sabbath-school," of course, I realized my situation, *curtailed my eloquence*, and escaped from my dilemma by singing a dear old gospel song.

However much attached to Belfast, yet my duty called me to go forward to give my services at Carrickfergus, and to go thence by steamboat to St. Helen's, Wallesey, Shrewsbury, Leominster, Burton, Walsall, Smithick, Birmingham, Atherton, Kidderminster, Worcester, Hereford, Swansea and Pembroke Dock, the great ship-building station of England, where I was greeted with an enthusiastic audience of rising twelve hundred persons. I next visited

Gloucester, the home and the birth-place of Robert Raikes and the Sunday-school. Notwithstanding I had sung here once before, and that the night was very stormy, I was greeted by a good house, and felt that the singing of my Sunday-school songs was most appropriate here on the very ground of the initiatory labor of the great instructor who sowed the seed upon this hallowed spot which has blossomed into a great harvest over all the civilized earth.

My next objective point was Taunton, where I stopped with that noble Christian gentleman, William Rawlins, who has a great number of men working in his large silk factory. I was told by one of his neighbors that for the last thirty years he had held morning prayers in his great mill, and that many of his operatives had became Christians through the influence of his prayers. He gave me £1 for my Mission Hall fund and a God bless you, and thus I left William Rawlins never to meet again on earth; but my present memory of him will live while I do.

My last services in the country were given at Barnstable, Davenport, Exeter, Yeoville, Guilford, Eastborn, Hastings, Ashford, Faversham, Shearness, Maidstone, Barnett and Luton. My remaining ten services were to be given in the metropolis of London and would conclude my third engagement with the London Sabbath-school Union.

INCIDENTS OF SONG SERVICES IN LONDON.

One of the most memorable occasions in my services in London, was at Conference Hall, where the good William Pennefather presided. Having assured the Sabbath-school Committee that if they would waive the admission fee at the door, he would see that a collection would equal the amount to be procured by the sale of tickets, of course the committee yielded to his request. The result of this plan was that every seat in the hall was filled quite early, while many hundreds of people had assembled at the great gateway unable to gain entrance. In my endeavor to pass through this crowd, and being personally unknown to them, I came near being crushed in my attempt to reach the gate-way, and entered the hall in a somewhat frustrated condition consequent upon the struggle with and the pressure of the people. As I at last came up the steps into the hall, the Rev. Mr. Pennefather said to me, "Is this Mr. Phillips?" to which I replied, "all that is left of him." He said, "come with me," and escorted me into a large private room and seated me in a cozy chair, and still holding my hand, fell upon his knees before me, and in the following simple words of faith prayed:

"Oh God, Mr. Phillips is weary and nervous from the press outside, and needs strength. Give it to him now and let thy blessing rest upon this service of song. Amen."

"Come," said he, "the hour has passed when we should commence;" and thus I was quickly ushered in before an audience of three thousand people, to whom I sang with more than usual composure and success. As I look back upon this occasion, I cannot but feel that my success was attributable to God's help in answer to the prayer of the righteous, uttered by one who has now passed from death into life, but whose influence is still felt and whose works are seen and do follow him.

My last public service in London, was held at the City Temple, at which the eloquent and noble divine, Dr. Joseph Parker, presided, who, after a few words commendatory of my humble efforts, introduced me to an elite audience of all denominations, to whom I sung as well as I was capable for more than an hour. At the conclusion of the service a special collection was tendered my Mission Hall fund, by the London Sunday-school Union, which amounted to about $100, after which resolutions of thanks were passed, and the meeting adjourned with the doxology and benediction.

A few days later my farewell meeting was held at Old Bailey Jubilee Hall, the following words being engraved on the ticket of invitation:

SUNDAY-SCHOOL UNION.
Farewell to Philip Phillips.

Mr. Phillips having spent the last twelve months in England, in the interests of sacred song, and in completion of his journey around the world, a meeting will be held to bid him farewell, on Tuesday evening, July 10, 1877.

Sir Charles Reed, L.L. D. (President of the Union), has kindly consented to preside.

Tea and coffee will be served in the Library at 6 o'clock. Meeting in the Lecture Hall at 7 o'clock.

ADMIT ONE.

W. GROSER, F. J. HARTLEY, } *Hon. Sec's*
A. BENHAM, J. E. TRESSIDER, }

After refreshments had been served, to the great pleasure of all present, we repaired to the hall where the farewell words and good bys were to be uttered. The chairman called the meeting to order, and, in befitting words, stated the object for which it had assembled, introducing the several speakers in their order, all of whom seemed to be in their happiest vein as they discoursed on the subject in hand in the most earnest and complimentary manner, among whom were Mr. F. J. Hartley, Mr. Shrimpton, Mr. Benham, Mr. T. B. Smithers, Rev. Dr. Rust, of Cincinnati, and Rev. W. T. Van Meter, of Rome.

The chairman presented Mrs. Phillips and myself with an elegant silver tea set (sterling), with some thoroughly appreciated remarks, to which I responded as well as I could.

Among the choice sayings on this occasion, were the playful remarks of Rev. Van Meter, when he added to his speech these words: " I like this tea business. There was a time when we would not have your tea; but it has since improved, and we know and love each other better, because we have worked shoulder to shoulder in the battle against sin and the devil."

This gathering at the conclusion of my third engagement of one hundred nights with the committee, was peculiarly gratifying to me, marked as it was from its opening to its close, with genuine heartiness of appreciation of my labor, in which I had been so signally blessed in perfect fulfillment of the engagement, with large audiences, and, more than all, by bearing home to my native land the kind regards and best wishes of all with whom I had come in contact.

The next day we took train for Liverpool, where I gave my farewell service in Hope Hall, which was thoroughly filled, and sung my songs with a happy heart seemingly to the delight of all present. Embarking on the "City of Richmond," of the Inman line, the next day, the shores of Old England soon faded away, and tender, grateful memories of love and thanksgiving filled our hearts. Next morning my little family quartet awaken from refreshing slumber in a large state-room, which we have all to ourselves, and while pacing the deck to discover who were our fellow passengers, we were made glad to find among them Mr. William Noble, the John B. Gough of England, whose companionship we greatly enjoyed during the entire voyage. Nine days spent after the usual programme of a sea voyage, and one beautiful July morning, we sight the shores of our loved native land, are met on shore by our dear friends and driven away to our quarters at the St. Dennis hotel, where, after a few days rest, we depart for

OUR OWN CHAUTAUQUA,

Which place we left three years before. Here the great Sunday-school Assembly, headed by that princely worker, Rev. Dr. J. H. Vincent, was in session, and as I appeared in front of the platform, he exclaimed therefrom, "I now have the privilege of introducing and welcoming home again, Philip Phillips, who has just returned from his singing tour around the world. Since he left this Assembly, three years ago, he has sung five hundred and seventy-four nights in the countries he has successively passed through. Let us give him a right hearty welcome 'home again,' after which he will sing you a song." Thousands of hands came together as one at the close of this announcement, and as the echoes of applause died away, they were succeeded by the strains of music of the well-known song:

>Come, and hear the grand old story,
> Story of the ages past,
>All earth's annals far surpassing,
> Story that will ever last.
>
>Christ, the Father's Son eternal,
> Once was born a Son of man;
>He, who never knew beginning,
> Here, on earth, a life began.
>
>Words of truth and deeds of kindness,
> Miracles of grace and might,
>Scatter fragrance all around Him,
> Shine with heaven's most glorious light.
>
>In Gethsemane behold Him,
> In the agony of prayer;
>Kneeling, pleading, groaning, bleeding,
> Soul and body prostrate there.
>
>On to Golgotha He hastens,
> Yonder stands His cross of woe;
>From the hands, and feet, and forehead,
> See the precious life-blood flow.
>
>It is finished! see His body
> Laid alone in Joseph's tomb;
>'Tis for us He lieth yonder,
> Prince of Life, enwrapped in gloom.
>
>But in vain the grave has bound Him,
> Death has barred its gates in vain;
>See, for us the Savior rises,
> Lo! for us He bursts the chain.
>
>Hear we, then, this grand old story,
> And in listening, learn to love;
>Flowing through it to the guilty,
> From a pardoning God above.

CLASSIFIED INDEX OF PERSONAL MENTION.

Anderson, Rev. J. H.,	289
Armstrong, Rev. Dr.,	91
Allan, Robert,	210
Anthony, Capt.,	232
Ames, Bishop,	79
Baily, J.,	291
Benham, Mr. A.,	457, 60, 464
Bliss, P. P.,	152, 351
Boole, Rev. William,	73
Bewley, Henry,	373, 355
Bonar, Rev. Dr.,	379, 376
Bane, Rev.,	377
Burns, Rev. Dr.,	377
Bainbridge, Thomas,	379
Bliss, Rev. Dr.,	458
Beer, Arnold,	301
Butler, Dr. William,	295, 302
Badley, Rev. B. A.,	303
Bowen, Rev. George,	315, 306
Butts, Miss,	307, 308
Burton, Rev.,	316
Barring, Judge,	332
Bee, John,	193, 248
Baugh, Rev. George,	256, 260
Brittan, Miss,	271
Blair, Robert,	220
Burrows, Mr.,	228
Bickford, Rev. James,	235

INDEX OF PERSONAL MENTION.

Bucklin, V. M.	134
Birkshall, Mr.,	239
Baker, Rev.,	176
Burnett, Mathew,	195
Barker, Rev. George,	202
Burns, Kit,	73
Bryant, William Cullen,	78
Brown, Mr.,	104
Braden, Rev. John,	118
Bradbury, William B.,	39
Borgart, Bishop,	321
Cushing, C. H.,	110
Carhart, Mrs. L. H.,	114
Clay, Henry,	120
Crane, Rev. E. F.,	45
Cook, D. J.,	51
Clark, Miss Olive M.,	53
Clark, Harvey,	53
Cookman, Rev. Albert,	85
Clark, Dr. Alexander,	457, 127
Cole, Major,	146
Colfax, Vice President,	150
Cole, Dr. R. E.,	159
Cunningham, Dr. Thomas F.,	160
Cook, Captain,	215, 172
Crouch, Ex-Mayor,	246, 186, 177
Crisp, Rev.,	190
Curmon, Rev. William,	220
Cope, John,	246
Carter, Rev. Mr.,	263
Conder, Mr. Henry,	306
Carey, Rev.,	309
Clark, Rev.,	319, 316, 310
Curtiss, Mr.,	346
Cook, Paul,	359, 358

INDEX OF PERSONAL MENTION. 469

Chalmers, Dr.,	379
Curruthers, Mr.,	383
Carp, Mr.,	459
Clements, Mr.,	233
Daniels, Mr.,	197, 348
DeHass, Dr.,	320
Duff, Rev. Dr.,	310
Dodson, James D.,	248
Dare, Joseph,	133, 248
Dewer, J. S.,	266
Davis, Mr.,	222
Deans, Wm.,	225
Damon, Dr.,	168
Douglass, Dr.,	141
De Paw, W. C.,	151
Davis, Adams,	43
Davis, H. S.,	53
Deems, Rev. Dr.,	95
Davis, Jefferson,	100
Davies, Rev. Dr.,	115
Doggett, Bishop,	92
Edsall, William,	61
Edgerly, Mr.,	109
Eggleston, Edward,	152
Eaton, Hon. J. H.,	457, 338, 265
Edwards, Rev. James,	348
Frazer, Dr.,	312
Froist, Hon.,	313
Fisher, Mr.,	314
Fox, D. O.,	212, 314
Fogo, Rev.,	346
Francis, Hon. J. M.,	268
Firth, Rev. F. F.,	219
Field, Cyrus W.,	231
Franklin, Sir John,	238

Friers, Dr.,	168
Fletcher, Captain,	199
Flockhart, Rev.,	205
Fitchett, Rev.,	208
Fribley, Jacob,	134, 123
Farwell, John V.,	152
Fisher, Joel,	34
Forbush, Mabel,	34
Gillett, Dr. Philip L.,	153
Grant, Benjamin W.,	35
Grant, Mrs.,	36
Grant, Henry,	39
Grant, General U. S.,	153
Grover, William,	457, 60
Godman, James H.,	123
Gurley, Rev. Dr. L. B.,	123
Glass, Mr.,	137
Gelling, Rev. James,	313
Guthrie, Dr.,	379
Gough, John B.,	465
Hartley, F. J.,	60, 457, 358, 464
Herkloltz, William Gregory,	351
Havelock, Sir Henry,	457
Horsley, Rev. J. F.,	209, 457
Havelock, General,	300
Hard, Rev. C. P.,	313, 302
Harcourt, John,	182, 228, 248
Hunter, Rev.,	214
Hastings, Hon. L. D.,	218, 214
Hurst, Rev. George,	220
Hardie, George,	224
Hardie, John,	225
Hancock, Captain R. V.,	232
Hobbs, Rev.,	234
Hart, Mr.,	246, 240

INDEX OF PERSONAL MENTION. 471

Hemme, A.,	162
Hastings, Dr. Thomas,	168
Henderson, Rev. Dr.,	185
Hitchcock, G. M. H.,	195
Hutchinson, Dr. H. B.,	205
Heard, Mr.,	139
Hicks, Dr.,	103
Hurst, A. C.,	120
Haine, John,	121
Hayes, President,	88
Hammer, Mr.,	90
Howard, Samuel,	38
Holland, Rev. Mr.,	282
Ick, Mrs.,	203
Ittman, P. G.,	351
John, Rev. Dr.,	310
Johnson, Miss,	330
Jones, Rev. T. W. S.,	338
Jones, Rev. J. I.,	264
James, Rev.,	199
Jolley, J. C.,	126
Jacobs, B. F.,	152
Janes, Bishop,	79
Johnson, Mary C.,	88
Johnson, President,	119
Johnson, Henry,	123
Jennings, Romina,	28
Jubilee Singers,	118
Kelynack, Rev. William,	221
Kling, Amos,	123
Kingsley, Dr.,	124
Kean, S. A.,	152
Kittridge, Rev. Dr.,	340
King, S. G.,	248, 186, 177
King, Rev.,	212

Kidder, Rev. Dr.,	234
Kimball, Miss,	271
Knox, Dr. Robert,	461, 374
Lawrence, Rev. Thomas C.,	250
Leslie, Miss,	280
Law, Joseph,	213
Livingston, Dr.,	375
Le Fevre, Miss,	335, 316
Lansing, Rev. Dr.,	332, 329
Leena, Dr.	338
Langley, Rev.,	339
Lyman, John C.,	248
Landon, Rev. I.,	262
Leslie, Miss,	274
Lipsett, E.,	234
Lincoln, President,	156, 56
Lewis, Captain,	116
McCauley, Jerry,	73
McEchron,	194
McCabe, Chaplain,	92
Moran, Rev. Dr.,	95
Menhall, Dr.,	97
Monnett, Abraham,	122
McGruder, T. J.,	123
Muller, Mr.,	59
Moody and Sankey,	63, 64, 135, 152, 157, 159, 184, 186, 194, 354
Murphy, Francis,	88
Meade, General,	126
Mathewson, James S.,	140
McLean, David,	145
McCarty, Rev. J. H.,	147
Murray, John,	177
Mayor of Melbourne,	182
McCartney, Rev. H. B.,	186

INDEX OF PERSONAL MENTION. 473

Marsh, W. G.,	186
Miller, Mr.,	213
McCoy, J. S.,	224
Musgrove, Lady,	231
Murdes, Thomas,	235
Marshall, Captain,	237
Marsh, Henry,	244, 243
Miller, Louis W.,	244
Moore, Hon. M.,	244
Millard, John L.,	248
Myers, Williams,	279, 273
Muir, Sir Richard,	274
Muckagee, Rev.,	276
May, Mrs.,	280
Milus, Rev. Dr.,	282
Mudge, Rev. J. M.,	299
Miller, Rev. Donald,	342
Millard, E.,	344, 343
Miles, A. H.,	374
McComas, Samuel,	373
Moody, Rev. A.,	345
Newton, Rev. Isaac,	54, 381
Newton, Thomas,	381
Newland, Brother,	314
Northcote, Lord,	283
Nichols, Adam,	248
Nicholson, Rev. William,	207, 258
Noland, Rev.,	225
Newman, Dr.,	88
Naylor, Dr. N.,	281
Noble, William,	465
Olmstead, E. B.,	52
Owen, Rev. Griffith,	87
Ounch, J. P.,	248
Oakes, M. E.,	280

INDEX OF PERSONAL MENTION.

Osborne, Mrs. S. C.,	123
Phillips, Sawyer, Sen.,	18
Phillips, Alonzo,	18, 20
Phillips, Thomas D.,	20
Phillips, Williston,	20
Phillips, Rosina,	20, 21
Phillips, William,	20
Phillips, Charles,	20
Phillips, Sawyer, Jr.,	21
Phillips, Joshua,	21
Phillips, Philip,	21
Phillips, Benjamin C.,	21
Phillips, Alphonzo,	21
Phillips, G. Harry,	21
Phillips, Z. Barney,	21
Punshon, Dr. William M.,	144
Priggen, Mr.,	343
Pratt, Orson,	157
Peckham, Rev. William,	25
Peck, Bishop,	124
Punshon, Dr.,	141
Preston, David,	146
Paulding, Mrs.,	44
Pitts, Rev. Dr.,	111
Philip, Captain,	216
Price, Hon. James,	233
Parish, Commodore,	268
Prince of Wales,	301, 282
Porter, Rev. J. L.,	322
Proemore, Dr. G. D.,	347
Pratt, Daniel,	358
Pennefather, Rev. William,	463
Parker, Dr. Joseph,	463
Reed, Henry,	240
Rust, Rev. Dr.,	464

INDEX OF PERSONAL MENTION.

Reed, Sir Charles, . . . 457, 464
Rawlins, William, . . . 462
Raikes, Robert, . . 462
Rosenthal, Rev, W., . . . 349
Richards, M. W., 60, 355, 360, 370, 374, 457, 458
Robinson, Rev. J. E., . . . 312
Richardson, Rev. Dr., . . . 287
Rogans, Mr., ... 234
Richards, Rev. J. B., . . . 246
Reed, J. S., ... 123
Root, Dr. George F., . . . 151
Reynolds, William, . . . 153
Radensburg, Mr. J., . . . 195
Sharland, W. H., ... 235
Smith, Aunt Sally, . . . 38
Sankey, Ira D., ... 127
Sutherland, Dr., . . . 141
Sanford, J. E., . . . 143
Smart, Rev. J. S., . . . 147
Studebaker Brothers, . . . 150
Simmons, Rev. J. C., . . . 207, 177, 161
Smith, A. J., ... 186
Smith, George, . . . 189, 188
Snyder, Asa, ... 92
Standing, Rev. George, . . . 99
Spence, Rev. Dr., . . . 119
Sumner, William, ... 54
Seward, William H., . . . 56
Shrimpton, Alfred, ... 60
Stewart, A. T., ... 78
Stokes, E. H., ... 79
Sewart, Geo. H., . . . 83
Smith R. Pearsall, ... 84
Sellors, Rev. Richard, . . . 220, 215
Steele, Rev. Dr., ... 224

476   INDEX OF PERSONAL MENTION.

Stephenson, T. Bowman, . . 231
Scott, A. A., ... 235
Stephenson, T. B., . . . 243, 235
Scott, Rev. John, ... 261
Scott, Miss, ... 261
Silva, S. Isaacs, ... 267
Spaar, Rev. J. A., . . . 267
Sherring, Rev. M. O., . . . 286
Smith, Supt., ... 294
Smith, Rev. James, . . . 297
Shaw, Rev. James, . . . 314
Spencer, O. M., ... 342
Smithers, T. B., . . . 464, 356
Scott, Sir Walter, ... 379
Stanley, Hon. A. P., . . . 383
Smith, Alderman C., . . . 459
Slade, Robert, ... 459
Sutherland, Thos., . . . 460
Shrimpton, Mr., ... 464
Tressider, J. E., . . . 60, 457
Thoburn, Miss, ... 299
Thoburn, Dr., 271, 274, 275, 280, 281, 282, 299, 302
Taylor, Rev. Wm., . 205, 206, 275, 306
Tebb, Rev., ... 264
Tasman, A. J., ... 237
Thurston, Miss, ... 168
Tiffany, Dr. O. H., . . . 141
Tynge, A. G., ... 153
Usher, Rev. P. R. C., . . . 211
Vincent, Dr. J. H., 64, 152, 156, 157, 159, 162, 352,
    353, 354, 357, 358, 359, 465
Van Diemen, Anthony, . . 237
Van Meter, W. C., . 404, 359, 358, 338
Vernon, Dr., . . 339, 340, 342, 338

INDEX OF PERSONAL MENTION.

Van Scheltema, Adama,	350, 349
Varley, Henry,	360, 358
West, Prof.,	456
Wilson, Mr.,	365
Wheelock, Rev. A.	51
Walton, Rev.,	324
Wheatley, Miss,	330
Waugh, John S.,	248
Watsford, John,	185, 203, 248
Willenberg, Rev. William,	255, 260
Wilkins, S. R.,	267
Wilson, Vice President,	269
Woolnough, Rev. George,	217, 227
Watkins, Rev.,	221
Webb, Hon.,	221
Waterhouse, Rev. Jabez,	223
Wells, Rev. W. P.,	231, 232
Wilson, J. R.,	94
Wightman, Rev. J. A.,	95
Wadsworth, Rev. J. A.,	95
Wadsworth, Rev. Dr.,	102
Wright, Rev. Samuel P.,	112
Wheat, J. H.,	120
Wallace, T. P.,	123
Wright, John R.,	54
Willard, Mrs. Francis,	88
Whittenmeyer, Mrs.,	88
Wood, Captain,	164
Webb, Mrs.,	168
Whitney, H. M.,	171
Waterhouse, John,	171
Watkins, Rev.,	191
Williams, Rev. M.,	196
Williams, Captain,	198

Watson, John, ... 198
Wetmore, W. C., . . 139
Way, Rev. L. P., . . . 32
Woodbury, I. B., . . . 39
Willoughby, Rev. B. C., . . 39
Yule, Rev. Dr., . . . 332

THE END.

www.ingramcontent.com/pod-product-compliance
Lightning Source LLC
Chambersburg PA
CBHW022104300426
44117CB00007B/576